The Experience of Reading

The Experience of Reading
Louise Rosenblatt and
Reader-Response Theory

Edited by John Clifford
The University of North Carolina at Wilmington

Boynton/Cook Publishers
Heinemann
Portsmouth, NH

For Joan

Boynton/Cook Publishers, Inc.
A Subsidiary of
Heinemann Educational Books, Inc.
361 Hanover Street, Portsmouth, NH 03801-3959
Offices and agents throughout the world

The following chapters were first published in the special issue on Louise M. Rosenblatt, *Reader* 20 (Fall, 1988) and are reprinted by permission of *Reader*:

"Louise Rosenblatt and Theories of Reader Response" by Carolyn Allen

"Democratic Practice, Pragmatic Vistas: Louise Rosenblatt and the Reader's Response" by Ann E. Berthoff

" 'First Steps' in 'Wandering Rocks': Students' Differences, Literary Transactions, and Pleasures" by Kathleen McCormick

"The Aesthetic Mind of Louise Rosenblatt" by Alan C. Purves

Excerpts from *The Reader, the Text, the Poem: The Transactional Theory of the Literary Work* by Louise M. Rosenblatt (1978) reprinted by permission of Southern Illinois University Press.

Every effort has been made to contact the copyright holders for permission to reprint borrowed material. We regret any oversights that may have occurred and would be happy to rectify them in future printings of this work.

Library of Congress Cataloging-in-Publication Data
The experience of reading : Louise Rosenblatt and reader-response
  theory / edited by John Clifford.
     p.   cm.
  "Bibliography of Louise M. Rosenblatt": p.
  ISBN 0-86709-262-9
  1. Rosenblatt, Louise M. (Louise Michelle)   2. Reader-response
criticism.   I. Clifford, John.
PN98.R38E97   1990
801'.95–dc20   90-37177
                                                                    CIP

Text design by Hunter Graphics.
Cover design by Virginia Evans.
Printed in the United States of America.
91 92 93 94 95   9 8 7 6 5 4 3 2 1

Contents

Introduction:
Reading Rosenblatt

John Clifford

When histories of the reader-response movement are eventually written, Louise Rosenblatt's *Literature as Exploration* (1938) is sure to be cited as the inaugural text. That many informed theorists after four editions and an international audience still do not know this impassioned defense of real readers is either an indication of the myopia of a lingering formalism or the literalness of the ivory tower. A rereading of this important book in our current poststructural climate is a bit odd, *déjà vu* with a rhetorical twist, as if someone were writing a lucid overview of how the ideas of Fish and Iser might be clarified and made relevant to students, without elaborate theoretical scaffolding. The reason for this familiarity is not mysterious: Rosenblatt's ideas about the dialectical simultaneity of the reading process, about the contextual complexity of language in its social and private dimensions, about the multiplicity of interpretation, and about the inextricable link between reading and democracy were simply a generation ahead of their time. Unfortunately, she was a victim of such circumstances as the dislocations of World War II, the impact of Sputnik, and her own pellucid discourse. And by victim, I simply mean the absence from critical discussion in university English departments of the theoretical merits of her argument. Her book was, however, always a vital and valued guide among progressive educators in America and England frustrated with the aridity and remoteness of formalist reading.

After having been trained as a close reader in the mid-sixties, I was rapidly becoming just such a frustrated instructor.

I heard little sustained conversation in graduate school about readers, beyond a passing reference to catharsis or the affective fallacy. Even in the late sixties, in the waning of the formalist paradigm, a serious interest in readers, especially the messy, untrained responses of students, was still a slightly perverse activity, perhaps a symptom of an even greater eccentricity—a commitment to democratic teaching. As a novice scholar and instructor, I had been socialized to believe that associating one's reading with the actual world, or worse, with one's passionate inner life, was emotionally self-indulgent, solipsistic, and unscholarly (I think unmanly was also lurking in the background). Subjectivity and objectivity both seemed clearly definable and separate. The former was to be extirpated, root and branch; the latter was to be rigorously cultivated. How hermetically sealed this New Critical notion of textual autonomy now seems, how repressive was the seemingly neutral and precise methodology of close reading. And, of course, how oblivious to the implications of contradiction, how unconcerned with the real reasons for difference.

Along with this philosophical naïveté and political suppression came inevitable constraints on teaching, constraints that denied the relevance and authority of experience. I felt acutely the irony that a professional approach to reading that was originally conceived of as an antidote to the diminution of humanistic values in an increasingly bureaucratic culture would itself become a source of fragmentation and alienation. How was it possible to discuss Whitman and Shelley while also ignoring the upheaval swirling in and around the working-class high school I taught in in the sixties? What innocuous role in society was already carved out for those instructors who privileged the textual artifact over the experience of reading?

I think it was finally a pervasive distrust of authorities of all sorts that led academics first to a skepticism about and then a rejection of rigidly constructed systems of official policy in government and in the university. The old ways just would not serve any longer; consequently, traditional notions of reading and meaning were intensely problematized. Eventually, the *a priori* authority of the text became widely suspect, and the way was thereby open for thinking hard about how reading actually proceeds. All of this foreshadowed the rejection of formalism, the rise of various participatory reception theories, and the rediscovery of Louise Rosenblatt. As the social and political consensus went sour, so too did my ability to teach or read in the old ways. It was simply too frustrating, too pedagogically detached, too politically unconscionable. I shared Louis Kampf's disappointment that the New Criticism "affected no one."

I longed for a new perspective. Fortunately, I discovered *Literature as Exploration*, and my reading and my teaching have never been the same. That neither I nor anybody I talked to in graduate school had ever heard of this text is, I think, a representative anecdote for the insularity of graduate training in English before 1970. Rosenblatt's belief that a spontaneous, emotional reaction to literature was "an absolutely necessary condition of sound literary judgment" had the immediate ring of truth to it.

In the Preface to the First Edition of *Literature As Exploration*, written some fifty years ago, for example, Rosenblatt announces a recurring and still pressing concern of English teachers "to demonstrate that the study of literature can have a very real, and even central, relation to the points of growth in the social and cultural life of a democracy" (ix). In the progressive context of the politically sophisticated thirties there was much sympathy for this position. That was to change, of course, under the pervasive influence of the cold war and the New Criticism, only to reappear during the late sixties with a force Rosenblatt probably did not intend. The conservative reaction to the perceived excesses of the sixties considerably dampened interest in a socially conscious pedagogy; yet once again English teachers are seeing what Rosenblatt knew a half a century ago, that reading is inescapably a social act.

This is also Frank Lentricchia's Deweyan insight from *Criticism and Social Change* (1983), a text that is often regarded as the theoretical catalyst for recent attempts to see schools once again as reformers of a flawed social order. To begin such a project, Lentricchia invokes Kenneth Burke's advice that we must first interrogate our own identities, which Lentricchia sees in terms of our political complicity as members of educational institutions. In the first chapter of *Literature as Exploration*, Rosenblatt anticipates this insight by claiming that the reader "needs to understand himself . . . he must achieve a philosophy, an inner center from which to view in perspective the shifting society about him" (3). Then, in the next sentence, she again sounds especially contemporary by asserting that the resulting knowledge should be "assimilated into the stream of his actual life," a primary concern of academics with a sociopolitical focus.

In the following paragraph, Rosenblatt makes a deconstructive move, claiming that school is not an enclosed sphere, opposed to the real world, since the student is always "already part of the larger world, meeting the impact of its domestic and international tensions" (3). In a recent theoretical text on the critic's political responsibility, James Merod also urges teachers of literature to see their task in this larger, less modest perspective, as a discipline capable of making a difference in the world. Merod and Rosenblatt are concerned with the constraining influence ideology has on our reading behavior. Interestingly, only a few paragraphs into *Literature as Exploration,* Rosenblatt acknowledges that teachers have not always realized their ideological role in fostering "general ideas or theories about human nature and conduct" (4), nor their role in affecting moral and political attitudes. But since it is in the very nature of literature to deal with "everything that man has thought or felt or created" (5), writers and readers themselves must inevitably be enmeshed in "a scheme of values, a sense of a social framework" (6). It is, she notes, impossible for the writer, the reader, or the teacher to avoid assuming some attitude toward the values encountered in the text. In this context, Rosenblatt advocates that teachers should bring this questioning of values "into the open for careful scrutiny" to raise the consciousness of the classroom community. Inevitably, in a response-oriented pedagogy, we all come to see that we read into texts our ideological presuppositions, that we judge Othello "in the light of our own assumptions about human nature" (11). These were important ideas in the sixties and are becoming increasingly influential today. When there is an active participation of the reader in the making of meaning, political domination seems less possible. And if the reader sees "the important molding influence in his own past . . . if he becomes aware of alternative social patterns or alternative types of happiness, he will be better able to make choices . . ." (156). Rosenblatt's goal here is for readers to understand and to change the world, not just to understand texts, so she hopes to create readers who might choose, citizens who might act, teachers who might empower.

As through a glass darkly, I began to see that I had been studying and teaching literary criticism, substituting the authority of the text for an exploration of the experience of reading. Instead of allowing myself and my students to confront our own varied responses to texts, I was making us all invisible, forcing students to repress deeply embedded values, ideas, emotions, and sociopolitical beliefs out of an allegiance to a critical tradition. The irony, of course, was that this repression was only for the masses: New Critics still read with their isolationist values intact; they still privileged aesthetics and devalued the sociopolitical. So, finally, it was everyone else's values that were ignored. Is it any wonder that this trained incapacity to be fully engaged alienated students from reading literature?

The pedagogical beliefs that followed my adaptation of Rosenblatt's transactional dynamic between the text and the reader were immediate and empowering. The voices of an evolving canon could now be put in dialogue with the voices of my students. Poems became less artifacts than sources for potential works of art, not discovered but dialectically created in the classroom. And what I have never forgotten, what lingers still in the intertextual crevices of all my critical reading, is the sense of psychological wholeness that I felt when I realized I did not have to split my inner life and my work, my sociopolitical values and my professional ethos. I could simply read the text as I read the world, with the same personal commitment, the same desire and need to understand, but without the certainty that it all needs to make sense, that there must be eventual coherence, that there is an ultimate intentionality one needs to uncover. After the stunning epiphany that the process of reading was parallel to larger perceptions of the world, reading began to seem crucial, an important way of being in the world. And for students it was a way to make meaning of their lives. They soon realized that whose meaning prevailed had social and political consequences as they read about the riots in Watts, the violence in Vietnam, the complex motivations involved in university demonstrations, as well as in their reading of Shakespeare, their judging of Gatsby, or their evaluation of rock lyrics. Rosenblatt simply allowed me to believe in the transformational potential of reading, writing, and discussing texts with students. Now some twenty years later, after the profession has exhibited an intense interest in theory and has developed a renewed concern for our political responsibilities, I see even more vividly the rich intellectual and psychological possibilities of response-oriented reading and teaching. Louise Rosenblatt's transactional theories of reading offer us the best chance to do serious intellectual work with a democratic conscience. As do some of the contributors to this collection, we may want to supplement her basic principles with theoretical issues from the richness of our current intellectual concerns. But when we do blend cultural, ideological, feminist, political, or psychological theories, it bears remembering that the foundation, the essence, and spirit of the reader's importance were championed first in her work. More than anyone, Louise Rosenblatt provides us with the necessary critical and ethical apparatus for significant transactions with texts. The essays collected in this volume attest to the theoretical richness of that transaction when the text is her work and the readers are an international mix of educators, theorists, and researchers. The diversity and sophistication of viewpoints about Rosenblatt's work are an exciting and encouraging indication that her work will endure.

Carolyn Allen's essay, which was first given as an informal talk at MLA, gives us a much-needed retrospective of Rosenblatt's career and some of the problems involved in her academic acceptance. She also reminds us of Rosenblatt's early insistence on the connections between the text and the social, psychological, and cultural life of readers. Although the long-standing bias against practical application of theory, that is, actual classroom teaching, has diminished in recent years, I think Allen is cogent in locating Rosenblatt's isolation in the academy in the pragmatism of *Literature as Exploration*. In fact, many of the contributors make note of the powerful influence the American pragmatists have had on her work, from John Dewey to C. S. Peirce and William James. It must be amusing to Rosenblatt that progressive thinkers as diverse as Richard Rorty, Frank Lentricchia, and Henry Giroux are now focusing on the contributions of Dewey some fifty years after she affirmed his centrality for democratic reading and teaching.

Gordon Pradl's essay on Rosenblatt's long-standing belief in the democratic possibilities of transactional reading uses a quote from a little-known piece Rosenblatt wrote some fifty years ago: "To what extent . . . is . . . literary study in the schools contributing to the persistent hold of habits of thought and images of behavior no longer appropriate to our present-day knowledge and our aspirations for a more democratic way of life?" Although she has recently focused on the nuances of the transactional experience and on characteristics of the aesthetic and efferent, Pradl maintains that social vision and activism in the service of "the democratic enterprise" have been life-long commitments and perhaps her enduring legacy to English education in America.

Pradl begins his essay with an analysis of editorials Rosenblatt wrote in college for the *Barnard Bulletin*. He uncovers clear harbingers of themes crucial to her thinking right up to the present. She saw early on the need for active self-expression, echoing Dewey's concern for the intellectual effort needed to earn self-expression. Pradl perceptively sees the connection with responding to texts within a testing social context. Other editorials announce the need for an open forum of ideas against insular thinking, the interdependence of the individual and the community, and the need for education to prepare us for life, not the "punctiliously accurate administration of our complex industrial machinery." Pradl is also able to see that her dissertation written at the Sorbonne continues these ideas as she focuses on how the education of readers could improve the social life of the community.

Reading has consequences. And Pradl argues that in *Literature as Exploration*, Rosenblatt focuses on the individual reader "only within a dynamic social context which fosters the values of a democracy." In that text Rosenblatt develops a dialectical method for teaching that asks the student to return to the text again and again to validate or disturb initial responses, all the while negotiating, as Pradl notes, "outward to the social context of other readers and other texts." This is an important point in today's brouhaha about the value of the great masterpieces of Western literature. Rosenblatt holds that the benefit that derives from these works flowers in the lively interaction of readers and not somehow in the isolated works themselves.

Although some readers may think that Pradl overstates the negativity of the attack on Western ideology from those on Rosenblatt's left, his essay is perhaps the clearest and most careful reading in the literature of the democratic spirit that imbues Rosenblatt's transactional theories.

Mariolina Salvatori's essay on Rosenblatt and pedagogy is indicative of the profession's growing interest in and commitment to the serious study of teaching. Rosenblatt's concern for informed pedagogy was simply a generation or two ahead of its time, for it is only recently that theorists have charted the inevitable connections between a theory of reading and classroom methodology. William Cain, for example, is convinced that the New Criticism became so enormously popular primarily because of the accessible pedagogy so clearly and appealingly inscribed in Brooks and Warren's *Understanding Poetry* (1938). Although it is usually not planned for, theory invariably works its way into pedagogical practice. The New Critics, for example, privileged the harmony of art only by denigrating the chaos of subjectivity; consequently, this retreat from the social was mirrored in classrooms, where the instructor was installed as textual authority, the student as novice explicator. Students were not expected to discuss their lives, and so they conformed to the hegemony of reading along very narrow paths.

Salvatori is a leader in the reconceptualization of that diminished instructional drama, taking her cue from Rosenblatt's critique of formalism's anemic theory of knowing. Both hope to rescue the reader as well as pedagogy itself from their marginal status in our profession. In a close reading of the various editions of *Literature as Exploration*, Salvatori uncovers Rosenblatt's evolving theory of reading, from one that slightly favored the text, to her present commitment to a transactional conception that allows readers to be active and fully attached to their felt experiences and real lives. In affirming the centrality of the reading experience, Rosenblatt also opened the way for literature to play an important role in the lives of readers by clarifying, challenging, and disturbing deeply held values. Text and readers affect each other, thus avoiding the theoretical and practical fragmentation of our intellectual and emotional lives so endemic in the academy. Both Salvatori and Rosenblatt have developed sophisticated notions of reading and teaching that help us be more integrated knowers.

Emrys Evans's useful report of Rosenblatt's influence in England, Australia, and elsewhere also has some parallels in the United States. Even though Rosenblatt's work was largely ignored by English professors here, her ideas on the connections between democracy and literature and the benefits of a response-oriented pedagogy have been important themes for progressive education professors and a number of high school teachers for decades. Of course, Evans is correct in noting that interest in more participatory reading strategies grew significantly after the Dartmouth Seminar. It was shortly after that conference, in fact, when I first read *Literature as Exploration* and realized that without a dialogue between one's own experience and the world of the text, teaching literature would be deadly for both teacher and student.

Evans cites an *English Journal* essay by Rosenblatt that seemed to have some influence in combating the New Critical emphasis on genre and textual analysis. He raises important questions about the lack of emphasis on the reader's creative contribution, inquiries that are still being addressed today. Evans notes that it has not been until quite recently that Rosenblatt's ideas have become widely known outside America. Evans himself, in an important Boynton/Cook collection, *Readers, Texts, Teachers,* becomes a key player in making Rosenblatt's ideas more accessible to teachers. He hopes that response has finally become a standard term in literary education, as a sign that Rosenblatt's emphasis on the reader's active possession of the literary work will be widely accepted.

Ann Berthoff's essay is yet another example of the vitality of Rosenblatt's texts and the humanistic energy of Berthoff's reading. After the long and depressing reign of positivist educational theory, Berthoff needs to remind us that it was not always so: that some educators were always concerned with the life of the mind. The Rosenblatt seminars I was in during the early seventies, for example, were about ideas, about philosophical inquiry, about multiple meanings, intention, and democratic values. And Berthoff recognizes this because her work is also about the mind, about the necessity of the reader to mediate between the symbol and the referent, between the word and reality. Since this is a constant theme in Berthoff's own reading and writing theories, she knows that Rosenblatt is also concerned with triadicity as a corrective to dyadic formalism. Both theorists are positing active, engaged readers, situated in a social world badly in need of thinkers who can tolerate ambiguity and who understand the cultural seriousness of their meaning-making responsibilities.

John Willinsky's rumination on what he sees as a shift in Rosenblatt's career from an emphasis on the political to a concern with the private raises interesting questions about the interpretation of theory. Willinsky praises *Literature as Exploration* for its explicit attempts to create through literature sensitive, critical readers alert to the needs of a democratic society. He also notes that Rosenblatt's affirmation of the reader as a force for democratization has been a source of inspiration for progressives for decades. Willinsky gives us an interesting overview of the milieu in which Rosenblatt developed her ideas. He is probably right in believing that in the enthusiasm and optimism of that time Rosenblatt overstates the liberating potential of literature, even when it is transactionally taught. Her belief in the benefit of science also seems innocent in the context of our current malaise about the power of both ideology and technology.

Nevertheless, it might also be that Willinsky himself exaggerates the extent to which Rosenblatt eschews communal democratic principles in favor of the individual reader. In *The Reader, the Text, the Poem* her focus on the transaction between reader and text can indeed be interpreted to be her intervention into the current critical conversation. As Allen, Salvatori, and Berg suggest, she had for some time been unfairly excluded from that dialogue, so her eagerness to be considered seriously is certainly understandable, even admirable.

But simply because the focus of a particular text shifts is no reason to assume that her ideas about the political importance of literature have changed. In fact, I think her democratic commitments are stronger than ever. Willinsky's example of how her recent work has been adapted to a "skills instruction setting" is unconvincing as evidence that her new work has had a conservative influence on curriculum. Theories, as Edward Said notes, are often used for notoriously different purposes than the originator intended. How others use our work is beyond our control and responsibility. I could also cite examples of theorists who have extended Rosenblatt to the left more than she would wish. Kathleen McCormick, for example, blends Rosenblatt with poststructural ideas, focusing in her textbook, *The Lexington Introduction to Literature,* on critiquing the ideological baggage students bring to texts. And composition specialists have adapted her work in ways that she would applaud, ways that enhance participatory and democratic involvement. Willinsky's essay is interesting, cogently argued scholarship, and further proof that each of us looks at literary and theoretical texts from unique and therefore invaluable perspectives.

Russell Hunt gives us a perceptive overview of various ways into texts, specifically, four methods of reading that critics have championed over the last few generations. Before the New Criticism took hold of English departments in the fifties, most of the attention was focused on literary history. Instead of being drawn into a world of passions and ideas, thousands of students were taught to subordinate literature to history, to the details of chronology and philology. The rise of the New Criticism, with its emphasis on close reading and textual autonomy, did free inexperienced readers from the burdens of history and authorial intention. However, although it was touted as a democratic pedagogy, it also created new problems for all of those not familiar with the techniques of explication most prized by proponents of organic unity, irony, and resolved tensions.

Hunt sees the recent popularity of the new historicism as more promising for readers. In his conception, the often "frozen conversations" of literary texts are thawed when readers are able to participate in their implicit dialogue. We better understand texts and ourselves if we can bring our own values and assumptions into the textual conversation. This, Hunt points out at different phases of his essay, is just what Louise Rosenblatt has been saying since 1938. Transactional reading, Hunt's fourth approach, does not separate object and subject, but rather sees writer, reader, and text as a contextual whole. The transaction among all of them is grist for the mill of Hunt's collaborative investigation. Reluctant to specify a dominant approach to reading, Hunt encourages dialogue and social transaction, thus building on Rosenblatt's work in original and exciting ways.

Kathleen McCormick's reading of Rosenblatt represents a significant gesture for the response movement, since she clearly represents a new generation of scholars comfortable with poststructural literary theory. Instead of Dewey and Peirce, her influences are more likely to be deconstructionists, neo-Marxists, French feminists, and other proponents of rigorous, eloquent, ideal constructions of the reader. Yet, because she is also interested in teaching, McCormick can see how critical Rosenblatt's real reader is, how much the quality of the literary experience depends on authentic responses from that quiet young woman by the window. And so McCormick reads her theory dialectically, Barthes in dialogue with Rosenblatt, the result being that Barthes's textual preoccupations are modified by shifting pleasure, bliss, and *jouissance* to the reader—Rosenbarthes! McCormick's study of her students' active, self-conscious critique of their meaning-making capabilities is intrinsically interesting, but in a larger sense it demonstrates yet again Rosenblatt's belief that "[t]he transactional concept can only reinforce interest in the dynamics of the relationship between the author, the text, the reader, and their cultural environments" (*The Reader, the Text, the Poem* 174).

Bill Corcoran's essay critiques Rosenblatt's transactional theories from the left. Most of the objections to reader-response criticism and its resulting pedagogies have come from traditionalists, those on the right who value textual integrity and the great literary tradition over the responses of novice readers. Rosenblatt's pedagogical purpose— to enfranchise readers of all abilities—was a democratic gesture not in keeping with the hierarchical inclinations of many formalists. Corcoran, however, is even more liberal than Rosenblatt and faults her for not seeing the hegemonic intent of schools, for not stressing the social constructedness of texts, students, and teachers. His perspective about the need for informed opposition to the class, race, and gender bias of institutions is currently quite popular, and, it seems to me, quite reasonable.

In 1938, Rosenblatt's *Literature as Exploration* was considered by many to be quite radical. Her opposition to antidemocratic forces was vigorous and unequivocal. It is somewhat ironic that now some fifty years later she would be seen by some as politically naive and innocent of the powerful molding forces in our culture. However, I doubt that she was then or is now unaware of the political implications of schooling in general and literary education specifically.

Corcoran uses two Australian publications to illustrate the opposition between Rosenblatt's celebration of "evolving evocations" and the more radical journey from the "merely personal" to textual resistance and cultural interrogation. *A Single Impulse* privileges the individual, while *The Connecting Conversation* focuses mainly on cultural connections between language and power. Corcoran worries that readers will think they can unproblematically own texts, as if language already wasn't imbued with powerful cultural values. He worries that they will feel too autonomous, too concerned with personal growth. He worries that they will not understand the ways their own subjectivities are constructed, that they will ignore the details of their cultural and institutional contexts.

Because Corcoran agrees with Henry Giroux that schools are sites of contestation as well as instruction, he wants students to be able to read against the grain, confronting the text's values with their own. Rosenblatt, never considering herself a radical, has been concerned that the kind of ideological critique Corcoran suggests might be too negative, might, in fact, jeopardize democratic values that are still strong and valuable. At the risk of oversimplifying both positions, I would suggest that both are right. Rosenblatt provides a pedagogical environment conducive to the critique Corcoran proposes, and if that interrogation is balanced, is able to oppose domination and to affirm existing democratic values, I think Rosenblatt would think her ideas are being built on in fruitful and challenging ways.

Elizabeth Flynn's essay builds an important bridge between contemporary feminism and Rosenblatt's transactional ideas. Although Rosenblatt does not situate herself within the camp of feminist literary theory, her work is certainly compatible with much of current feminist thinking, especially the emphasis on the need for the reader's active confrontation of the text. Of course, Rosenblatt does, as Flynn points out, affirm the equality of women; she just doesn't explicitly take a feminist stand, even though her attempts "to disrupt the traditional hierarchy" (Flynn) certainly sound *au courant*. And in her astute comparison of Iser and Rosenblatt, Flynn shows us how the text is in masculine control in Iser, while in Rosenblatt the relationship between the text and the reader is more organic and sharing. In other words, Rosenblatt enacts in her theory of reading feminist impulses that can be seen as a fertile ground for more explicit feminist ideas to grow and flourish.

Rosenblatt's objective, of course, is not just to empower women but all readers, of all abilities. To achieve this end, she is concerned with developing readers, not just with the informed or ideal readers one encounters in most theory. *Literature as Exploration*, for example, is often cited as the major pedagogical text for the teaching of literature. Flynn notes that context plays a crucial role in the classroom environment Rosenblatt tries to create. There is an intellectual and emotional ecology at work in learning that Rosenblatt is quite attuned to: reader and text interpenetrate each other so that the subjective and the objective become irrelevant. The concepts of reader and text thus become shifting categories, tied to the evolving context of classroom dynamics. Texts can be resisted, à la Judith Fetterley, or embraced, à la Roland Barthes; everything depends on the "transactions, contexts, processes, positions" (Flynn) of the reading as an event in time. In her emphasis on connections, on contextual webs, and on taking strong stances with texts, Rosenblatt, as Flynn notes, easily becomes a model of lived feminism.

Temma Berg's detailed essay actually has a simple theme: female scholars like Louise Rosenblatt have been excluded from the conversation men have been having about literary theory since Plato. Canonical theory has misrepresented or mistreated the significant contribution of women theorists. To substantiate this claim, Berg convincingly provides us with both historical and anecdotal evidence that should reinforce feminist suspicions of an academic discipline dominated by men and their masculine assumptions and values.

Berg sees Rosenblatt's work as part of that excluded history, especially her insistence that literature is not detached from life, that reading interconnects with the emotional and personal as well as the intellectual. In fact, in attempting to give all readers the right to create their own meaning, Rosenblatt demonstrates through her refusal to separate the knower from the known that the boundaries between the subjective and objective are not clear at all. This epistemological break with the traditional reading theory of the New Critics is entirely in harmony with current feminist thinking. Berg further suggests that Rosenblatt's empathy for her students, her desire to empower them, as well as her interdisciplinary range and inclusiveness all situate her within a feminist theoretical tradition that needs to be recognized and valued.

John Rouse begins his careful explication of the pedagogical dynamics involved in Rosenblatt's response theory by reminding us of the erotic dimensions implicit in the relationship between teacher and student. If students are to take that relationship seriously, the distance and apparent objectivity of the New Criticism will not do. Rouse gives us an interesting reading of Rosenblatt's pedagogy with its delicate balance of patience and prodding. The group dynamic in which Rosenblatt's questioning occurs signals a change from the traditional authority of the teacher who knows the inquiring members of the group as they actively compare, discover, revise, and clarify their individual readings. Since Rosenblatt has always held that both literature and the reader are embedded in the social, Rouse's perceptive notion that transactional readings are about possibilities helps us to hope for a society made more critically aware through the transactional study of literature.

Alan Purves has long been interested in the ways the human mind experiences art. In his consideration of the significance of Rosenblatt's psychological aesthetics, he touches on several provocative themes, including offering a corrective to I. A. Richards's protocol studies in *Practical Criticism*. Purves maintains, correctly I believe, that texts are "mediated experiences" that can be used to challenge the mind and its values, and by extension, our professional values and our unexamined cultural presuppositions. I. A. Richards assumed that his students erred in their reading, instead of seeing the more significant lesson that his students could not avoid using the knowledge already in their heads. They had not yet been trained to read as dutiful members of an interpretive community by adhering to some *a priori* formulation of a correct reading. Purves is keenly aware of the impact training can have and bemoans our culture's obsession with propositional reading and its concomitant disregard for the aesthetic. I especially like his emphasis on stance and its power to determine how we read. Since stance is largely responsible for the formation of our currently limited canon, it is one of those seminal concepts that we need constantly to interrogate. For, after all, we read texts not only for what they tell us about the world and ourselves, but also because by being attuned to their aesthetic possibilities, we are more fully engaged, more fully alive to the possibilities of our existence. It is this aspect of Rosenblatt that renews my belief that the vitality of the transactional experience can be the basis for the important work reading, writing, and teaching must do in the world.

Works Cited

Lentricchia, Frank. *Criticism and Social Change*. Chicago: U of Chicago P, 1983.

Rosenblatt, Louise. *Literature as Exploration*. 1938. New York: Noble and Noble, 1968.

———. *The Reader, the Text, the Poem: The Transactional Theory of the Literary Work*. Carbondale, IL: Southern Illinois UP, 1978.

1

Louise Rosenblatt and Theories of Reader Response

Carolyn Allen

Several years ago, while investigating the role of the reader in literary interpretation, I found myself running across footnotes and parenthetical references to the work of Louise Rosenblatt. There was Wayne Booth referring to her "unfortunately neglected works"; Steven Mailloux mentioning her in a footnote to a chapter that summarized the work of Iser, Bleich, Fish, and Culler; and David Bleich acknowledging her early work but criticizing it for being allegedly moral and pragmatic rather than theoretical (Booth 442; Mailloux 37n; Bleich 110). Suspecting a phallic plot to overlook the work of a woman scholar, I read through two anthologies of what had come to be called "reader-response criticism," hoping for enlightenment from their female editors. Neither included articles by Louise Rosenblatt, though both mentioned her in their summary introductions, one by noting her "pioneering work in the field of subjective criticism," but saying it came to her attention too late to be included (Suleiman and Crosman 45). Finally, I turned directly to Rosenblatt's work to reach my own conclusions about her contributions to reader-response theory.

This chapter was originally a paper read at the Modern Language Association meeting, December, 1983, at a session honoring pioneering women scholars.

I retrieved her 1938 book, *Literature as Exploration*, from the farthest reaches of our library stacks, the shelves where books have been kept so long that they still have Dewey decimal call numbers.

My first response to *Literature as Exploration* was, "This is wonderful." In 1938 she had already written a philosophy of literary teaching that had taken me ten years of practice to work out. She stressed the relationship between literature and the students' social, psychological, and cultural worlds and the need for the teacher to have an interdisciplinary knowledge of the social sciences. She also delineated what happens in the act of reading, declaring that the novel or poem exists in interaction with specific minds, and that reading any literary work is a unique experience involving the mind and emotions of some particular reader. Those ideas, elaborated throughout the book, led to her later, more fully developed theoretical considerations of the contributions of the reader to the literary work.

From that beginning she went on to develop what she calls the transactional theory of reading. In it she conceives the poem (or any literary work) not as an object, but as an experience shaped by the reader under the guidance of the text, which she defines as "printed signs in their capacity to serve as symbols" (*The Reader, the Text, the Poem* 24). The poem is an event in time that comes about through a transaction between the reader and the text. Her theory shares with Iser's a conception of the text as a set of "clues" (Iser calls them reading instructions) to guide the reader's performance. But unlike Iser's theory, the details of her work are not particularly well known among literary theorists. I'd like to suggest why that might be by sketching the critical reception of her two best-known books: her pedagogical study, *Literature as Exploration*, and her theoretical work, *The Reader, the Text, the Poem*.

From the beginning of her distinguished career, Louise Rosenblatt has had two reputations: one as a literary historian and critic, the other as a shaper of pedagogical philosophy. Her first book, *L'Idée de l'art pour l'art dans la littérature anglaise*, on theories of art for art's sake in nineteenth-century French and English writers, was her comparative literature dissertation at the Sorbonne. Published in French in 1931, it has remained a classic in the field for more than fifty years. In its final pages she noted the "need for a public of readers able to participate fully in the poetic experience" (quoted in *The Reader* xi). From that closing observation came the interest in the reader's role that, together with her pedagogical philosophy, is central to *Literature as Exploration*. These two books, one scholarly, the other largely pedagogical, treat topics that culminate in the theoretical work of *The Reader, the Text, the Poem*. Ironically, the very success of these earlier works has prevented her later theoretical ideas from receiving the attention they deserve.

Only after I reread *Literature as Exploration* and learned more about its publishing history did I see that the appearance of Rosenblatt's work in footnotes rather than in chapters of theoretical studies of reader response was at least in part a result of the continuing unfortunate split in our profession between pedagogy on the one hand and literary criticism and theory on the other. In fact, that split has not always been so acute. When *Literature as Exploration* was first published, it was widely praised not only by teachers and teachers of teachers, but also by leading literary critics as well. Howard Mumford Jones was so impressed when he read the book in manuscript that he invited Rosenblatt, then a young literature instructor at Barnard, to join with him and other established scholars to draw up a statement on the teaching of literature for *PMLA*. It was published in 1938, the same year as her book. Since that time *Literature as Exploration* has never been out of print. It has gone through three editions, has long been available through the National Council of Teachers of English, and since 1976 has been distributed by the MLA, which in 1983 reprinted it as an official MLA publication. Thus it is only those of us working recently in literary criticism and theory who feel we have made a significant discovery on the back shelves of the library. Earlier scholars and those who worked in pedagogical method have known all along where to find it.

Recent critics who acknowledge that Rosenblatt was "the first among the present generation of critics in this country to describe empirically the way the reader's reactions to a poem are responsible for any subsequent interpretation of it" (Tompkins xxvi) generally attribute the lack of attention given her theoretical ideas to the all-pervasive influence of New Criticism in the years following the publication of *Literature as Exploration*. Clearly any book that claimed that "the novel or poem or play exists . . . only in interactions with specific minds" (*Literature* 32) was not championing "the poem itself" or celebrating impersonality or avoiding the affective fallacy. Certainly, the hegemony of the New Criticism in the years following World War II turned critical attention away from the emphasis on the reader's experience, and it is to Rosenblatt's credit that she continued to pursue and refine her ideas when it was so unfashionable to do so.

But that is, I think, not the only reason why her contributions to reader-response theory have not been accorded the attention given her literary scholarship and her ideas about teaching literature. Rosenblatt developed her transactional theory in articles in *College English, Educational Record*, and the *Journal of Reading Behavior*, and so her work may not have been well known to literary theorists doing similar study. Or, more likely, articles published in these journals may have been deemed of interest only to the practitioner and not to the theorist, even though *College English*, an official journal of the NCTE, has often contributed substantially to literary critical debates. Similar divisions between applied and theoretical scholars exist in a number of disciplines including linguistics, anthropology, and sociology. Yet other critics who share her interest in pedagogy have gained their measure of theoretical fame. Stanley Fish, Norman Holland, and David Bleich all cite their teaching and describe the responses of their students. In Bleich's work, in fact, the literary text nearly gives way to student responses as the focus of the interpretive act. So if it isn't her empiricism per se that has kept her from being better known as a theorist, what is it? First, she is a woman seen as addressing a stereotypic woman's profession about the importance of emotional response. Her interest in English education, her pedagogical emphasis in *Literature as Exploration*, and the very acclaim this work has received from secondary classroom teachers and from leading members of the NCTE each have militated against a more serious understanding of her theoretical work—in short, politics, both sexual and academic. Second, there is the question of her theoretical sources. Though her wide-ranging knowledge of continental philosophy is evident throughout *The Reader, the Text, the Poem*, it is primarily to American rather than European theorists that she looks—to Charles Peirce, George Santayana, William James, and John Dewey. It is they rather than Husserl or Ingarden who speak most obviously through her work. She follows her own philosophical path, and it leads her to an American rather than a continental allegiance, equally weighty, but less theoretically fashionable. Finally, she refuses to use the discourse that we have come to associate with recent critical theory. In the preface to *The Reader, the Text, the Poem*, her culminating theoretical book, she says that she has "avoided the current tendency to create new terminology" and held citations to a minimum (xi). All these facts have kept her theoretical work from being as well known in contemporary MLA circles as her pedagogical writing is among members of the NCTE. That she has not had a voice in the Fish-Iser or Bleich-Holland debates is again a consequence of politics. Fortunately, she has spent forty years pursuing her own line of inquiry undaunted by the stream of critical fashion running in other directions. It is heartening to see that she is now, however belatedly, recognized as "a pioneer" and "the first among the present generation." Better late than never.

Critical reception of *The Reader, the Text, the Poem* demonstrates some of these considerations. Reviewers for the *English Journal*, the *CEA Critic*, and *College English* all praised it without reservation

Douglas; Miller). Alan Hollingsworth's *College English* review is typical. It begins, "*The Reader, the Text, the Poem* is a major contribution to literary and critical theory. It should be read, re-read, and reflected on by anyone involved with the activity of reading" (223). Reviewers for the *Sewanee Review* and the *Yale Review*, though they praised many of the book's ideas, were more critical. Monroe Beardsley who, as a principal proponent of the affective fallacy could hardly be expected to agree with her emphases, nevertheless says it "deserves much praise for its contribution to our understanding of reading as response" and finds her illuminations "especially helpful to the teacher of literature." But he criticizes her lack of separation between "elements of the [literary] experience . . . under [the] control [of the text], and . . . [the reader's] feelings and personal associations that may be present and allowable but do not belong to the work" (642). Terence Hawkes also criticizes her treatment of the concept of "text." Yet Rosenblatt's ideas about the degree of determinacy in the text are no more problematic than they are in, say, Iser, whose *The Act of Reading* was published in English the same year as *The Reader, the Text, the Poem*. Like Rosenblatt, Iser is not clear where the determinacy of the text supplied by the author ends and where the production of meaning by the reader begins. Yet Iser has been acclaimed as an important theorist in a way that Rosenblatt has not.

The imbalance in some of these critical assessments may stem in part from the conscious stylistic differences between the two critics. In describing how the reading process works, Iser writes,

> The reader's part in the gestalt consists in identifying the connection between the signs; the . . . 'autocorrelation' will prevent him [sic] from projecting an arbitrary meaning on the text, but at the same time the gestalt can only be formed as an identified equivalence through the hermeneutic schema of anticipation and fulfillment in relation to the connections perceived between the signs. (120)

Of a similar moment Rosenblatt says,

> What the reader has elicited from the text up to any point generates a receptivity to certain kinds of ideas, overtones, or attitudes. Perhaps one can think of this as an altering of certain areas of memory, a stirring up of certain reservoirs of experience, knowledge, and feeling. As the reading proceeds, attention will be fixed on the reverberations or implications that result from fulfillment or frustration of those expectations. (*The Reader* 54)

I make this comparison of discourse not to disparage Iser, from whom I have learned a great deal, but to suggest that perhaps Rosenblatt has not been taken as seriously simply because she made a conscious decision to eschew jargon and use a straightforward style.

In their incomplete attention to Rosenblatt's literary theory, commentators have failed to see how her departure from her colleagues empowers her work. Part of the strength of her professional contribution comes from her testing of theory by practice. Her work differs most markedly from other reader-response work in its understanding of the reader. She is not caught up in the construction of characterized, ideal, informed, implied, or intended readers because her interest is in what happens when particular people read a particular text at a particular moment in time. Having declared for real readers, however, she is not much concerned with analyzing their psyches, but with the readers' becoming self-aware, self-critical, and self-enhancing. She emphasizes their transaction with the text and argues that they "crystallize out from the stuff of memory, thought, and feeling a new experience which [they] see as a poem." Thus, she conceives of "the concept of the poem as the experience shaped by the reader under the guidance of the text" (*The Reader* 12). It is this last idea of the poem as a reader's experience of it that she has, over the years, championed most strongly against the competing definitions posed by the New Critics. Ironically, she now finds herself defending, as they might have, the propriety of close reading against the versions of reader criticism that draw on ego-psychology or psychoanalytic theory to analyze individual responses. While Rosenblatt stresses the importance of the reader's emotional response, she rejects pure subjectivity in interpretation.

Her current theoretical work contributes in a new way to the old debate about the nature of literature. She accounts for poeticity by formulating a continuum to describe the stances that the reader might take or be encouraged to take during the reading process. At one pole is the *aesthetic*, the full absorption in the rich experience of thought and feeling during the reading itself. At the other is the *efferent*. In efferent readings, the reader reads through the text, seeking only to take away specific bits of information at its conclusion, as one would do when reading instructions on a bottle or a recipe. Thus she focuses on the shifting stance of the reader rather than on the language of the text as the source of "literariness." Consideration of this idea allows us to think more carefully about why we read and how our differing reading stances help create different literary experiences as we select various strands of the text for attention. No other reader-response critic considers such stances as part of a theory of reading.

Indications are that her work is quietly making its way. *The Reader, the Text, the Poem* is being read in graduate courses in criticism, rhetoric, and literary theory, and the book appears on Lawrence Lipking's highly selective bibliography of literary criticism in the MLA's *Introduction to Scholarship in Modern Languages and Literatures*. Another such sign was the session on her transactional theory at a recent convention of the International Comparative Literature Association.

Louise Rosenblatt has waited through forty-five years of shifting critical winds to see attention finally focus where she knew all along it ought to be: on the relationship between the reader and the text. She has given us a theoretical ground for our pedagogical practice, and she deserves as much credit as we can bestow, not only for being a pioneer, but for moving throughout her scholarly life from theory to practice and back. By steadfastly refusing to countenance the split between theory and application, she continues to exert a healing influence on our profession. With her long-standing reputations in both literary and pedagogical study, and with her growing reputation as a theorist, she truly is one of our most versatile and eminent scholars.

Works Cited

Beardsley, Monroe. "Reader Meets Text." *Sewanee Review* 87 (1979): 639–46.

Bleich, David. *Subjective Criticism*. Baltimore: Johns Hopkins UP, 1978.

Booth, Wayne C. *The Rhetoric of Fiction*. 2nd ed. Chicago: U of Chicago P, 1983.

Douglas, Wallace. "Rosenblatt's Theory of the Literary Transaction." *CEA Critic* 41.4 (1979): 34–38.

Hawkes, Terence. "Taking It as Read." *Yale Review* 69 (1980): 560–76.

Hollingsworth, Alan. Rev. of *The Reader, the Text, the Poem*, by Louise Rosenblatt. *College English* 41 (1979): 223–27.

Iser, Wolfgang. *The Act of Reading*. Baltimore: Johns Hopkins UP, 1978.

Lipking, Lawrence. "Literary Criticism." *Introduction to Scholarship in Modern Languages and Literatures*. Ed. Joseph Gibaldi. New York: MLA, 1981.

Mailloux, Steven. *Interpretive Conventions*. Ithaca: Cornell UP, 1982.

Miller, James E. Rev. of *The Reader, the Text, the Poem*, by Louise Rosenblatt. *English Journal* 69.3 (1980): 82–83.

Rosenblatt, Louise, *L'Idée de l'art pour l'art dans la littérature anglaise pendant la période Victorienne*. Paris: Champion, 1931. New York: AMS Press, 1976.

———. *Literature as Exploration*. 1938. New York: MLA, 1983.

———. "The Poem as Event." *College English* 26 (1964): 123–28.

———. *The Reader, the Text, the Poem: The Transactional Theory of the Literary Work*. Carbondale: Southern Illinois UP, 1978.

———. "Towards a Transactional Theory of Reading." *Journal of Reading Behavior* 1.1 (1969): 31–51.

———. "A Way of Happening." *Educational Record* 49 (1968): 339–46.

Salvatori, Mariolina. "Reading and Writing a Text: Correlations Between Reading and Writing." *College English* 45 (1983): 657–66.

Suleiman, Susan, and Inge Crosman, eds. *The Reader in the Text*. Princeton: Princeton UP, 1980.

Tompkins, Jane, ed. *Reader-Response Criticism: From Formalism to Poststructuralism*. Baltimore: Johns Hopkins UP, 1980.

2

Reading Literature in a Democracy: The Challenge of Louise Rosenblatt

Gordon M. Pradl

Although Louise Rosenblatt's transactional model of reading appears to be gaining increasingly wide influence, the force of its original intent has been significantly blunted by its inclusion in the realm of reader-response criticism. While discussions of such theory concentrate on the active mental processes involved in reading, they usually fail to question the attitudes and social relations fostered by the way literature is taught. The story that needs telling here concerns the broader campaign Rosenblatt has been waging since the 1920s on behalf of a critical literacy that is embedded in the values of democracy. To tell this story requires focusing attention on *Literature as Exploration* and its persistent challenge to the literary establishment.

The themes developed in that pioneering work have steadily marked Rosenblatt's writings over a sixty-five-year period. The earliest source we have for charting her thinking about education and its role in promoting the values of a democratic society are the editorials she wrote during her tenure as editor-in-chief of the *Barnard Bulletin* from April 27, 1923, to April 11, 1924, a position previously held by her friend Margaret Mead. During the heady intellectual days when Rosenblatt attended Barnard College (1921–1925), a debate was quickening over the students' responsibility for more active participation in their own education. In one of her editorials, Rosenblatt captured the changes afoot both in knowledge and academia: "We are even now passing through a period of readjustment. Authoritarianism no longer holds full sway in matters of intellect. New attitudes in politics, in economics, in art, in education, are manifesting themselves. New values are seeping into the thought of the time." According to Rosenblatt, such a period of intellectual ferment provided students a rich "opportunity to gain a comprehensive view of our culture." Further, she urged, "The college student can contribute toward the development of standards by which to measure these new trends of opinions, and can prepare herself to participate intelligently in the formation of new values." Learning, in other words, called for a moment of openness to new experience in order to advance a student's understanding, and clearly Rosenblatt relished the challenge:

> Periods of change, of transition, appeal to the imagination of youth, and we of to-day should be able to understand why Wordsworth said,
>
> > "Bliss was it in that dawn to be alive,
> > But to be young was very Heaven!"
>
> To seek out ideas, to interest oneself in the trends of thought in all fields of activity, is to see the college course in broader perspective, and to escape the "sins" of dullness and boredom. (February 29, 1924)

The list of speakers at Barnard as reported in the pages of the *Bulletin* confirms the range of social, cultural, and educational issues that distinguished the intellectual milieu in which Rosenblatt studied as an undergraduate: Roger Baldwin, Walter de la Mare, Alexander Meiklejohn, A. F. Pollard, Bertrand Russell, George Macaulay Trevelyan, Carl Van Doren, Stark Young. During her junior year, while editor-in-chief of the newspaper, Rosenblatt also chaired the executive committee in charge of the Forum Luncheon Series, which featured speakers such as Franz Boas addressing "Cultural Environment and Race" and John Dewey talking about "Education and Freedom."

Dewey's remarks, as reported in the *Bulletin*, strike a resonant progressive chord, which Rosenblatt was to take up in her own work a decade later. After attacking the idea that freedom was merely a "natural endowment," a state where restraint was absent, Dewey argued that freedom was something deliberately attained:

> The counterpart of this false conception of freedom is found in those educational theories which believe that self-expression will come simply as the result of "laissez-faire" policy. . . . "Self-expression" can come only as the result of intellect and effort.

Although Dewey agreed that intellectual freedom in higher education was a desirable end, he argued that achieving such freedom would remain difficult as long as there was so much discontinuity between ideals and methods across the various educational levels from elementary schools to the university.

> The student cannot spend sixteen or eighteen years in . . . habit formation and then expect habits of intellectual freedom to suddenly appear. If intellectual curiosity and freedom are to be the dominating principles of higher education they must be equally prevalent in the lower schools. (March 28, 1924)

When Dewey's words come under close scrutiny, we see the extent to which his original ideas behind the progressive movement have been misrepresented: freedom and self-expression do not occur in a vacuum, but must be earned; intellectual curiosity must be encouraged from the earliest stages of development if it is in fact to be valued later. Rosenblatt's transactional theory parallels these key themes in the area of literature education. For a student's response to a text will not grow and mature if the teacher never allows it to be expressed in the first place. Nor can a student's response be validated in isolation without testing and negotiating other responses.

Another participant in the Forum discussions on educational problems was William Kilpatrick, professor at Teacher's College, who spoke on "The Signs of Good Teaching." In his talk, as reported by the *Bulletin*, Kilpatrick began by asserting that one can't describe *teaching* without also describing the *learning* that is attached to it. As part of his emphasis on the student's learning, Kilpatrick underscored that people "learn much more and much faster where they are interested." This principle he illustrated by telling of the superior results achieved by a teacher who threw out the formal curriculum and focused on only "four types of activity: games, story-telling and reading, excursions and construction. The problems of arithmetic, geography, history, and spelling which can be found in these natural activities would be dealt with as they arose." Kilpatrick then concluded with his two basics of good teaching: "First, that students learn in direct proportion as they have a definite aim which they wish to follow and do follow, and, secondly, some criterion must be furnished for telling them whether they succeed or not" (April 4, 1924). His message reinforces a primary progressive theme: the student's intentions and ideas need an avenue of expression, but always in a questioning verbal context, which, while encouraging self-reflection, provides meaningful criteria for their evaluation.[1]

The editorials Rosenblatt wrote during this period reflect her youthful exuberance and progressive idealism as she consistently hammered away at the theme of public dialogue. She was committed to such dialogue because she saw it as providing the necessary means of testing and refining the ideas and opinions of the individual. This active process was, in fact, prerequisite for reaping the rewards of a democracy. At the core of her faith in democracy was her belief that "free" speech had not only to exist, but had also to be exercised. In this way only would the true benefits of democratic practice unfold: the continual improvement both of our understanding of the world and of our social relations within it.

In her inaugural editorial, Rosenblatt revealed the perspective that would underlie much of her later thinking. Recognizing that our representations of the world would only be as accurate as the kinds and sources of information we sought, she noted the special responsibility of the newspaper:

> Walter Lippman [sic], in his recent book *Public Opinion*, speaks of the fact that, since we are not able personally to investigate everything in the world about us, the "Pictures in Our Heads" correspond to the "World Outside" only in proportion to the correctness of the information presented to us. Newspapers, as conveyors of information, thus contribute much to our mental images of the world, and so should give as true an idea of the reality as possible.

Then after promising a *Bulletin* that "will reflect a student life even more active, intelligent, and constructive than ever before," Rosenblatt considered the issue of "insulated ideas." Skeptical of the "quite general belief in the omnipotence of 'systems,' " her vision focused on the kind of social relations which encouraged both a sharing and a scrutiny of the values which propelled the larger community. What she saw around her, however, seemed

> to be a tacit agreement between members of different groups to refrain from any inquiry into one another's ideas. . . . we have a large number of small group standards. Each group . . . engages in its own activities and is usually indifferent to—if not contemptuous of—the ideas and standards of the other groups. This insulation of ideas naturally vitiates the growth of a general college standard of values. (April 27, 1923)

In her very next editorial, Rosenblatt continued with this theme that education depended on an open community continually engaged in the testing of its ideas and opinions. While one should hold opinions enthusiastically, one needed to be

> self-analytical enough to understand the basis for the enthusiasm, so that if new facts present themselves a change in opinion is still possible. The ideal of open-mindedness is too often translated into indifference or a continual postponement of decision. The higher ideal would be open-mindedness which meant the ability to change or modify one's enthusiasms. (May 4, 1923)

In commenting on a series of faculty-student curricular meetings Rosenblatt emphasized the value of public discussion because she saw college as a joint student-faculty venture, with both contributing their varying viewpoints. This ideal of collegiate intellectual life rested on a "partly unconscious desire to make of college and the experience it offers a unified, cohesive whole—a place where the various activities and studies are subordinate to, and the result of, some major idea or purpose." A unity of purpose vitalized education by "connecting it more definitely with actual life." But compartmentalization is an ever-present and powerful countervailing force:

> Students come to college, acquire knowledge in various fields, and keep the types of information isolated in separate compartments of the mind, without ever correlating them, or realizing their inter-relationships. Educators have been relying on the assumption that the students would make the necessary correlations for themselves, but, evidently, for some reason or other, students have generally failed to do this.

Accordingly, Rosenblatt made a plea for a kind of college "learning" that is directly connected to the individual's attempt to understand the immediate demands of living. Education, in other words, must bear on what is required of individuals if they are to play a constructive role in the larger society which makes their gains and achievements possible:

> "To understand life"—vague, general, perhaps, but broad enough to include all types of personality, interested in all phases of human activity, and worthy enough to induce into the college community the much-needed spirit of a common purpose, of enthusiasm for the experiences which it offers. If this purpose were but made a more integral part of college thinking, if, instead of being taken for granted, it were offered to the students, not in the form of a pre-digested course, but as the spirit, the motive for presenting all courses, methods for stimulating students to think would be less needed, and the students would necessarily attempt to correlate and connect up with actual life, the information which they were getting. Under such conditions, college would indeed be a community in which all felt themselves part of a common enterprise. (June 1, 1923)

The importance of public expression was again underscored when Rosenblatt extolled the virtues of debating because it "develops practice in the technique of acquiring information, fosters an interest in social questions, and gives students training in expressing themselves forcefully." Later in the same editorial she considered the "prevalent misconception" that college was "a place where experts are trained for the punctiliously accurate administration of our complex industrial machinery."

It is not enough that the college student be made an effective part of
the machine, an eliminator of friction in the industrial world. He
should be able to comprehend the machine in its entirety, to understand the significance of his relationship to other men, and above all,
to enjoy and appreciate all that our culture may offer. The college of
liberal arts should develop people who can live more fully, and with
greater intensity of appreciation, than if they had not been members of
a college for four years. (November 2, 1923)

Although the organization of college life perhaps only mirrored the
fragmentation of the larger society and the occupational pressures
faced by students, such fragmentation needed resisting. For if the
ideals of a liberal education were lost, where, Rosenblatt wondered,
would the overarching vision and integrating values come from that
made democracy possible by mediating the diverse and competing
elements of society?

In another editorial, Rosenblatt supported diversity, yet she wor-
ried about how special interest groups kept insulating individuals
(students) from its benefits:

We find a number of small, internally homogeneous groups, which
tend to nullify much of what Barnard does offer in the way of valuable
personal contacts. The Freshmen usually drift into a number of groups
and develop within the small circles interests and standards of values
which become more intensified each year. . . . It is only natural that
people who are interested in the same things should see much of one
another. The danger lies in letting one's membership in a distinct
group interfere with one's having wider experiences. It is appalling to
realize how little the students in the various circles know about one
another. The groups have a tendency to become insulated; the principle of "Osmosis," of interchange of elements should be applied. Much
of our vaunted individualism at Barnard loses meaning and value if
there is not to be the interaction between people of different interests
and ideas.

In concluding, Rosenblatt once more emphasized the importance of
a common purpose: "Undergraduate life might become extremely
interesting if instead of being an aggregate of groups, it became a
community where individualities reacted upon one another" (December 21, 1923).

In her penultimate editorial, Rosenblatt looked for a more vital
and positive status for the role of "student." Students should be
responsible for inquiring into the nature of their culture, for seeking to
understand and appreciate what it had accomplished so far. The
learning environment that best supported such students recognized
the necessary but creative tension that existed between individuals
and the community:

> Those who desire a community feeling appeal for it usually on the
> grounds of institutional tradition, or college spirit. A more valuable
> community feeling, free of objectionable sentimentality, might be
> based on the sense of belonging to a definite group who, as students,
> have a common impulse to think, and learn, and act. The thinking and
> learning and action may take varied forms, as temperaments and per-
> sonalities vary, but they will have in common an intensity of
> interest in something of intellectual value. This is a community feel-
> ing in which even the most consciously individualistic might share.
> (April 4, 1924)

Because Rosenblatt returned to this theme of the interdependence of
the individual and the community consistently throughout her editorials, it seems reasonable to underscore the importance of such a social
perspective to the theory of literature that she subsequently developed. If we ignore her concern for the conditions of public dialogue,
we also fail to appreciate fully the weight she places on the real world
consequences of how a person reads.

After graduating from Barnard, Rosenblatt went on to study at the
University of Grenoble, before eventually ending up at the Sorbonne,
where in 1931 she completed a dissertation for her doctorate in comparative literature entitled *L'Idée de l'art pour l'art dans la littérature
anglaise pendant la période Victorienne*. We might, naturally, expect that
scholarly work in a literary discipline would have caused Rosenblatt
to leave behind the social concerns expressed in her earlier editorials.
Instead, she continued her project of exploring the dialogue conditions that best encouraged a vital democratic culture—in this instance,
the crucial relation between writers and their reading public. Specifically her dissertation focused on "the theories of art for art's sake
developed by nineteenth-century English and French writers to com-
bat the pressures of an uncomprehending or hostile society" (Rosenblatt, *The Reader* xi). And it was in this study that Rosenblatt saw her
life's work in literature education as unfolding:

> In the concluding pages, I stated the need for a public of readers able
> to "participate fully in the poetic experience"—readers able to provide
> a nurturing, free environment for poets and other artists of the word.
> Their texts possess, I believed, the highest potentialities for bringing
> the whole human personality, as Coleridge had said, "into activity."
> Here already was the germ of an increasingly intense preoccupation
> with the importance, to the arts and to society, of the education of
> readers of literature. (xi)

In one published offshoot of her dissertation, Rosenblatt charted
the compromised artistic course taken by Robert Louis Stevenson.
Bowing to the prudishness of the Victorian English reading public,
Stevenson produced a fiction based in "romance," a region of the

embodied imagination where "the writer need never meet the challenge of a moral issue; in which indeed, to avoid moral choices is an artistic merit" ("The Writer's Dilemma" 204). Such a strategy, while ensuring his financial success, meant that he failed to apply his artistic talents and vision to explore any realm of intimate relations. In this sense Stevenson would be classed with those authors who out of expediency disavow their "artistic freedom." He chose rather to cut himself "off from almost all the most significant and most profound materials of human life, consciously restricting himself to those aspects of experience which were safe precisely because of their lack of moral significance for his time" (207).

Such a denial of will was significant to Rosenblatt because it also denied society those critical voices that could imaginatively embody and survey the ethical landscape, the space within which a community's values are tested, refined, and extended. Without this moral attention, living reduces to a matter of behavior as opposed to responsible conduct. The fundamental conversation between conscience and action is severed when a society's artists are rendered mute. Rosenblatt again suggested the importance of the circumstances that made artistic expression or response possible. Public education, in other words, could help create the necessary audience for literature, an audience that should be open and receptive even as it is critical, able to connect the writer's vision with the reader's private concerns. As Rosenblatt explained,

> The only guarantee against the necessity for the artist's flight
> from the most vital materials of his time is an aggressive public sense
> of the artist's right to tread seemingly dangerous ground, and a willingness on the part of the reading public to have its fundamental prejudices and presumptions challenged. Only under such circumstances
> could we feel sure that art might flourish with complete honesty and
> the writer seek out the materials entirely congenial to his mind and
> talent. (210)

Still, Rosenblatt acknowledged, numerous obstacles block the road to a society where such freedom might exist that institutions and traditions, both public and private, would be continually open to scrutiny.

> Such propitious conditions will be created only when we become conscious of the automatic tendencies of our culture, when we see what
> taboos are imposed upon the artist, what intellectual barriers set up,
> and when we seek to counteract those automatic pressures. Otherwise,
> as we saw in the case of the Victorian attitude toward sex, excess and
> irrationality in one direction will stifle the free play of mind, and
> inevitably bring an equally excessive and irrational reaction. (210)

And though society might never become completely self-critical, citizens need enough self-consciousness to avoid becoming complacent about their tolerance for diversity. For without "a social atmosphere that welcomes challenge," art has difficulty flourishing (211).

Given her unique combination of social and literary concerns, her doctorate in comparative literature, her undergraduate and graduate studies in anthropology,[2] and her experience of teaching undergraduates at Barnard, Rosenblatt was especially well prepared to write a book that would attempt to offer a positive and practical demonstration of literature teaching, rather than the usual negative progressive attack on the existing traditional arrangements that dominated the schools. *Literature as Exploration* contained a deliberate social agenda for teaching literature in the schools, one that had been evolving in Rosenblatt's mind since her editorials at Barnard. Specifically targeted for teachers of adolescents in college and secondary school, the book turned out to be equally appropriate for teachers at all levels.

If an author's stated intentions are to be given any weight, it will pay to mark the words she wrote in her preface to the first edition:

> My aim in this book is to demonstrate that the study of literature can have a very real, and even central, relation to the points of growth in the social and cultural life of a democracy. (ix)

Having tactically deployed the word "democracy," she continued:

> Viewing literature in its relations to the diverse needs of human beings, this book will seek to answer the questions: "How can the experience and study of literature foster a sounder understanding of life and nourish the development of balanced, humane personalities?" "How can the teacher minister to the love of literature, initiate his students into its delights, and at the same time further these broader aims?" (x)

With these questions in mind, an educational proposal would only be appropriate if it included some kind of transactional process that began with the individual student and then had that student participate in sharing and contesting with other students as part of a dialogue of inquiry and interpretation. And although values are the province of literature, how they are understood, finally, depends very much on the way they are evoked and considered.

Like any text, *Literature as Exploration* can, of course, be interpreted from a variety of perspectives. Typically, when Rosenblatt speaks in the following tone, she is seen as offering a universal appeal for the importance of literature as a way of "exploring" and celebrating human experience:

> The literary works that students are urged to read offer not only "literary" values, to use a currently favored abstraction, but also some

approach to life, some image of people working out a common fate, or some assertion that certain kinds of experiences, certain modes of feeling, are valuable. (20)

In turn, passages such as the following are pointed to as revealing her wisdom, with its characteristic "progressive" stamp, as to how literature should be taught in the schools:

A situation conducive to free exchange of ideas by no means represents a passive or negative attitude on the part of the teacher. . . . Certainly, lively, untrammeled discussion bespeaks an admirable educational setting. The fact that the student is articulate and eager to express himself is a wholesome sign. (71, 75)

Finally, when Rosenblatt directs our attention to an educational issue, as in her statement that "the problem that the teacher faces first of all . . . is the creation of a situation favorable to a vital experience of literature" (61), her central lesson is seen as accentuating the teacher's obligation to respect and encourage the individual reading responses of the students.

The alternate interpretation that I am proposing does not deny these emphases; rather, it seeks to establish the social reasons behind her discovery of the reader. Rosenblatt's choice to emphasize "evocation and response" is not based on the results of some independent, "objective" investigation of a reader's processes of reading; instead, she privileges the individual reader *only* within a dynamic social context that fosters the values of a democracy. Indeed it is crucial that we do not lose sight of this word *democracy* in any discussion of Rosenblatt's work, though this is precisely what happened in the revision of the index of *Literature as Exploration*. This key word (and also words such as *freedom* and *character*), although figuring prominently in the index of the 1938 edition, is not listed in the second edition (1968). Similarly, when one looks up "values" in the 1938 edition one finds "in a democracy, 191–263," but under the same word in the later edition, the closest entry is "development in modern society, 164–165." We might question the extent to which this second index in fact represents a "re-reading" (or "mis-reading") of Rosenblatt.[3]

Throughout *Literature as Exploration* Rosenblatt never sees literary training as existing in isolation, but instead stresses that what goes on in the literature classroom involves furthering "the assimilation of habits of thought conducive to social understanding" (22). The entire argument of the book, in fact, centers on the responsibility of the English teacher, who

can play an important part in this process, since the student's social adjustments may be more deeply influenced by what he absorbs through literature than by what he learns through the theoretical materials of the usual social science course. (22)

This inevitably is what can happen in a transactional literature classroom where the teacher is never the sole and dominating reader. For, "when the student has been moved by a work of literature, he will be led to ponder on questions of right or wrong, of admirable or antisocial qualities, of justifiable or unjustifiable actions" (17). The literary work, in other words, concretely embodies the abstractions of other human disciplines and thus provides a direct means for students to entertain considerations of human actions and motives.

What can seem at times a ponderous dwelling on ethics and social values is only Rosenblatt's insistence that democracy is a function of the quality of life and relationships earned from below, not a result of privileges dogmatically dispensed from above. And naturally she fears for the fragility of these social arrangements, which the human temperament seems always on the verge of relinquishing. It is easier to be told what to do, yet if resistance to this urge is not developed early and often in our educational institutions, the risk of externally imposed "solutions" is great:

> Obviously, a rigid set of dogmatic ideas and fixed responses to specific conditions is the worst kind of equipment for the contemporary youth. As soon as actual conditions prove that his passively acquired code is useless or even harmful, he has nothing else to cling to. Having been made dependent upon ready-made props, he will be precipitated into painful insecurity. This kind of insecurity, this craving for some easy, reassuring formula, makes the youth of other countries and sometimes our own a ready prey to those enemies of democracy who hold out the delusive bait of ready-made solutions to all problems. Unprepared to think independently, the young man and woman seek to return to the infantile state in which there is no responsibility to make decisions; they are thus willing to blindly follow some "leader" whose tools and prey they become. (129)

The best educational defense against the "true believer," against the mechanically automated student, is a transactional program of teaching/learning, which reinforces one's faith in one's own judgments, even as these judgments are open to question. This is always the delicate balance, how to keep belief from degenerating into dogma.

The deepest tension that Rosenblatt identifies as animating the American experience is between "voluntarism"[4] and "social determinism."[5] The course of our behaviors can be plotted against the perils of these two shores, as on one occasion we cultivate personal interest and ignore the group and on the next we bow to social constraints and pledge blind allegiance. The danger, Rosenblatt points out, lies in our losing the ways of mediating those forces within any democratic society that would prefer vision from a single angle:

> The individualistic emphasis of our society builds up a frequent reluc-
> tance to see the implications for others of our own actions or to under-
> stand the validity of the needs that motivate other people's actions.
> The fact that the success of the individual must so often be at the
> expense of others places a premium on this kind of blindness. Teachers
> of literature need to take this cultural pressure into account, since it is
> so directly opposed to the attitude of mind they are attempting to fos-
> ter. For literature by its very nature invokes participation in the experi-
> ences of others and comprehension of their goals and aspirations.
> (92–93)

Ideally, Rosenblatt keeps stressing, citizens in a democracy have the convictions and enthusiasms of their own responses, yet are aware of how these responses reflect their affiliation with particular groups. Although democrats know there will be conflicting responses because of these competing groups in society, they are willing to keep an open mind as to these various points of view, and finally are able to nego-tiate meanings and actions that respect both individual diversity and community needs (184–85, 193, 223).

As we know, societies in the past have typically solved the prob-lem of individualism by denying its existence—hierarchies and vari-ous forms of autocracies have dominated in recorded history. So individuals weren't really serving the community, they were serving some kind of master. Democracy on the other hand presents a new range of opportunities, but not without the price of a new set of burdens. Chief among these is the feeling of alienation from the group. Such alienation we often compensate for by exhibiting "other-directed" type behavior, a phenomenon perhaps first described by de Tocqueville. To overcome this tendency to follow authority blindly, individuals must be inspired to have confidence in their own feelings about experience and objects in the world. But after such individuals are turned loose, there also needs to be in place a tradition of conduct for reeling back in these individual responses to some sort of publicly tested consensus. In light of this characteristic dilemma of life in a democracy, Rosenblatt's unique contribution to English education is especially salient: the dialectical method of back and forth mediation between reader and text and then the reach outward to the social context of other readers and other texts.

Further, Rosenblatt's transactional approach to the teaching of literature has important implications for text selection when interper-sonal classroom dialogue is of paramount importance. Writing in 1940, two years after the publication of *Literature as Exploration*, Rosenblatt argued for a balance between contemporary works and "the classics." Wishing to avoid "the feeling that literature is something remote, academic, something to be approached with all the decorum of the classroom," she asserts that judgment only grows through use—in a democracy it "cannot be legislated [or] imparted from above." Individuals must continually experience for themselves and be responsible for their own reflections.

> The development of the power to discriminate, to accept what is good and to reject what is valueless in literature and in life, is frustrated by any view which sets up a body of works as "timeless classics," hence passively to be accepted as *ipso facto* valuable, without the necessary struggle to perceive values in terms of life and literature as the student himself experiences them. ("Moderns" 103)

In the transactional classroom, modern works figure centrally. Not only do they confront students with artistic representations of the basic problems of living, they also encourage independence in matters of valuation since questions regarding the worth of a work remain open. As Rosenblatt suggests, "Not from the works in themselves, but from lively interaction with them, may flower heightened sensitivities, and powers of judgment based on an ever more human scale of values" (109).

Yet the pattern of reading behaviors, of the "lively interaction," is not objective or preexistent in a scientific sense; rather, these behaviors grow out of a set of socially constructed values—namely, how citizens in the American democracy *ought* to act if we are to continue this shared experiment of *rational* development. But this is where the confusion comes in. Academics narrowly concerned with literature, with the psychological dynamics of response or isolated aesthetic issues, choose to ignore the social project for the reading of literature that Rosenblatt has launched. Instead they continue with "objective" research trying to determine precisely the features and parameters of their models of reading. In doing so they provoke endless quarrels over what is the "real" transactional model. When reader-response critics attempt to be totally descriptive (whether of their own processes of reading or of someone else's) what they forget is that the construct itself is finally prescriptive. In other words, the research goal here can never be to discover the "natural" process of interpretation and any argument about whether the transactional model is sufficiently accurate in a descriptive sense misses the point. Indeed, the whole history of literacy is one of constraint and liberation. Only recently has it even occurred to people to emphasize their "personal" connection with the text they were reading, let alone that such a connection might figure in the social scheme of things (Graff 265,

275–76, 315). Further, if we lived under a different set of social values, such as the absolute subordination of the self to the family that is characteristic of the East, our research and educational agenda would not be the same. Transactionalism is not for all societies, and indeed the different sides in the "reader-response" debates reflect not "reality" but alternate "socially constructed" experiences and traditions.

The transactional model does, of course, describe how many people in contemporary times seem to go about reading—it has construct validity. Indeed, it settles the contest over how much "meaning" resides in the reader and how much is text-governed by revealing such arguments to be futile exercises in the first place, since neither category exists in isolation of the other. Such enervating, and false, dilemmas, including outlandish claims as "the words on the page offer no constraints to interpretation," only come about when the context of social vision—democracy in this case—is forgotten or conveniently ignored. When we examine phenomena, we tend to have a synchronic perspective, and thus we frequently forget that the phenomenon came from someplace, has a history that is the result of certain value choices. If we try to look at the reader/text relationship as a stationary absolute, we ignore that the relationship is an artifact of a particular set of socially constituted values. It's never just reader/text/poem, but readers testing readings in a public arena and then modifying accordingly—the essence of the democratic process. With respect to the interpretive maneuver, it's the individual as part of a social game and the kinds of character and behavior this engenders that's important, not any actual spoils of victory (some absolutely determined "meaning"). For what matters, Rosenblatt demonstrates over and over, is the balance or moderation that must be reinforced as part of the education of the young, as part of their coming to terms with the collaborative role of the text. And what better way than through the reading of literature, which yokes the self with the group by beginning with the wellsprings of the individual reader and ending with the dynamics of public validation, including the respective cycles of consensus and change.

Reader-response criticism that stops short of dialogue is not worthy of the name; it is something other than education for democracy. But critics and teachers get nervous when talk shifts to citizenship, democracy, or character development, so they retreat to the aesthetic back alleys of individual readings.[6] Because Rosenblatt never wants to lose sight of our need for a verifying community to participate in, one that serves as an anchoring referent point for our readings, she separates herself from Holland and the other "egocentric" reader-response approaches to literature (*The Reader* xiii; see also "The Transactional

Theory"). On the other hand, it seems appropriate to ask to what extent other critics in the reader-response domain—say someone like Wolfgang Iser, perhaps the leading Reception theorist—share a common agenda with Rosenblatt, since on the surface at least their work appears to be similarly engaged, even if there are disagreements as to specific features of the reading act. Yet despite the fact that both have long concentrated on the reader and the reader's processes of reading, one resides in the fiction of the compartmentalized individual, an "implied reader" dominated by the conditions of *indeterminacy* provided by the text, while the other manifests a concern for the reader in a dynamic social matrix, one which forms the space wherein individual responses and interpretations emerge and evolve. Iser, in other words, at most offers the reader a dyadic conversation with an author and in doing so ignores the process of group "problem solving." In contrast, Rosenblatt sees such group effort as supportive of individual human agency. Indeed it characterizes reading in nonhierarchial, democratic classrooms where students are continually part of the circle of praxis, moving from understanding to decision to action.

One reason Rosenblatt refuses to see reading and a literary education in isolation lies in her awareness of the forces inimical to the democratic traditions in America. In her remarkable essay on Whitman's *Democratic Vistas,* published in 1978, the same year as *The Reader, the Text, the Poem,* Rosenblatt carries forward her preoccupation with the kind of social relations required to mediate American pluralism successfully. Consistent with the points she has been driving home since her 1923 editorials—the need through public forums for individuals to assert their unique positions and yet simultaneously to listen to and try to understand the beliefs of other groups—in this essay, she squarely faces the opportunities and dilemmas of democracy. While in 1923 she was promoting communication among the cliques surrounding her at Barnard, in 1978 she is still trying to encourage, with Whitmanesque largess, a rational conversation across the ethnic mixtures that make up America. Specifically, Rosenblatt addresses the question: "Is there room for the new ethnicity in Whitman's view of the state as an aggregate whose prime justification is that it creates the stable environment within which the individual can freely and fully develop?" (197). If we are to maintain the creative tension of our culture, we must always be clear what it is competing against and how literature itself embodies a range of conflicting values:

> . . . although Whitman accepts the perennial, universal elements derived from earlier literatures, he again and again reminds us that these older cultures embody much that is alien to, and inimical to, the ideal of democracy. Thus, he enjoins upon us an active selectivity, a

testing, a rejection of all derived from our ancestry that is alien to the special needs of a free society, all that cramps and confines the individual.

Through this aspect of his vision Whitman warns us against a
possible danger in the new ethnicity, the danger that membership in
the group may impose its own kind of rigid conformity upon the
individual. (199)

The transactional teaching of literature becomes a primary way of
protecting against the dangers of the new ethnicity, for by beginning
with an individual reader's response the teacher establishes a countervailing force to work against the later constraining of interpretation by
the group as a whole. If students are to experience the entire cycle of
interpretation, it is important that the teacher not immediately con-
taminate or direct students toward preordained answers or meanings.

This need for the teacher to create a community that fosters individuality, not stifles it, Rosenblatt finds growing out of "Whitman's
other fundamental principle of democracy":

> . . . the need for unity, for an American identity that, though com-
> posite, pluralistic, including multitudes, still creates the solidarity
> which makes possible the freedom of each segment, and of each indi-
> vidual within it. (201)

Rosenblatt is, of course, aware of how much and how often we fall
short of the goals of democracy in our classroom, but she maintains
her spirit of optimism in closing her essay:

> Whitman can be listened to because he, too, looked squarely at the
> distortions and defections of the society about him, and nevertheless
> could predict the ability of our democratic institutions to surmount
> them, to persist, and to advance. His vistas extend far beyond the cen-
> tury that separates us from him. . . . Whitman calls equally on each of
> us to be ready to listen to those who, sharing his faith in the demo-
> cratic idea, and refusing either complacency or despair, would seek to
> inspire us to create the symphony of a society of free, varied, mutually
> respecting men and women. (203–4)

This optimism characterizes an American faith in progress and the
future, a feeling that we are part of an experiment that is continually
unfolding. As Whitman spoke prophetically: "[Democracy] is a great
word, whose history, I suppose, remains unwritten, because that
history has yet to be enacted" (1157). Typically, Rosenblatt expresses
this faith in ways such as, "There is the recurrent theme of aspiration
toward an ever more democratic and humane way of life" (*Literature*
270). In the light of this kind of aspiration, her vision for literature
education in a democracy remains steadfast: it must inevitably influence the character patterns citizens will need to exhibit if the possibilities of democracy are to continue.

In *Democratic Vistas* Rosenblatt found an inspiring formulation of her transactional view of the reading process, and used it to conclude *The Reader, the Text, the Poem.*

> Books are to be called for, and supplied, on the assumption that the process of reading is not a half sleep, but, in the highest sense, an exercise, a gymnast's struggle; that the reader is to do something for himself, must be on the alert, must himself or herself construct indeed the poem, argument, history, metaphysical essay—the text furnishing the hints, the clue, the start or framework. Not the book needs so much to be the complete thing, but the reader of the book does. That were to make a nation of supple and athletic minds, well trained, intuitive, used to depend on themselves, and not on a few coteries of writers. (175)

In the essay on Whitman we would naturally expect Rosenblatt's social agenda to be manifest. Yet even in two of her most recent articles, which address specific and localized issues regarding her transactional model of reading, these themes continue to predominate. In "Viewpoints: Transaction Versus Interaction—A Terminological Rescue Operation," she again affirms her holistic view of reading.

> Instead of breaking the subject matter into fragments in advance of inquiry, the observer, the observing, and the observed were to be seen as aspects of a total situation. . . . Recent developments in ecology have made this way of thinking clearer to many people. *Transaction,* then, designates an ongoing process in which the elements or parts are seen as aspects or phases of a total situation. (98)

She defends her use of the word "transaction" by locating a 1460 OED usage—"*Roman and Civil law:* The adjustment of a dispute between parties by mutual concession; compromise"—and concludes that "from the very beginning evidently, transaction carried overtones of mutuality, a blending of components" (98). Then she emphasizes that reading does not exist outside of historical time and circumstances but resides "in a particular social and cultural setting, and as part of the ongoing life of the individual and the group" (100). Consistently, she hammers home this thesis:

> *Literature as Exploration* underlines the importance of seeing any reading event in its personal, social, cultural matrix. Not only what the reader brings to the transaction from past experience with life and language, but also the socially molded circumstances and purpose of the reading, provide the setting for the act of symbolization. The reading event should be seen in its total matrix. (104)

Finally, after discussing what her model implies for research, especially for studies carried out under the new ethnographic paradigm,

Rosenblatt again asserts the primacy of the social context for her work: "The transactional theory, with its sense of the individual reader and the individual text as bearers of culture creating new cultural events in unique transactions provides a critical framework" (106).

Similarly, in *Writing and Reading: The Transactional Theory*, published in 1988 by the Center for the Study of Reading, Rosenblatt bases her consideration of the reciprocity of reading and composing on the fact that language in whatever mode does not "function in isolation, but always in particular verbal, personal, and social contexts" (3). As she continues, she stresses that personal meanings evolve out of social dialogue:

> The individual's share in the language, then, is that part, or set of features, of the public system that has been internalized in the individual's experiences with words in life situations. The residue of such transactions in particular natural and social contexts constitutes a kind of linguistic-experiential reservoir. Embodying our funded assumptions, attitudes, and expectations about the world—and about language—this inner capital is all that each of us has to start from in speaking, listening, writing, and reading. We make meaning, we make sense of a new situation or transaction, by applying, reorganizing, revising, or extending elements drawn from, selected from, our personal linguistic experiential reservoir. (3)

On the reading side of the equation, after noting her distinction between efferent and aesthetic reading stances and the mixing of private and public meanings in each case, she uncovers a crucial reason why a broad-based reading of literature is foundational to a democratic society: "Someone else can read a text efferently for us, and acceptably paraphrase it. No one else can read aesthetically, that is, experience the evocation of, a literary work of art for us" (6). Literary texts are central to education for democracy because they affirm and confirm, through the personal acts of aesthetic evocation that are necessary to access them, the uniqueness of the *individual* even while insisting that such acts inevitably relate to sharing and participation in the action of a larger community—because literature is never merely knowledge or propaganda, one reader can never be substituted for another. And it is within this community, when we make our underlying assumptions explicit, that we come to understand "the tacit sources of disagreement. Hence the possibility of change and of revision of the criteria. Such self-awareness on the part of readers can also foster communication across social, cultural, and historical differences between reader and author, and among readers" (6–7).[7]

Rosenblatt's social agenda for the reading of literature continues to place her outside of traditional academic literary concerns even with the rise of reader-response criticism, because she has refused to separate acts of interpretation from their social implications. As Jane Tompkins argues in her provocative analysis, the focus of reader-response criticism has for the most part only been an excuse for a new formalism, not a campaign for emphasizing how words are marshalled by authors to bring about specific social effects on readers. As Tompkins elaborates:

> Literature [during the Renaissance] exists in order to serve its clientele and is subject to the audience's judgment. In the modern period, on the other hand, the work is not written for a known constituency, nor is it intended to have such well-defined results. Instead of moving the audience and bringing pressure to bear on the world, the work is thought to present another separate and more perfect world, which the flawed reader must labor to appropriate. The work is not a gesture in a social situation, or an ideal model for human behavior, but an interplay of formal and thematic properties to be penetrated by the critic's mind. (210)

When both the reading and teaching of literature are disconnected from any vital relationship with how the forms of social life in a democracy are to be determined, "the art product loses its power to influence public opinion on matters of national importance" (213). In tracing the history of literature's declining influence, from the ancients to the present time, Tompkins sees the cultivation of the individual in splendid isolation, rather than in constant dialogue with others. For instance, the literature of feeling—sentimental and Gothic novels or the poetry of sensibility—can be viewed as having been "designed to give the reader certain kinds of emotional experience rather than to mold character or guide behavior, and is aimed at the psychic life of individuals rather than at collective standards of judgment on public issues" (215). By shifting the reader's attention from a course of action to "meaning" divination, most modern literary theorizing has created a safe zone away from any practical concerns regarding life in a democracy.

Not surprisingly, Tompkins herself, despite her radical position, is still steeped in a literary critical tradition that has found it convenient to ignore Rosenblatt's message. Rather than representing her with an essay in the collection *Reader-Response Criticism*, Tompkins only provides an afterthought footnote in her introduction:

> Louise Rosenblatt deserves to be recognized as the first among the present generation of critics in this country to describe empirically the way the reader's reactions to a poem are responsible for any subsequent interpretation of it. Her work . . . raise[s] issues central to the debates that have arisen since. (xxvi)

Then, in her essay that concludes the collection, Tompkins uncritically lumps Rosenblatt with Fish and Holland when she remarks, "For although reader-oriented critics speak of the 'poem as event' and of 'literature as experience,' meaning is still for them the object of the critical act" (206). This reference to Rosenblatt's *College English* article, "The Poem as Event," fails to distinguish the context that would clearly separate her from these other critics, namely that there are important pedagogical consequences for a democracy when a student is not encouraged to join in the evocation and interpretation of the poem. Critics like Holland and Bleich do, of course, permit students the opportunity to evoke and interpret; however, their extreme focus on the reader's identity pattern serves to retard the more complete reading cycle that the transactional model represents, and thus the student is frequently left with no bridge to the social consequences of a "reading" (see "The Transactional Theory").

Tompkins's essay also foreshadows the triumph of the "cultural critics" whose approach Rosenblatt's own work both anticipated and transcended. With the sociopolitical emphasis that has emerged in the current post-deconstructionist phase of criticism, it is popular (especially among Marxists) to use the techniques of reading to disclose underlying assumptions, the network of ideological constraints that determine both a reader's reading and being. Such a maneuver, however, is seldom innocent or neutral; its main interest is attacking "Western" ideology. Rosenblatt's anthropological background and the frequency with which, in *Literature as Exploration*, she refers students to the social, moral, and psychological assumptions that are implicit and taken for granted in the literary work as experienced might initially lead us to include her with this group of critics. But there is a crucial difference: Rosenblatt has never fostered the notion that the individual is solely created, "written," by the culture, by its codes and conventions. Unlike those critics who want "disclosure" to paint a negative picture of "Western" values, values which they see as subjugating individuals to subservience under capitalism, she insists on helping students to *discriminate* between what should be rejected and what should be retained and strengthened. This kind of critical discrimination requires, of course, some set of values, in this instance the values of democracy:

> Any system of values can be scrutinized in terms of its consequences for human life. Any form of conduct, any social mechanism, any custom or institution, should be measured in terms of its actual effect on the individual personalities that make up the society. To use the culturally sanctioned terminology, every human being is entitled to "life, liberty, and the pursuit of happiness." . . . This rests upon the belief in the fundamental dignity and worth of the human being. It sets up

the well-being and fulfillment of the individual in opposition to any abstractions for which might be claimed a superior reality or value such as the Elect, the Superman, the Proletariat, the Nation, the Race, or the State. This basic postulate of value is obviously one that receives support from many elements present in our cultural heritage. Implicit in various religious philosophies or in the democratic philosophy, it applies not only to our political but also to our social and economic life. (*Literature* 165–66; see also "Language" 72–74)

Rosenblatt answers the "cultural critics," who justify their covert indoctrination of antidemocratic, anti-American attitudes by insisting that all teaching ultimately indoctrinates political attitudes, when in her writings she challenges us to openly "indoctrinate" the basic concepts of a democratic system. This avowed presentation of democratic principles helps to protect students from covert indoctrination of completely negative attitudes toward our society and to preserve students' freedom to make up their own minds about what to accept and what to reject. Further, it sees literature study as part of a broader movement to foster constructive social transformation, while avoiding the "alienation" and antihuman values unwittingly invited by the "cultural critics."

As I hope is now evident, the intention and force behind Rosenblatt's ideas are most starkly revealed when she addresses broad cultural/social issues in order to provide a context for dwelling on specific problems of reading and the teaching of literature. What we read in such passages, beginning with her editorials at Barnard in 1923, allows us to see a consistent picture of her lifelong social vision and activism. Her readers are generally misled if they think they can understand the meaning and significance of her work by only concentrating on "objective" considerations of the reading act. While the interpretive and aesthetic processes of individual readers have been a central preoccupation of hers, this inquiry has always been in the service of her social/educational mission, one that has focused on her fundamental concern for how best to characterize and shape the citizenship roles required to further the unique democratic experiment that continues to take place on American shores. Her guiding question has consistently remained: "To what extent . . . is . . . literary study in the schools contributing to the persistent hold of habits of thought and images of behavior no longer appropriate to our present-day knowledge and our aspirations for a more democratic way of life?" ("Moderns" 106).

Teachers of English, Rosenblatt keeps reminding us, can contribute in an important way to creating the character of future citizens. They can model and encourage a social script for students who in turn must become members of a larger society, which, because it will never have all the answers, depends on rational discourse as the basis for decision making and action taking. This is a society continually trying to understand how it is that an individual's freedom and possibilities are most expanded when there is a creative balance between self and group. In this sense Rosenblatt's seminal contribution to English education derives from her social concerns as they are translated into an agenda for individual readers. Unfortunately, a narrow research focus on "reader response" has deflected us from recognizing both the greatness of her work and its peculiarly American character. For as she has declared,

> If we only do justice to the potentialities inherent in literature itself, we can make a vital social contribution. As the student vicariously shares through literature the emotions and aspirations of other human beings, he can gain heightened sensitivity to the needs and problems of others remote from him in temperament, in space, or in social environment; he can develop a greater imaginative capacity to grasp the meaning of abstract laws or political and social theories for actual human lives. Such sensitivity and imagination are part of the indispensable equipment of the citizen of a democracy. (*Literature* 274)

Rosenblatt's theory, like the democratic enterprise itself, seeks the benefits of the relationship that grows out of the tension between freedom and discipline. While other political configurations would deny this tension by submerging the "self" in hierarchical shackles, it is the American genius to try to respect the diversity of minority rights and views even as these appear to threaten the hegemony of dominant values. If such an American clearinghouse is to continue, there must be citizens with sufficient confidence to value and proclaim their own interpretations even as they tolerate and rationally discriminate among the interpretations of others. And further, in dialogue, such citizens must be willing to keep reexamining their own structures in the light of new and rational information. The transactional model of reading literature, the lived-through experience of the text, provides a self-renewing framework for realizing this goal.

Notes

1. "I was amazed to read your account of the reports of the Dewey and Kilpatrick lectures in the *Bulletin*. I have no recollection of hearing either. My recollections of Dewey date back to the thirties, but not before. Perhaps this documents the fact that my interest in teaching (rather than general social theory) dates from the time when I started teaching. Before then, I took what went on in classrooms pretty much for granted." (letter from Rosenblatt to the author, January 12, 1989)

2. As early as her sophomore year at Barnard, Rosenblatt was studying anthropology in a course taught by Franz Boas.

3. "Sidney Ratner did the first index. Noble and Noble had someone do the second—without any ideological 'influence,' but simply an impersonal indexer, I suspect." (letter from Rosenblatt to the author, January 12, 1989)

4. "This view is based on the idea that any behavior can be interpreted as having been willed by the actor. The assumption is that in all situations the individual is free to accept or reject various modes of behavior" (144).

5. ". . . the individual is merely a kind of automaton entirely at the mercy of external pressures" (155).

6. Of course, it is important to emphasize here that Rosenblatt herself never means to imply any mechanistic notion of influence. As she remarks in *Literature as Exploration*, "This view of literature study is completely alien to the old notion of 'character building through literature,' which consisted in giving the student, without any regard for his own needs and state of mind, a series of models of behavior to imitate. Equally unacceptable are attempts to treat literature as a body of documents that may be brought forth to illustrate various subtopics under the heading of human relations. Lists of books dealing with topics such as family, war, labor relations—let alone such moralistic topics as noble characters or great deeds of the past—will not in themselves do the job that has been formulated in this book" (247).

7. It is interesting to note that in this article Rosenblatt also speaks directly to the central role of public speaking in developing readers and writers: "In a favorable educational environment, speech is a vital ingredient. Its importance in the individual's acquisition of a linguistic/experiential capital is clear. Moreover, it can be an extremely important medium in the classroom. Interchange, dialogue, between teacher and students and among students, can foster growth and cross-fertilization in both the reading and writing processes. Such transactions can help students to develop metalinguistic insights in a highly personal and, hence, instructive way. The aim should be, not simple 'correct' or 'excellent' performance, but metalinguistic understanding of skills and conventions in meaningful contexts" (13).

Works Cited

Graff, Harvey J. *The Legacies of Literacy: Continuities and Contradictions in Western Culture and Society.* Bloomington: Indiana UP, 1987.

Rosenblatt, Louise. "Language, Literature, and Values." *Language, Schooling, and Society.* Ed. Stephen N. Tchudi. Portsmouth, NH: Boynton/Cook, 1985. 64–80.

———. *Literature as Exploration.* 1938. Rev. ed. New York: Noble and Noble, 1968.

———. "Moderns Among Masterpieces." *English Leaflet* 39 (1940): 98–110.

———. "The Poem as Event." *College English* 26 (1964): 123–28.

————. *The Reader, the Text, the Poem: The Transactional Theory of the Literary Work*. Carbondale: Southern Illinois UP, 1978.

————. "The Transactional Theory of the Literary Work: Implications for Research." *Researching Response to Literature and the Teaching of Literature*. Ed. Charles Cooper. Norwood, NJ: Ablex Press, 1985.

————. "Viewpoints: Transaction Versus Interaction—A Terminological Rescue Operation." *Research in the Teaching of English* 19 (1985): 96–107.

————. "Whitman's *Democratic Vistas* and the New 'Ethnicity.' " *Yale Review* (Winter 1978): 187–204.

————. "The Writer's Dilemma: A Case History and a Critique." *International Journal of Ethics* 46 (1936): 195–211.

————. *Writing and Reading: The Transactional Theory*. Technical Report No. 416. Urbana-Champaign: Center for the Study of Reading, U of Illinois, 1988. 1–17.

Tompkins, Jane P., ed. *Reader-Response Criticism: From Formalism to Post-Structuralism*. Baltimore: John Hopkins UP, 1980.

Whitman, Walt. "Democratic Vistas." *Major American Writers*. Ed. Howard Mumford Jones, Ernest E. Leisy, Richard M. Ludwig. 3rd ed. New York: Harcourt, Brace and Co., 1952. 1150–68.

3

On Behalf of Pedagogy

Mariolina Salvatori

> Pedagogy always echoes epistemology: the way we teach reflects
> the conception we have of what knowledge is and does, the way
> we think about thinking.
>
> Ann E. Berthoff, *The Making of Meaning*

In his foreword to the third edition of *Literature as Exploration* (1976),
Alan Purves writes: "The nearly forty years since the first publication
of *Literature as Exploration* have seen a number of shifts in literary
theory and the practice of teaching literature in schools and colleges in
the United States. Through these permutations, Louise Rosenblatt's
magnificent discussion of the relationship between reader and literary
work has remained the major document on that subject. Critical and
pedagogical theory being two fields noticeably subject to vicissitudes,
one might be surprised that a book that bridges the two would have
so long a life" (iii).

Indeed, I agree with Purves, one of the strengths of *Literature as
Exploration*, and in fact its most significant feature, is the consistent
integration of theory and practice, both in terms of what the text
proposes and of how that is enacted.[1] One might say, following Ann
E. Berthoff, that Rosenblatt's work lucidly demonstrates that theory is
not the antithesis of practice, and in fact it serves an authentic purpose
because it is continually brought into relationship with practice so that
each informs the other. Yet, I will suggest, possibly because critical
and pedagogical theories, for complex historical, ideological, and
institutional reasons have been and still largely continue to be conceived as separate from, if not in opposition to, one another, this

47

integration—or, more accurately, transaction—has not been sufficiently acknowledged. I want to address myself to a particular manifestation of this lack of acknowledgment because I see it as a
nonaccidental omission that needs to be recognized and analyzed as
both a symptom and a cause of unnecessary and deleterious divisions
in the discipline of English studies.

Susan R. Suleiman and Inge Crosman's *The Reader in the Text:
Essays on Audience and Interpretation* and Elizabeth Freund's *The Return
of the Reader* are valuable and scholarly contributions to the current and
healthy investigation of the reading process. As far as Louise Rosenblatt's "pioneering work" in this field is concerned, however, both
texts make a similar gesture: as they acknowledge Rosenblatt's contribution, they relegate it to a marginal position.

At the very end of her excellent introduction to *The Reader in the
Text*, Susan R. Suleiman quite candidly states:

> To my regret, Louise M. Rosenblatt's pioneering work in the field of
> subjective criticism came to my attention only after this essay was in
> proof. A footnote will therefore have to replace the discussion her
> work deserved in an earlier section. Rosenblatt's book, *Literature as
> Exploration* (New York: 1938), challenged the objectivist assumptions of
> the New Criticism as they affected the teaching of literature in high
> schools and colleges. Rosenblatt first proposed the term *transaction* to
> designate the relationship between text and reader (*Literature as Explo-
> ration*, paperback edition, p. 27). Although her work was influential
> among those most concerned with questions of pedagogy, its relevance
> for literary theory was recognized only recently, when it was rediscov-
> ered by Bleich and others. (45n)

As she acknowledges the originality and longevity of Rosenblatt's
influence, Suleiman indirectly offers a clue for her oversight: Rosenblatt's work exercised its influence on "those most concerned with
questions of pedagogy."

A more recent survey/interpretation of reader-response theories
repeats the same move. In 1987, Elizabeth Freund (*The Return of the
Reader*) acknowledges the "historical and pragmatic" significance of
Rosenblatt's work, but covers it, together with Slatoff's work, in a
footnote.[2]

Suleiman's and Freund's gestures are marked by a peculiar dou-
bleness: they are, simultaneously, a gesture of inclusion and exclusion. Because this gesture can be read as a reenactment of the historical
and institutional lack of transaction between those most concerned
with questions of pedagogy and those most concerned with literary
theory, such a gesture can unwittingly reinscribe and perpetuate the
marginal position of pedagogy in our profession as it disseminates a
reductive view of its function and consequently of its practitioners.[3]

L as E was indeed addressed to those most *concerned* with pedagogy. But to adduce this as the reason why its influence did not extend to the field of literary theory is to perpetuate the assumption that pedagogy has been and remains the exclusive concern of elementary and high school teachers or, within colleges and universities, of composition faculty and literature faculty who devote themselves "essentially" to teaching at the expense of research and publishing.[4] It is also not to acknowledge that *L as E* proposes and illustrates a radical and unsettling reconceptualization of pedagogy—one that constructs the classroom as the site for theory and practice to face and to interrogate each other, cogently and relentlessly, so that each may test and expose its own as well as the other's gaps, contradictions, and need for revision. It is from within this reconceptualization of pedagogy that I wish to offer a reading of Rosenblatt's work. Specifically, I want to analyze a particular set of changes that mark an important difference between the 1938 and the 1968 version of *L as E*. Disturbing a commonly accepted hierarchy of influence (theory directs/determines practice), I wish to argue that Rosenblatt's revision of her theory of reading was reciprocally directed/determined by her practice as a teacher.

In the Preface to the third edition of *Literature as Exploration* (1976), Rosenblatt argues that "research in reading, no matter what else it has demonstrated, has found the teacher to be a most important—perhaps *the* most important—factor in the educational process" (xi). In the paragraph from which I have excerpted this quotation, Rosenblatt is addressing herself to the issue of teachers' participation—both in terms of their having something to say about curricular reforms and of their having the appropriate training to carry them through. In the larger context of her work, she is addressing the issue of a teacher's participation in and responsibility for preparing students for life.[5] But, as readers often do, I want to use this quotation to make a different point—a point about Rosenblatt the theorist practitioner, that is, Rosenblatt the pedagogist.

Before writing the first version of her book, Rosenblatt had written a critique of the "art for art's sake" movement. As I read, in the prefaces to her two major works and in her various articles, her descriptions of her cultural formation, particularly her interest in and study of the social sciences—sociology and anthropology especially— I cannot help but infer that the ways of knowing of these disciplines both made possible and necessitated her critique, a critique that called for an artist's *social* responsibility and accountability. Her writing of *L'Idée de l'art pour l'art* in 1931 was itself the responsible enactment of a critic's social role. But an even greater act of responsibility was her subsequent extension of that critique into a critique of those classroom

practices that would invalidate or pay lip service to a student's experience of a literary text. The result of that critique was *Literature as
Exploration*. Her focusing the critical attention on the student necessitated that she test, revise, *re*theorize her theory of reading so that it
could account for and grant authority to the ways in which all readers,
not only expert readers and literary critics, make meaning.

When she was chosen by the Commission on Human Relations to
represent and to enact a way of teaching literature that would enforce
the commission's commitment to promoting "social understanding"
through "literary appreciation" (1938, xi), Rosenblatt began, I believe,
where she was later to claim teachers and students should begin. She
began the exploration that would produce her work with an exploration of, a look inward to, her own experience. She reflected on the
shaping influences on her intellectual life. She interrogated her relationship to Boas and Mead, Santayana and Dewey, Richards and
James, and others. And having realized how her own way of thinking
had structured, and been structured by, her understanding of their
ways of thinking, she urged teachers to focus on and to learn to make
manifest the intricate web of influences that shaped their own and
their students' understanding. Thus, she argued for the fundamental
similarity between experienced and inexperienced readers' ways of
thinking.

Since the very beginning, central to her pedagogy was an understanding of the act of reading as an analogue for the act of knowing
that tried to take into account the reciprocally transforming relation
between a reader and a text, a knower and a known (or knowable) as
well as the influence of the various psychological, social, and historical forces affecting readers' ways of thinking. In the first formulation
of her theory, the key term she used to describe her novel conceptualization of reading was *interaction*. But this term did not quite serve her
purposes; in fact, I believe, it curtailed the power of the theory of
reading she was in the process of formulating and invalidated the
teaching practices she advocated. *Transaction*, as a term (and as a *fully*
articulated concept), was not yet available to her. As she has repeatedly pointed out, the term was first proposed by Dewey and Bentley
in 1949. She adopted the term for the revised edition of *L as E* (1968),
but she introduced it, as we shall see, almost as an afterthought. In
the preface to the revised edition she claimed to have "been diffident
about making substantial changes in [the] general pattern, despite
considerable revision in *presentation* and *illustrative materials*" (vii,
emphases mine).

On behalf of pedagogy, I dare disagree with Rosenblatt herself,
and I wish to argue that her adoption of the term *transaction* made it
possible for her to transform in fundamental and important ways her

theory of reading in accordance with the acts of reading she thought the students she was teaching did and could perform. Let me highlight some of those changes.[6]

In the Preface to the First Edition, for example, Rosenblatt suggests some of the questions that teachers need to ask of their theory and practice so they can make their teaching of literature an activity that honors the "sense of literature as first of all a form of art" (v) while at the same time transforming it into something that connects with readers'/students' lives. The questions that as a theorist and teacher she posed and tried to answer were

> How can *the experience and study of literature foster* a sounder understanding of life and *nourish* the development of balanced, humane personalities?

> How can the teacher *minister to* the love of literature, *initiate his students into* its delights, and at the same time *further* these broader aims? (v)

The task facing Rosenblatt at the time was to propose a method that would avoid "on the one hand, the tendency to treat literary works merely as sociological documents or moral tracts, on the other, the 'purely aesthetic' point of view" (v–vi). But she was also faced, I imagine, with the delicate task of following the commission's directives toward fostering "appreciation" at the same time that she was undertaking a theoretical critique of "appreciation."[7] The metaphor for reading she suggested—one that would balance and reintegrate such extremes into a "responsible" appreciation of a literary text, and that would avoid the trap of passive absorption—was *exploration*. In this process, she stated, "the reader counts *at least* as much as the book or poem itself" (vi). In so far as her book called for a teacher's responsibility to foster this exploration, she urged reflection on "the habits of mind, the general approach to other people and to life, the fundamental concepts about human nature and society, that are engendered by the experience and study of literary works" (vii). For this reflection to be made possible, she argued,

> we need to find out what happens when specific human beings, with their interests and anxieties, *participate* in the emotional and intellectual life that *books make possible*. We need to know what human insight, what knowledge, what habits of mind, will enable our students to attain ever richer literary satisfactions, and to derive from them the equipment to embark on increasingly fruitful explorations of literature—and of life. (vii)

Extending the Progressivist tradition to the teaching of literature in high schools and colleges, Rosenblatt then, long before it became again popular and imperative to do so, was arguing for making the student the agent, the focus, the means and the end of instruction.

Long before the dissemination of Freire's influence made it for many an almost tacit assumption, she was urging teachers to begin with their students, and to approach students' work as a text worthy of sustained critical inquiry. The term *interaction*, however, and the conceptualization of the method of reading that the term represented, inevitably seemed to tilt the balance, however slightly, in favor of the text, the teacher, the author's authority. *Interaction* structured the role of the teacher as one who *ministers to, initiates, furthers,* and the role of the reader/student as counting *at least as much as* the book or poem itself, since the reader at most *participates* in the emotional and intellectual life they make possible. Moreover *art* was recognized as having a "multiplicity of powers," and *in books* was located the spring of "emotional and intellectual life," the source of nourishment that can lead to "the development of balanced, humane personalities" (v).

In the Preface to the Revised Edition (1968), there is no mention of the term and the concept of *transaction*. Reading is again described as a *relationship* between text and student. However, the role Rosenblatt now assigns to the teacher is neither to minister to nor to initiate, but rather to guide "students to responsible reading" and to acknowledge that "it is essential to develop programs relevant to what students bring to the printed page" (vii–viii). Here, read in light of the main text it prefaces, and of some of the changes therein, *relationship* is a synonym for *transaction*.

A comparison of the first paragraph of chapter 1, "The Challenge of Literature," in the 1938 and 1968 versions, foregrounds certain differences that are essential to my argument.

> In an unsettled world, our *schools and colleges are confronted with the demand that they prepare the student directly for living. He must be helped to develop* the intellectual and emotional capacities for a happy and socially useful life. *He must be given* the knowledge, the habits, the flexibility, that will enable him to meet unprecedented and unpredictable problems. *He needs to understand himself;* he needs to work out harmonious relationships with other people. Above all, he must achieve some philosophy, some inner center from which to view in perspective the shifting society about him; he will influence for good or ill its future development. To have pragmatic value, any knowledge about man and society that school can give him must be assimilated into the stream of his actual life. (1938, 3)

> In a turbulent age, our schools and colleges *must prepare the student to meet* unprecedented and unpredictable problems. *He needs to understand himself;* he needs to work out harmonious relationships with other people. He must achieve a philosophy, an inner center from which to view in perspective the shifting society about him; he will influence for good or ill its future development. Any knowledge

about man and society that schools can give him should be assimilated into the stream of his actual life. (1968, 3)

It could be argued that the differences in these two passages are superficial or the result of a more mature writer's handling of prose. To do so, however, would be to undermine their nexus with the theory of reading and the revision of the theory that demanded them. In the second edition, more sharply than in the first, the human picture in the center of attention is a student *initiating* an understanding of himself, of society, and of himself in relationship to society, rather than of a student *being initiated* ("he must be helped to develop," "he must be given the knowledge") into such understanding by the teacher. In light of what has been deleted out of the second edition, the force of such sentences as "He needs to understand himself; he needs to work out harmonious relationships . . . He must achieve a philosophy . . . " makes the student the agent of change.

In so far as the study of literary works can prepare the student "to meet unprecedented and unpredictable problems," that study must reinforce, *not undermine,* a student's sense of agency. This awareness, at work, with greater clarity, in the second edition than in the first, can be construed to be the driving force for the following remarkable revision:

> *The novel or poem or play exists, after all, only in interactions with specific minds.* The reading of any work of literature is, of necessity, an individual and unique occurrence involving the mind and emotions of some particular reader. We may generalize about similarities among such interactions, but we cannot evade the realization that there are actually only innumerable separate responses to individual works of art. (1938, 32)

> *A novel or poem or play remains merely inkspots on paper until a reader transforms them into a set of meaningful symbols. The literary work exists in the live circuit set up between reader and text:* the reader infuses intellectual and emotional meanings into the pattern of verbal symbols, and these symbols channel his thought and feelings. Out of this complex process emerges a more or less organized imaginative experience.
> When the reader refers to a poem, say, "Byzantium," he is designating such an experience in relation to a text. (1968, 25)

The live circuit is set in motion by the reader whose function is not only to initiate it but also to do it *responsibly,* acknowledging that the transformation of inkspots into meaningful symbols depends on what a reader can elicit from a text as much as what a text can evoke in a reader.

Not incidentally, the "live circuit" scientific metaphor in the second edition replaces "the interaction of two complex chemical compounds" (34) from the first edition. But let me turn now to what I consider *the* crucial revision, the actual insertion of the term *transaction* into her text. The fact that the site where she introduces the term is the scene of instruction is especially relevant to my argument. Here are the two versions:

> The teacher of literature, above all, needs to keep a firm grasp on the central fact that he is seeking always to help specific human beings— not some generalized fiction called THE STUDENT—to discover the pleasures and satisfactions of literature. *The teacher's job,* in its fundamental terms, then, *consists in furthering a fruitful interrelationship* between the individual book or poem or play and the individual student. The teacher is dealing with a necessarily fluctuating and dynamic problem. *His material is no less than the infinite series of possible interactions between individual minds and individual literary works.* (1938, 32–33) (I have capitalized Rosenblatt's italics.)

> The teacher of literature, then, seeks to help specific human beings discover the satisfactions of literature. *Teaching becomes a matter of improving the individual's capacity to evoke meaning from the text by leading him to reflect self-critically on this process.* The starting point for growth must be each individual's efforts to marshal his resources and organize a response relevant to the stimulus of the printed page. *The teacher's task is to foster fruitful interactions—or, more precisely, transactions—* between individual readers and individual literary works. (1968, 26–27)

A footnote is appended to this paragraph. I will reproduce it in its entirety because, I think, it marks an important moment—a moment in which Rosenblatt simultaneously looks ahead (to the formulation of what will be *The Reader, the Text, the Poem,* in which the "poem" is no longer a genre but an act of production) and back (to her 1938 early formulation of her emergent transactional theory of reading):

> The usual terminology—e.g., "the reaction of the reader to the literary work," "the interaction between the reader and the work," or references to "the poem itself"—tends to obscure the view of the literary experience presented here. Hence at times the need to differentiate between *the text,* the sequence of printed or voiced symbols, and *the literary work (the poem, the novel,* etc.), which results from the conjunction of a reader and a text. In various disciplines *transaction* is replacing *interaction,* which suggests the impact of distinct and fixed entities. *Transaction* is used above in the way that one might refer to the interrelationship between the *knower* and what is *known.* The *poem* is the transaction that goes on between reader and text. Cf. John Dewey and Arthur F. Bentley, *Knowing and the Known* (Boston, Beacon Press, 1949). (27n Rosenblatt's emphases)

Though, even as early as 1938, Rosenblatt's work demonstrates that she shared Dewey's rejection of "the epistemological dualism that would place the human being over against nature as two separate or autonomous entities" ("The Reading Transaction: What For?" 120), the first version of *L as E* is traversed by numerous traces of that very "dualism." Dewey and Bentley's reflections on the difficulty of imagining a language that would not reinscribe the old problem help us understand the difficulty of the task facing Rosenblatt:

> Our position is that the traditional language currently used about knowings and knows (and most other language about behaviors, as well) shatters the subject matter into fragments in advance of inquiry and thus destroys instead of furthering comprehensive observation for it. (68)

This is not to suggest that the use of the term *interaction* had shattered Rosenblatt's "subject matter into fragments" and had incapacitated her inquiry. To the contrary, this is to propose considering that her steady focus on students' reading and her "comprehensive observation" of their contribution to the act of reading may have enabled her to further her inquiry *in spite of* the inadequacy of traditional language.

"The field of knowings and knowns in which we are working requires transactional observation, and this is what we are giving it and what our terminology is designed to deal with," wrote Dewey and Bentley.[8] Rosenblatt's revision of her own text records and makes manifest the effects of both her own transactional observations of reading and of the language necessary to describe it accordingly. Now, a teacher's job changes from "furthering a fruitful interrelationship between the individual book or poem or play and the individual student" (1938) to "improving the individual's capacity to evoke meaning from the text by leading him to reflect self-critically on this process." Now, a student's "capacity to evoke meaning from the text" is more than just acknowledged. It is posited as the *sine qua non* for the self-critical reflection on the process of meaning making a teacher leads and facilitates: "The starting point for growth must be each individual's efforts to marshal his resources and organize a response relevant to the stimulus of the printed page" (1968, 26).

The more transactional role of the reader, in turn, necessitates a revision of what a text contributes to the reading process. Thus a text's verbal stimuli are no longer "present in the literary work" (1938, 35); because they are virtual in character, a mere potentiality, they remain "inkspots on paper until a reader transforms them into a set of meaningful symbols" (1968, 25).

> Just as the personality and concerns of the reader are largely socially acquired and socially patterned, so the literary work, like language itself, is the result of the fact that man is a social being. *The importance of literary tradition and the crystallization of particular literary forms and techniques of communication is in no way denied by our insistence on the*

psychological nature of any specific literary experiences. Anything that we
do learn about these general social factors, however, must eventually
be brought to bear upon actual literary experiences. Hence, *the essential
consideration* at this stage of our inquiry *is that anything we call a literary
experience gains its significance and force from the way in which the stimuli
present in the literary work interact with the mind and emotions of a particular
reader.* (1938, 34–35)

Just as the personality and concerns of the reader are largely socially
patterned, so the literary work, like language itself, is a social product.
The genesis of literary techniques occurs in a social matrix. Both the
creation and reception of literary works are influenced by literary tradition. Yet ultimately, *any literary work gains its significance from the way in
which the minds and emotions of particular readers respond to the verbal stimuli offered by the text.* (1968, 28)

Though Rosenblatt has acknowledged the crucial difference that
the use of one term instead of the other makes for our understanding
of reading and the teaching of reading,[9] she has not (yet?) commented
in detail on the remarkable theoretical advancement that the change
of terminology made possible for her:

When in 1949 Dewey called for *transaction* in place of *interaction,* he
was drawing on a theoretical position he had long espoused. And if I
may be forgiven the inescapably personal character of these remarks,
in adopting Dewey's terminology for the relationship between reader
and text, I was finding a new designation for a theory of reading that I
have been developing since 1938. . . . In the following decades, I presented this view of the dynamic relationship of reader and text (e.g.,
1964, 1968, 1969, 1977). In the second and later editions of *Literature as
Exploration* (1968, 1976, 1983), I indicated that I preferred *transaction* to
my use of *interaction,* and in the Winter, 1969, issue of *Journal of Reading Behaviour,* published "Towards a Transactional Theory of Reading."
("Viewpoints" 100–101)

Why does Rosenblatt so insist that her revision be seen as no more
than "a new designation" for a theory of reading *she* had been developing? What does this insistence mask? These are sensitive questions
to raise. Their intention can easily be misconstrued. But because here,
as elsewhere, I have chosen to speak on behalf of a pedagogy that calls
into crisis the theory/practice division, and sees that division as "both
the cause of the barrier and the means for its removal," I cannot
suppress them.[10] Let me then try to address them as cogently as I can.

As long as traditional assumptions about the nature and the function of pedagogy remain unexamined, any attempt to "return to" the
past in order to recognize the *place* of pedagogy in the discipline of
English Studies is doomed to be ineffective and inconsequential. From
this perspective, Suleiman's and Freund's return to the place in their

text that marks the omission of Rosenblatt's work functions as no more than a "historical supplement" that redoubles the exclusion. In their map of the profession, pedagogy remains at the periphery.

However, from within the same perspective, Rosenblatt's return to her own text performs a similar function. By insisting as she does on the origin of her transactional *theory* of reading, she fails to (or chooses not to) reclaim for herself the origin of a version of pedagogy that, in its subversion of the theory practice hierarchy, so radically transgresses the limits of the power and of the status that "the academy" has chosen to impose on it.[11] Those limits have forestalled and continue to forestall the possibility of change.

The alternative conceptualization of pedagogy that, I have argued, *L as E* illustrates, makes it possible to return to the past and to see it differently, and in light of that difference to theorize ways of transforming current understanding and practices of pedagogy.

From within this view of pedagogy, Suleiman's and Freund's readings, to say the least, would need to be much more carefully constructed, and Rosenblatt's insistence would not be necessary.

In *Reception Theory*, Robert C. Holub points out that

> the reason for the appropriation of a given theory at a particular time in a particular fashion is not simply a matter of availability of material. The editorial policies of publishing houses or the selections of libraries may very well have some effect on the development of theory, but they are never enough to determine impact. There must, in addition, be *some readiness on the part of the intellectual community to rethink its methods,* and this preparedness coupled with an influx of theoretical impulses may then lead to a productive reception. (14)

The fact that the first publication of *Literature as Exploration* was under the aegis of the Commission on Human Relations of the Progressive Education Association, and the latest by the Modern Language Association, seems to indicate a readiness on the part of the intellectual community MLA represents to retheorize the function and the place of pedagogy. However, what remains to be seen is how committed that community is to rethink its ways of reading the theory practice relation so as to transform it from "negative opposition" to a transaction that keeps both theory and practice vigilant about their "structured" resistance to each other.

Notes

1. Because "bridging" suggests the linking up of two separate activities, I prefer using the term "integration." By the integration of theory and practice I mean more than the cogent, rigorous, coherent application and extension of

the theories we practice in the production of the work that gives us status in the Academy. That is the *sine qua non* for our tenured membership in our profession. What I mean is the willingness, determination, and the courage to run the risk of making our classroom practice the actual testing ground for our theories. What I mean is relentlessly asking of ourselves and acting upon questions of this kind: What does our adoption of a particular theory reveal about our epistemological assumptions? How do we make those assumptions manifest to ourselves and our students? How do we map out with and for our students the particular "ways of knowing," the particular methods of inquiry of that theory so that both they and we can enact and test them knowing what we are doing and why? How do we use our students' "ways of knowing" to test and, if necessary, to expose a theory's gaps and contradictions? How do we learn to detect and to take responsible action for the gaps and contradictions between our theoretical understanding of teaching and learning and our actual practice? Within dominant reductive views of pedagogy—these questions—the instruction of teachers whose role it is to instruct their students, the doling out of methods, techniques divorced from their theoretical antecedents—are "structured silences."

2. I have given considerable thought to raising this issue about Suleiman's and Freund's work. Let me affirm my respect for their scholarship and let me offer a justification for what both to them and others might seem an arbitrary reading of their work. As Rosenblatt says in the Preface to the third edition of *Literature as Exploration*, "What readers make of a work will vary with different situations and at different times, as they *bring different preoccupations and interests to the text*" (vi, emphasis mine). The fact that "Bleich and others" should have recognized this book's "relevance for literary theory" clearly has a lot to do with their conception of pedagogy (see David Bleich's "Pedagogical Directions in Subjective Criticism" and "The Identity of Pedagogy and Research in the Study of Response to Literature"). And so does, of course, my reading of Suleiman's and Freund's reading of Rosenblatt's work (see "Towards a Hermeneutics of Difficulty" and "Pedagogy: From the Periphery to the Center"). My point is not about "the fact that" (I realize quite well the constraints that often lead us to "footnoting"; I am myself "footnoting" important names and titles), but rather about "the possible reason why" or how that reason can be construed.

For some time now, I have been doing research in pedagogy to pursue and provide answers to questions that have haunted me for a long time. The questions began long ago, when, as a foreign student pursuing a Ph.D. in English literature, I was disoriented, and occasionally silenced, by uneasy responses to my professed interest in pedagogy. In no unclear terms I was told to be careful about my choices, lest I be identified as a "school of education" person—a label that I did not quite understand. It was only when I became involved with the study and the teaching of composition that my interest in pedagogy became both valued and expected. Its being valued and expected, however, signified something different to composition and literary theorists and practitioners. Moreover, my conceptualization of pedagogy, of what it could and should be, usually struck most (with the notable exception of Ann Berthoff and a few others) in both fields as being either idealistic or foreign, eccentric.

When I was about to conclude that my questions were both anachronistic and nonautochthonous, that I was approaching the issue of pedagogy with speculative and evaluative criteria determined by my foreign cultural formation, I discovered an undercurrent tradition, within the history of American education, that made possible, indeed called for, the very questions that I had risked silencing. This is a tradition of suspicion and scorn at worst, of omission at best. (The term "pedagogy" is hard to find in most encyclopedias and annals of American education. See note 4 for an explanation.) This tradition, both the source and the result of consequential institutional and programmatic oppositions (School of Education vs. English Literature Department; literature vs. composition, or in language departments, language instruction; literature vs. literary theory; research vs. teaching; and so on) seems to have been set aside, in the last two decades or so, by tacit consensus. I am not sure, however, that the reemergence of the term signals a changed understanding of pedagogy. With the exception of Marxist educators—for whom pedagogy means a political program—the term is generally being deployed as a euphemism for teaching methods, teaching techniques, classroom management, or as the application and extension of theory. The extent to which the use of the term and the practice of pedagogy by influential theorists like Berthoff, Bleich, Derrida, Freire, and Lacan might be responsible for its current ubiquity and "new status" in the discourse of English studies, particularly in the domain of literature and literary theory as opposed to composition (which, for political reasons, has been considered its "natural" domain), needs to be investigated, lest a new debased tradition of pedagogy be instituted, one that only pays lip service to a term now in vogue but that has not yet, clearly, been stripped of its negative traces.

3. In 1982, James Hoetker ("A Theory of Talking about Theories of Reading") suggested, as I also do in this essay, that Suleiman's "omission of a discussion of Rosenblatt's work" might have to do with disciplinary divisions. In 1986, David Bleich ("Intersubjective Reading") noted that although Rosenblatt's work "introduced concerns with the phenomenological experience of reading and of intersubjectivity that are absent from the present critical interest in 'reading' . . . for reasons that are not altogether clear—perhaps having to do with her being a woman in a School of Education—her work did not (or was not permitted to) enter the continuing critical exchange in academic literary communities" (401–2). I. A. Richards suffered a similar disregard. According to Ann E. Berthoff, Richards's reception was determined by historical views of linguistics. See her "I. A. Richards," *Traditions of Inquiry.*

4. According to Ernest N. Henderson, professor of philosophy and education at Adelphi College and author of the entry on pedagogy in the 1913 edition of *A Cyclopedia of Education,* the term *pedagogy* has carried with it the connotation of "lack of esteem, if not contempt" historically associated with both the status of the pedagogue and with the education of children. These negative connotations lingered on for centuries and across cultures and, it can

be argued, in various manifestations traces of them still surface in current views of pedagogy. Ironically, when in the last two decades of the nineteenth century pedagogy in North America finally gained status as a university subject, so resilient were the negative connotations attached to the term that it was deemed advisable to substitute the term *education* for *pedagogy*. "The newer 'education' differs from the old 'pedagogy' in two respects. First it includes more than method in teaching and school management; second, it is more scientific" (622). Writing at the beginning of the second decade of the twentieth century, Henderson sounded optimistic about the effects that such changes would bring about, particularly about the status that the adoption of scientific methods would grant education. The 1980s grant us a different perspective both on some of the consequences of education's adoption of scientific methods, and on the fact that the meaning of pedagogy as method of teaching (usually divorced from theory) and school management is still very much with us. (For various defenses of "education" as a university subject, see *Education in the United States: A Documentary History*, vol. 3, 1414–20. For much more positive views of the function and status of the pedagogue in Greek and Roman culture, views that call into question the uncritical dissemination of his negative reputation, see Frederick Beck, *Greek Education*; Henry Marrou, *A History of Education in Antiquity*; Stanley F. Bonner, *Education in Ancient Rome*. For an early critique of education's movement away from philosophy and toward science, see Robert R. Rusk, *The Philosophical Bases of Education*. For an early example of the scientization of education, see Charles C. Boyer, *Principles and Methods of Teaching*.

I would like to express my sincere thanks to Carolyn Ball, Christine Ross, and Lori Shorr for their help in my research on pedagogy. My warmest thanks to my colleagues David Bartholomae, Joseph Harris, and Paul Kameen for their comments on an early draft of this paper; to Jean Ferguson Carr and Steve Carr for their rigorous and generous reading of the final version; and to Ann E. Berthoff, for being pedagogy's "tutelary spirit."

5. Addressing this very issue, Stanley Aronowitz and Henry Giroux argue that the only way out of the "siege" is for educators to become Gramscian "intellectuals" (*Education Under Siege*). At present, more constructive reconceptualizations of pedagogy have been proposed by reader-response theorists and practitioners, psychoanalytical theorists (see the two issues on pedagogy edited by Robert Con Davis in *College English* and the work of Shoshana Felman, Barbara Johnson), deconstructive critics, and Marxist educators (see, for example, the work of Michael Apple, Paulo Freire, Ira Shor, Henry Giroux, Stanley Aronowitz, Peter McLaren).

6. Unless otherwise indicated, the "italicizing" in the excerpts from *L as E* is mine. Because my reading is not simply a matter of emphasis, but rather an attempt to make manifest and to register particular moments of transaction with the text, I wish to avoid the customary notation of "emphasis mine."

7. See Applebee on the reasons for the establishment and widespread adoption of this tradition of reading.

8. In the preface to their *Knowing and the Known*, John Dewey and Arthur F. Bentley wrote: "The difficulty attending dependability of communication

and mutual intelligibility in connection with problems of knowledge are notoriously great" (v). Of particular interest for an understanding of these terms are the following chapters: "The Terminological Problem" 47–78; "Postulation" 79–102; "Interaction and Transaction" 103–18; "Transactions as Known and Named" 119–43; "A Trial Group of Names" (287–306).

9. See also "Towards a Transactional Theory of Reading," and "The Transactional Theory of the Literary Work: Implications for Research."

10. See Michel Foucault, *Language, Counter-Memory, Practice*. See in particular "What is an Author?" For the reading it offers of acts of symptomatic forgetfulness.

11. I use "academy" to designate both the *site* and the *nature* of the opposition. The refusal to grant pedagogy university status was rationalized, in the last three decades of the 19th century, as an opposition to the "professional," the "vocational." This tradition is kept alive today by constructions of pedagogy that justify its being denied theoretical status.

Works Cited

Applebee, Arthur N. *Tradition and Reform in the Teaching of English: A History*. Urbana, Ill.: National Council of Teachers of English, 1974.

Aronowitz, Stanley, and Henry Giroux. *Education Under Siege*. South Hadley, Mass.: Bergin and Garvey Press, 1985.

Beck, Frederick A. G. *Greek Education*. New York: Barnes and Noble, 1964.

Berthoff, Ann E. "I..A. Richards." *Traditions of Inquiry*. Ed. John Brereton. New York: Oxford University Press, 1985. 50–80.

———. *The Making of Meaning*. Portsmouth, N.H.: Boynton/Cook, 1981.

Bleich, David. "The Identity of Pedagogy and Research in the Study of Response to Literature." *College English* 42 (1980): 350–66.

———. "Intersubjective Reading." *New Literary History* (1986): 401–21.

———. "Pedagogical Directions in Subjective Criticism." *College English* 37 (1976): 454–67.

Bonner, Stanley F. *Education in Ancient Rome*. Berkeley: University of California Press, 1977.

Boyer, Charles C. *Principles and Methods of Teaching*. Philadelphia: J. B. Lippincott Co., 1900.

Cohen, Sol. *Education in the United States: A Documentary History*. Vol. 4. Random House, 1974.

Davis, Robert Con, ed. "Psychoanalysis and Pedagogy I." *College English* 49 (1987): 621–769; 785–815.

———. "Psychoanalysis and Pedagogy II." *College English* 50 (1987): 749–769; 785–815.

Dewey, John, and A. F. Bentley. *Knowing and the Known*. Boston: Beacon Press, 1949.

Foucault, Michel. *Language, Counter-Memory, Practice.* Ed., Donald F. Bouchard. New York: Cornell University Press, 1977.

Freund, Elizabeth. *The Return of the Reader: Reader-Response Criticism.* New York: Methuen, 1987.

Hoetker, James. "A Theory of Talking About Theories of Reading." *College English* 44 (1982): 175–81.

Holub, Robert C. *Reception Theory: A Critical Introduction.* New York: Methuen, 1984.

Marrou, Henry. *A History of Education in Antiquity.* London: Sheed and Ward, 1956.

Monroe, Paul, ed. *A Cyclopedia of Education.* New York: The Macmillan Co., 1913.

Rosenblatt, Louise M. *L'Idée de l'art pour l'art.* Paris: Champion, 1931; New York: AMR Press, 1977.

————. *Literature as Exploration.* New York: Appleton-Century, 1938. Revised. New York: Noble and Noble, 1968. 3rd ed. New York: Noble and Noble, 1976. 4th ed. New York: MLA, 1983.

————. "The Reading Transaction: What For?" *Developing Literacy.* Ed. Robert P. Parker and Francis A. Davis. Newark, Del.: International Reading Association, 1983. 118–35.

————. "Towards a Transactional Theory of Reading." *Journal of Reading Behavior* 1 (1969): 31–67.

————. "The Transactional Theory of the Literary Work: Implications for Research." *Researching Response and the Teaching of Literature.* Ed. C. Cooper. Norwood, NJ: Ablex Press, 1984. 33–53.

————. "Viewpoints: Transaction Versus Interaction—A Terminological Rescue Operation." *Research in the Teaching of English* 19 (1985): 96–107.

Rusk, Robert R. *Philosophical Bases of Education,* New York: Houghton Mifflin Company, 1916.

Salvatori, Mariolina. "Pedagogy: From the Periphery to the Center." *Reclaiming Pedagogy: The Rhetoric of the Classroom.* Ed. Patricia Donahue and Ellen Quandahl. Carbondale and Edwardsville, IL: Southern Illinois UP, 1989.

————. "Towards a Hermeneutics of Difficulty." *Audits of Meaning.* Ed. Louise Z. Smith. Portsmouth, NH: Boynton/Cook, 1988.

Suleiman, S. R., and I. Crosman, eds. *The Reader in the Text: Essays on Audience and Interpretation.* Baltimore: Johns Hopkins UP, 1980.

4

Transactions Overseas: Louise Rosenblatt and the Pedagogy of Literature in Schools in the United Kingdom and Elsewhere

Emrys Evans

Literature as Exploration, republished in the United States in 1968, appeared in Britain in 1970, published by Heinemann and with a foreword by Denys Thompson. Thompson, who died in 1988, was one of the most influential figures in the field of English teaching in Britain during the 1950s and 60s. As early as 1933, he had been coauthor with F. R. Leavis of *Culture and Environment*, and he was for twenty years (from 1949 to 1969) editor of *Use of English*, the only periodical to concern itself exclusively with the pedagogy of English in schools before the appearance in 1964 of the *NATE Bulletin*, later retitled *English in Education*. Louise Rosenblatt's memoirs show that Thompson must have read her book soon after its first American publication, since he wrote to her about it in 1940, though it was 1965 before they first met each other. In any case, his advocacy of the book might have been expected to be important, and he makes it clear that the 1970 edition represented "the publication (in the United Kingdom) for the first time of Professor Rosenblatt's book" (vi).

Use of English was also at that time the main source of critical reviews of books that English teachers might find interesting. By 1971, when *Literature as Exploration* was reviewed, the editorship had passed into the hands of Frank Whitehead, with Christopher Parry as review editor. *Literature as Exploration* was reviewed alongside a work by Ruth Mock, *Education and the Imagination*, in a curious piece compiled, rather than written, by J. V. Davies, then lecturer in English and education at the University of York. After a brief introduction, in which he rather ambivalently stresses Louise Rosenblatt's "optimistic feeling for the collaboration between the literature teacher and the social scientist" (Davies 262), he contents himself with doing no more than excerpting quotations from each book alternately, seven from each.

It is an oddly unhelpful effort, which fails to present at all effectively the content and emphases of Rosenblatt's book. Moreover, it is extremely difficult to imagine more than a very few of those who bought or read *Use of English* at that time reading through all that small print, much less being encouraged to turn to either of the books.

I have not been able to find any references to Rosenblatt's work after this in British writing about English and literature pedagogy in the 1970s. References have been commoner in the 80s, however, and I shall list some of these later.

Between 1965 and 1980, considerable work was in progress in the UK in the development of new approaches to the teaching of language and literature in secondary schools. From 1966 onwards, as a result of the Dartmouth seminar, this work formed part of a continuing dialogue with teachers in the United States, Canada, and other English-speaking countries. Much, though not all, was consonant with the general spirit of Louise Rosenblatt's principles as these appear in *Literature as Exploration* and later in *The Reader, the Text, the Poem*. David Allen's survey of the whole field shows clearly how the precise importance given to the teaching of literature in the English curriculum as a whole was a regular point of difference between various writers and the schools of thought they represented. Among the most influential books of the period were John Dixon's *Growth Through English*, a commissioned account of the Dartmouth conference; James Britton's *Language and Learning; Patterns of Language* by Leslie Stratta, John Dixon, and Andrew Wilkinson; the "Bullock" report, *A Language for Life* (Department of Education and Science), and Douglas Barnes's *From Communication to Curriculum*. And, as Allen points out, there had been important "pre-Dartmouth" volumes, too, such as the works of David Holbrook, of which one of the earliest and most influential was *English for Maturity*, and Frank Whitehead's *The Disappearing Dais*.

Allen reminds us how all these writers, and the group represented at the secondary level by Peter Doughty, working under the guid-

ance of Professor M. A. K. Halliday to introduce a new consciousness
of the role of language in all aspects of individual and social culture,
offered, explicitly or implicitly, their own views on two basic questions: how important the place of literature was in the area of English
as a whole, and how the teaching of literature should be approached.
There is no room to examine these arguments in any detail here:
Allen's book, though admittedly and inevitably subjective, is a good
guide to what was going on. However, many views were expressed
that were in accordance with Rosenblatt's basic theses, so that in
retrospect the whole debate has served incidentally to prepare British
English teachers to understand and welcome her views as they
become more widely available. For example, John Dixon, in *Growth
Through English*, has a short paragraph that has been much quoted and
discussed by teachers and students throughout the '70s and '80s:

> The essential talk that springs from literature is talk about experience—
> as *we* know it, as *he* sees it (correcting our partiality and his; exploring
> the fullness of his vision, and ours). Conversely, only in a classroom
> where talk explores experience is literature drawn into the dialogue—
> otherwise it has no place. The demand for interpretation—was it this
> or that he meant?—arises in the course of such talk: otherwise it is a
> dead hand. (60)

Such a view of the relationship in the classroom between readers' own
experience and the experience offered by literary texts is well tuned to
the attitudes Rosenblatt explores in chapter 4 of *Literature as Exploration*, "What Brings Students to Literature?" In *The Reader, the Text, the
Poem*, however, Rosenblatt's precise enunciation of the nature of the
relationship between readers and texts takes us much further than
Dixon does, while to his emphasis on the importance of personal
experience in the reading of literature she adds much clearer and more
critical accounts of the processes teachers need to engage in. "Self-
awareness," she writes, "making articulate the assumptions and attitudes lived through . . . becomes even more important as the process
of evaluation takes over. The blandness and quiet dogmatism of much
literary criticism might disappear with such articulateness of criteria."
(157) She seeks a clarity of connection between "what the reader
brings" and what the text offers, which must indeed be derived from
talk, as Dixon says, but suggests means for its development and that
of those taking part in it.

One of the most interesting accounts of English pedagogy in
schools during the period we are looking at is to be found in *Patterns
of Language*, by Stratta, Dixon, and Wilkinson. Chapter 2, "Literature
and Interpretation," is, like most of this book, largely concerned with
offering practical approaches to teaching that involve young people in

the reading of literature. Various functions of literature are first described, after which a variety of "workshop" treatments are proposed, culminating in a principle described by the authors as "imaginative recreation," of novels in particular, as a way toward understanding and appreciating them more fully. In the opening paragraphs of this chapter, people who teach literature so as to suggest that it has "little or no relevance to life as [pupils] live it beyond the school" are strongly criticized. By contrast, literature is underlined as offering "the comfort and security of having our impressions of people and events confirmed," "visions of life as different from our own," and ways of temporary "escape . . . from our own world" (43). Rosenblatt's fuller description of "The Province of Literature" in Part I of *Literature as Exploration* develops and refines these views. She refers to one of her own students as singling out literature's "objective presentation of our own problems. It places them outside ourselves, enables us to see them with a certain detachment and to understand our own situation and motivation more objectively" (41). She shows how "the student who has lived through the experience of *Othello* . . . will have entered, for the time, into a world of strange moral values and responsibilities" (43). Many of the techniques suggested by Stratta and his coauthors for involving students in the experience of literature are well designed to produce the awareness of literary experiences that Rosenblatt desires, though it could only sharpen these techniques further to reconsider them in the light of her theoretical position.

So it seems that much of the development of English and literature pedagogy in the United Kingdom from 1965 to 1980 was quite well attuned to, though apparently largely or entirely conducted in ignorance of, Rosenblatt's work. The wider debate concerning the propriety of placing the study of literature at the center of the English curriculum as a whole (still evidently not exhausted, as Peter Medway's keynote address to the annual conference of the Australian Association for the Teaching of English, given at Melbourne in 1987, interestingly shows) also continued together with the question of how literature should be taught. Rosenblatt's contribution to this discussion most easily available in the United Kingdom is her article "Pattern and Process—a Polemic." This was first published in the United States in *English Journal* 58.7, and reprinted in *Use of English* 22.3 (1971). Its first concern is with the arguments over the American "Project English" curricula of the late '60s and early '70s, when curriculum designers, informed largely by the theories of Jerome Bruner, looked for the "basic concepts of a discipline," which should provide the foundations for "a spiralling increase of complexity during the subsequent course of the student's education" (Rosenblatt "Pattern and Process," 204). The close reading approach of the New Critics was used to attempt to structure English curricula on the same lines as those in the sciences and mathematics, and emphases on "genres" were offered as types for structure-providing theoretical concepts. (This, by the way, is another issue that won't lie down. See Michael Rosen's response to Francis Christie and others: "Will Genre Theory Change the World?").

As we would expect, Louise Rosenblatt, seeing "the human aspect" entering this style of literature teaching only in terms of the writer's creative task, asks, "What about the reader's creative task?" She proposes a sequential, rather than a spiral, curriculum, in which we look to "literary experiences to be participated in" rather than "concepts to be analytically apprehended." "Progression will be determined by what will constitute meaningful experience for the individual in the course of his development as a person" ("Patterns and Process," 210). And in the final paragraph of her article, she refers to the publications arising from the 1966 Dartmouth Seminar, which, she argues, "should give impetus to the development of programs that place the reader and the reader's life experience directly in the center of attention."

It is impossible to say how much notice was taken of this important article at the time of its publication in Britain. Its appearance in the same issue of *Use of English* as Davies's perfunctory review is ironic: in some ways, its appearance in that periodical at all is unexpected, and perhaps symptomatic of a potential shift in its stance that never actually took place. Possibly if things had developed differently at that time, American and British thinking might have flowed together more harmoniously, and one unfortunate result of this independence, among others, might have been avoided.

This unfortunate result is the occurrence of a clash in terminology, and particularly in the use of the term *transactional*. James Britton, referred to above as a major authority in this general field, developed with colleagues in London a convenient theoretical framework to describe the uses of language one might expect to find encouraged in the speech and, more particularly, the writing of children at school. Beginning from a generally conversational style of language (for which he borrowed from Edward Sapir the term *expressive*), it could move either in the direction of pleasure and self-consciousness in the use of words for their own sake (a usage described as the *poetic*), or toward a more practical, directional use (for which he unfortunately chose the term *transactional*). The use of that term clearly differs radically from, and, when both are known, seems likely to conflict with Rosenblatt's use of the same term to describe the relationship between reader and text. Rosenblatt herself has deplored this clash, in private correspondence if not publicly.

Two things, however, stand in her support. The first is that technical terms must overlap, with different meanings, in different disciplines, and Britton's attempt to describe language usage as a whole is a sufficiently different area of study from a concern with the nature of literary experience for the terms to be usable interchangeably by most intelligent students. The second is that, although Britton's labeling of this "continuum" had some success over a period of time in the education of teachers in Britain and elsewhere, it is being increasingly overtaken by more subtle and more precise descriptions, and his use is, I believe, less likely to survive than Rosenblatt's, whose roots are deeper in the thinking of other earlier scholars, notably John Dewey.

Apart from the British publication of *Literature as Exploration* in 1970, the only other appearance of Rosenblatt's work in this country in the 1970s seems to have been the reprinting referred to above of her article, "Pattern and Process—a Polemic." David Allen's bibliography of selected important titles for the history of English teaching in his period includes this article, but neither of her two volumes, even though it lists publications up to and including 1978. The other works I have mentioned, such as Britton (*Language and Learning*) and Stratta, Dixon, and Wilkinson, have no reference to her work at all.

In 1984, on the retirement of Harold Rosen from his chair at the London Institute of Education, some of his colleagues gathered together a collection of essays under the title *Changing English*. The final chapter, "Message and Text in Poetic Utterance," is by Rosen's former colleague, James Britton. In it he refers to Rosenblatt's work, but to one feature of it only—her distinction between *efferent* and *aesthetic* writing, taken from *The Reader, the Text, the Poem*. And there is one other reference in the same volume, in chapter 13, "Doing Teaching English," by Peter Medway. It is to exactly the same distinction, so that it appears that an older and a younger authority in the pedagogy of English in the United Kingdom had both read *The Reader, the Text, the Poem*, and had chosen this one offer of a new terminology as something of Rosenblatt's that was useful to them. (Medway was still finding it useful a year or two later, in his contribution to Andrew Wilkinson's *The Writing of Writing* [23]).

In 1985 and 1986 two volumes, originating respectively in the United States and Canada, became available in Britain, both of which include contributions by Louise Rosenblatt and references to her work. These are *Language, Schooling, and Society*, edited by Stephen N. Tchudi (the record of the International Federation for the Teaching of English seminar held at Michigan State University in 1984), and *The Creating Word*, edited by Patricia Demers (a collection of papers given at an international conference at the University of Alberta, also in 1984). It is possible that the appearance of Louise Rosenblatt's views in volumes also contributed to by writers more familiar in Britain, such as Anthony Adams and John Dixon (who has articles in both these books), may have made her name more familiar and persuaded people to turn to her own work, though it does not seem likely that either volume would have had a very wide circulation.

Probably the first deliberate attempt to stress for British readers the importance of Rosenblatt's views of the reading process and the relationship between readers and texts came with the publication in this country by the Open University Press of *Readers, Texts, Teachers,* edited by Bill Corcoran and Emrys Evans, in 1987. My own chapter in this volume, chapter 2, "Readers Recreating Texts," tries to show some of the parallels in thinking between Wolfgang Iser (about whom I had already written earlier in *English in Education*) and Louise Rosenblatt. I am aware, of course, that there are many dissimilarities between Iser's work and Rosenblatt's, that they stem from different traditions in European and American thinking, that (to put it mildly) their styles of writing are not easy to reconcile, and that they look to different areas of literature for examples to illustrate their theories. Nevertheless, it seemed to me that in their shared concentration on the role of the reader and the cardinal importance of the reader's own experience in the act of reading, they both offered teachers of English in schools new reasons for focusing on the literary development of their students at least as much as on the understanding and elucidation of texts. This view was shared by my Australian colleagues, Bill Corcoran and Clem Young, each of whom made Rosenblatt's work an important strand in the theoretical framework we tried to set up together in the opening chapters of *Readers, Texts, Teachers.* I believe, too, that although specific reference to Rosenblatt's work only occurs in two of the following eight chapters—Mollie Travers's chapter on responding to poetry and, in a rather different light, in Pam Gilbert's concluding "deconstruction"—attitudes favorable to various parts of both Iser's and Rosenblatt's ideas of literature inform the volume as a whole.

In the same year, 1987, there was published in Australia and simultaneously in the United States and Britain, another very important contribution to our understanding of how young people read and how we can help them to read better—Jack Thomson's *Understanding Teenagers' Reading.* Thomson's work is based on several detailed research studies of adolescent reading behavior conducted in Australia and Great Britain. He sets out to provide a systematic description of the stages through which readers pass in developing a sophisticated ability to interact with text, and to suggest the implications of such a description for the practice of teachers of literature. His theoretical groundwork, developed in detail in his third chapter, is chiefly based on reader-response criticism, with Iser's work firmly at the center. There are, however, several references to Rosenblatt, though unfortunately only to *Literature as Exploration*. One feels that *The Reader, the Text, the Poem* could have been very helpful to Thomson's position, and I hope that those who try to build on his work will take up Rosenblatt's later and fuller accounts of her position and use them.

Three other recent volumes illustrate how Rosenblatt's work appears to be becoming more understood and accepted and more widely seen as relevant to the teaching of English below university level in Britain. Since the first of these volumes was written by an Australian, and the second by a Canadian and an Englishman together, what is suggested for the UK should also be true in Australia and Canada.

Ken Watson's *English Teaching in Perspective* was first published in Sydney, New South Wales, in 1981. It has since been revised and published in the United Kingdom in 1987, by the Open University Press. Rosenblatt's view of the relationship between reader and text is strongly stressed on pages 60–61 (revised edition), and a connection is made between it and the work of David Holbrook on the one hand and Stratta and his colleagues' *Patterns of Language* on the other—a connection that I find convincing, as I have tried to show earlier. The fact that this is already present in the 1981 Australian edition makes it one of the earliest occurrences of Louise Rosenblatt's name in the literature under review.

In the same Open University Press series, Patrick Dias of McGill University, Montreal, and Mike Hayhoe of the University of East Anglia published, in 1988, *Developing Response to Poetry*. A total of eleven references to Louise Rosenblatt in their index, particularly to the distinction between aesthetic and efferent reading and to literary reading as a transaction, suggest that she is an important influence. *Literature as Exploration* is properly seen, not only as one of the earliest works to stress the active role of the reader in making meaning, but as seeing this as importantly a pedagogical concern (16). Her phrase "the lived-through experience of the work," isolated by Thomson (232), is again chosen out by Dias and Hayhoe (39). These writers also compare Iser's work with that of Rosenblatt (20–23) and find in Rosenblatt's concept of *transaction* a term that is helpful to their understanding of how poetry can be read and taught.

Also in 1988, Michael Benton, of Southampton University, with three secondary English department heads from the county of Hampshire, wrote *Young Readers Responding to Poems*. This is the most recent of the books and articles reviewed in this chapter, and Benton's account of Rosenblatt's transactional theory is brief, clear, and accessible. It appears in the first chapter of the book, where I. A. Richards's work is also reconsidered. Rosenblatt's position is offered partly as a corrective to what Benton sees as an unfortunately negative approach to the reader's task in Richards's *Practical Criticism*, and a more constructive series of "ten positive statements" describing the aesthetic of poetry reading is offered. Together these positions inform much of the practical research reported by Benton's colleagues in chapters 2, 3, and 4, while Benton himself proposes "a response-centered methodology" for the poetry classroom in his concluding chapter.

Perhaps the most recent evidence of the increasing international importance of Louise Rosenblatt's thought, especially in the pedagogy of literature, came in the program of the International Convention on Reading and Response held at the University of East Anglia in April, 1989. Some important presentations, notably those of John Squire from the United States and John Harker from Canada, refer to her by name in their titles or synopses. Others, such as those by Robert Probst (U.S.A.), Bill Corcoran (Australia), and Margaret Meek (U.K.), also made substantial reference to her.

It is evident, then, that the discovery and acceptance of Louise Rosenblatt's views in Great Britain and those parts of the English-speaking world where pedagogy for literature is influenced by British thinking has been slow and somewhat random. It should be equally evident that my own conviction is that she has much more to teach us than we have yet allowed ourselves to learn. In conclusion, I should perhaps try to make clear what I take the most important of those points to be.

First there is her constant stress on the vital importance of the reader's experience as he or she brings it to the reading of a text. This was the topic of chapter 4 of *Literature as Exploration* and is fundamental to the distinction between the kinds of activity involved in aesthetic and efferent reading; it also forms an important part of the conclusion of *The Reader, the Text, the Poem*, where the "self-awareness" of the reader is seen as vital to both enjoyment and evaluation.

This self-awareness is central to much recent writing about the pedagogy of literature in Britain, whether or not it is explicitly informed by Rosenblatt's theory. We see it in David Jackson's work (*Encounters with Books*, e.g.), where flow diagrams and reading journals maintain the reader's awareness of the processes of reading. Benton's colleagues (*Young Readers*) show their young readers annotating the texts of poems, tape-recording or writing down their reactions, and holding informed and lively discussions to compare their responses. Rosenblatt's own emphasis on the centrality of "meaningful experience" is, as we have already indicated, a main conclusion of "Pattern and Process—a Polemic." It has taken her ideas ten or

twenty years to become vital components of reading curricula in Great
Britain, and to begin to inform even such government documents as
the Kingman and Cox reports of 1987 and 1988, but it is interesting
and hopeful that "response" is now a key term in syllabuses and
curricula at this level.

With this goes Rosenblatt's stress on the experience of reading
while it is actually going on—"the journey itself," as Coleridge puts it
in *Biographia Literaria*. This seems to me to be one of the points where
a parallel exists between Rosenblatt's thought and Iser's, and where
Iser's description of the reader's "wandering viewpoint" develops
Rosenblatt's position valuably. Fortunately, new tendencies in the
assessment as well as the teaching of literature in the United Kingdom, where work done from day to day in the classroom is achieving
at least equal importance with end-of-course examinations in the
grading of pupils' work, have made room for this emphasis to be
further explored and experimented with.

The same trend has made teachers and examiners—now more
often than in the past the same people, or working more closely
together—readier to accept Rosenblatt's view of the text itself as a
constraint rather than a *norm*: "a pattern which the reader must to
some extent create even as he is guided by it" (*The Reader, the Text, the
Poem* 129). For example, it is now possible for many "advanced" Level
students of English literature in British schools (i.e., students mostly
of seventeen or eighteen years of age, intending to proceed to higher
education, though not necessarily to specialize in English language or
literature) to respond to their reading of a novel by writing in the
author's style, attempting alternative endings, experimenting with
the production of chapters that cover incidents or encounters implied
but not given in detail in the text, and by various other "re-creative"
or apprentice-style techniques. In these, the original text has to be
seen as an effective constraint. To write an alternative ending to *Tess of
the d'Urbervilles* in the style of Graham Greene would not (unless
perhaps the intention to do so was declared and justified) be a legitimate exercise. But an ending, such as I have recently seen and been
instrumental in grading highly, that not only plausibly and delicately
suggested the relationship between Angel Clare and Tess's sister 'Liza
Lu immediately after the death of Tess, but concluded by viewing
their parting from the point of view of a very characteristically Hardy-
like peasant figure chewing an apple, is not only good writing in itself
but also commendable and perceptive criticism. Fears that extremes of
reader-response criticism might lead to increasing disregard for the
very presence, let alone the precise detail, of the text can be allayed
by close attention to Rosenblatt's analysis, and there is room for this
to proceed further in the theory and practice of literature teaching.

When "students themselves ask the questions," as Louise Rosenblatt suggested ("Pattern and Process" 209), what we move toward is a new kind of "close reading," which "can become a source of increasing skill and subtlety of interpretation."

Somehow, we need to examine more closely, and perhaps in spite of what I have said earlier, to reword (in view of the confusion introduced by Britton's different use of the term) the concept of the literary *transaction*. Rosenblatt uses another metaphor when she says that "the reader's attention constantly *vibrates* between the pole of the text and the pole of his own responses to it" (*The Reader, the Text, the Poem* 129; my italics). As I have suggested in *Readers, Texts, Teachers,* there is a valuable analogy here between Rosenblatt's term *vibration* and the term *oscillation* used by Robert Witkin to describe the process involved in the creation and appreciation of works of art of all sorts. I have not mentioned Witkin's book, *The Intelligence of Feeling,* earlier, because it is not a work mainly concerned with literature or literary education. But there are many parallels between his thinking and Louise Rosenblatt's, on social as well as aesthetic topics: the very first paragraph of the first chapter of *Literature as Exploration* reminded me at once of the opening paragraph of Witkin's book. It may be that a development of their common ideas could be valuable to education in the arts generally, as well as in literature, in Britain and elsewhere.

"Fundamentally, the process of understanding a work implies a re-creation of it" (Rosenblatt *Literature as Exploration* [1938], 113). Good teachers will be concerned to provide their students with the tools for proceeding to such a re-creation. As I have shown, some of these have been suggested by Stratta, Dixon, and Wilkinson in *Patterns of Language;* others are offered by Peter Adams in his conception of "dependent authorship" in *Readers, Texts, Teachers,* and more will no doubt be devised in the future.

Finally, it seems to me that throughout her career Louise Rosenblatt has been a model for teachers of literature in her concern for all readers everywhere (though perhaps particularly in America and other democracies), above all for that universal human phenomenon she investigates in the final chapter of *The Reader, the Text, the Poem:* the "common" or "general" reader. In articles like "Pattern and Process—a Polemic," where she examines the place of literature in what were then described as "the Project English curriculums," she has shown her concern for pupils and students of all ages: in "The Literary Transaction" she places her own theory up against other schools of criticism, especially the deconstructionists, as investigated in the previous chapter by M. H. Abrams, and defines it in terms that I find more than convincing. The crucial problem of literary pedagogy, as it is practiced in a primary or secondary classroom, a university, or elsewhere, is clearly isolated in the final chapter of *The Reader, the Text, the Poem:*

> If readers are . . . to be helped to be "in possession of the literary work of art," the real problem is the maintenance of . . . spontaneity and self-respect while at the same time fostering the capacity to undertake relationships with increasingly demanding texts. (140)

This is the art we need to develop. Other writers—I might mention David Bleich in the United States; alongside Robert Protherough, David Jackson, Michael Benton, and others in Great Britain; and Jack Thomson in Australia—are increasingly offering teachers means to do this. But the aims and the reasons are set out by Louise Rosenblatt, and we in the United Kingdom and elsewhere owe her and ourselves increasingly close study of her writing to support and direct our activities.

Works Cited

Allen, David. *English Teaching Since 1965: How Much Growth?* London: Heinemann, 1980.

Barnes, Douglas. *From Communication to Curriculum.* Harmondsworth: Penguin Books, 1976.

Benton, Michael, and Geoff Fox. *Teaching Literature Nine to Fourteen.* London: Oxford UP, 1985.

Benton, Michael, et al. *Young Readers Responding to Poems.* London: Routledge, 1988.

Bleich, David. *Readings and Feelings.* Urbana, Ill.: National Council of Teachers of English, 1975.

Britton, James. *Language and Learning.* Harmondsworth: Penguin Books, 1970.

———. "Message and Text in Poetic Utterance." Meek and Miller. 235–61.

Bruner, Jerome. *The Process of Education.* Cambridge, Mass.: Harvard UP, 1960.

Corcoran, Bill, and Emrys Evans, eds. *Readers, Texts, Teachers.* Upper Monclair, N.J.: Boynton/Cook; Milton Keynes: Open University Press, 1987.

Davies, J. V. "Two Apologies for Poetry": Review of Louise Rosenblatt, *Literature as Exploration* and Ruth Mock, *Education and the Imagination. Use of English* 22.2, 261–65. 1971.

Demers, Patricia, ed. *The Creating Word.* New York and London: Macmillan, 1986.

Department of Education and Science (UK). *A Language for Life.* The Bullock Report. London: Her Majesty's Stationery Office, 1975.

Dias, Patrick, and Mike Hayhoe. *Developing Response to Poetry.* Milton Keynes: Open University Press, 1988.

Dixon, John. *Growth Through English.* 1967. Rev. ed. 1969. 3rd ed. London: Oxford UP, 1975.

Evans, W. D. Emrys. "The Art of Reading and the English Teacher: An Introduction to Wolfgang Iser and Others." *English in Education* 15. 3 (1981):
34–39.

Holbrook, David. *English for Maturity*. London: Cambridge UP, 1961.

Jackson, David. *Encounters with Books: Teaching Fiction 11–16*. New York and
London: Methuen, 1983.

Leavis, F. R., and Denys Thompson. *Culture and Environment*. London: Chatto
and Windus, 1933.

Medway, Peter. "Access to What? Reality, Play and Pleasure in English."
English in Australia, 82 (1987) 12–22.

———. "Doing Teaching English." Meek and Miller. 134–42.

———. "What Gets Written About." Wilkinson. 22–39.

Meek, Margaret, and J. Miller, eds. *Changing English—Essays for Harold Rosen*.
London: Heinemann, 1984.

Mock, Ruth. *Education and the Imagination*. London: Chatto and Windus, 1970.

Protherough, Robert. *Developing Response to Fiction*. Milton Keynes: Open
University Press, 1983.

Richards, I. A. *Practical Criticism*. London: Routledge and Kegan Paul, 1929.

Rosen, Michael. "Will Genre Theory Change the World?" *English in Australia*
86 (1988): 4–12.

Rosenblatt, Louise M. "Language, Literature and Values". Tchudi. 64–80.

———. "The Literary Transaction". Demers.

———. *Literature as Exploration*. 1938. 2nd ed. 1968. UK ed. 1970. 3rd ed. New
York: Modern Language Association; London: Heinemann, 1976.

———. "Pattern and Process—a Polemic." *Use of English* 22. 3 (1971): 203–11.

———. *The Reader, the Text, the Poem: The Transactional Theory of the Literary
Work*. Carbondale, Ill.: Southern Illinois UP, 1978.

Stratta, Leslie, John Dixon, and Andrew Wilkinson. *Patterns of Language*.
London: Heinemann, 1973.

Tchudi, S. N., ed. *Language, Schooling, and Society*. Portsmouth, N.H.: Boyn-
ton/Cook, 1985.

Thomson, Jack. *Understanding Teenagers' Reading*. New York: Nichols Publishing; Melbourne: Methuen; London: Croom Helm, 1987.

Watson, Ken. *English Teaching in Perspective*. 1981. Rev. ed. Sydney, New
South Wales: St. Clair Press; Milton Keynes: Open University Press, 1987.

Whitehead, Frank. *The Disappearing Dais*. London: Chatto and Windus, 1966.

Wilkinson, Andrew, ed. *The Writing of Writing*. Milton Keynes: Open University Press, 1986.

Witkin, Robert W. *The Intelligence of Feeling*. New York and London: Heinemann, 1974.

5

Democratic Practice, Pragmatic Vistas: Louise Rosenblatt and the Reader's Response

Ann E. Berthoff

For anyone old enough to have been a student before the midcentury mark, one of the pleasures of reading Louise Rosenblatt is encountering old friends—interesting minor figures like Maud Bodkin, Rosamond Lehmann, and Gordon Allport, as well as giants like John Dewey, Franz Boas, and Edward Sapir. It is not a matter of nostalgia but of recalling a time when the philosophy of education was more concerned with ideas than with data. It is inspiriting to read Louise Rosenblatt, because her conviction that critical theory and classroom practice are philosophical to the core is voiced on every page. For younger readers, one of the chief benefits is to be set straight about certain events and movements and schools which have been in recent times badly misunderstood and wantonly misrepresented. She was one of the first to recognize the significance of I. A. Richards' *Practical Criticism*, to understand what the purposes of the New Criticism were and how certain of the proponents of this critical practice derailed the enterprise. For all readers, there is the pleasure of reading straightfor-

ward prose about the importance of literature in our lives and the
logical, psychological, pedagogical, and political reasons for beginning with the reader's response.

Defining the context for Rosenblatt's theory of the reader's role
takes us to the heart of American philosophy. It would be salutary for
contemporary critics to turn to Rosenblatt's explanation of her principal ideas because they will find there a more authentic understanding
of C. S. Peirce and William James than they will get, say, in reading
one American academic's interpretation of another's redaction of a
British expositor's rendition of an idea gleaned from a European critic's
uninstructed reading of Peirce. Sometimes cross-cultural exchange
can be generative, as when Martin Luther King, Jr. found in Gandhi
what Gandhi had taken from Thoreau, who had gathered it, in part,
from Eastern mysticism. But the reheated, refiltered, decaffeinated
criticism currently available is neither generative nor instructive.
Reading Rosenblatt brings us closer to the genuine sources of some of
the most significant concepts in contemporary philosophy.

I want to claim that Rosenblatt exemplifies pragmatism at its best.
The student of John Dewey and a careful reader of William James, she
is attentive to both logical and psychological dimensions of theory and
practice. Further, she is at home with what I. A. Richards called
Peirce's "revolutionary doctrine of the Interpretant." The Interpretant
is the idea that mediates the symbol and its referent; it is part of the
sign, an element of the meaning relationship. It is held, generally
speaking, by an individual person, but Peirce was very reluctant,
except as "a Sop to Cerberus," to conflate the person and the idea
because he did not want to lose the point that interpretation is logi-
cally constitutive and not a psychological additive. In Peirce's semiotics (he reclaimed the term, which he spelled *semeiotic*), the meaning
relationship is three-valued, triadic: interpretation is entailed in signi-
fication. Saussure's signifier-signified, in contrast, is two-valued,
with interpretation seen as a psychological additive. Modern linguistics derives from Saussure and tends to be centrally concerned with
neither meaning nor interpretation. Understanding the two varieties
of semiotics is crucial to understanding how and why Rosenblatt's
theories differ from other varieties of what is generally called "reader-
response" theory.

Naming the theory which holds that the reader's response is
important in many different senses is not easy: "reader response" is
slightly pleonastic, for from where else would there be a response?
But, of course, the point is not what phrase we decide on but what we
mean by it. A pragmatic understanding takes active, interpretative
practice as the chief consequence of triadicity: if all knowledge is
mediated, then we must continually interpret our interpretations. If

there is no direct access to reality, truth, or any other absolute, then we must look to our practice to mediate our understanding. If we apply the pragmatic maxim—what difference would it make to our practice if we hold thus and so?—the advantages are immediately apparent. For the pedagogical implications of reader-response theory are very rich indeed, and it is for her careful exploration of them that we have chiefly to thank Rosenblatt. Three distinctions provide points of departure for that exploration: interaction/transaction, text/poem, efferent/aesthetic. In all cases, a triadic conception supplants a dyadic one: transaction, poem, and aesthetic stance are, in Rosenblatt's hands, thoroughly triadic, thoroughly pragmatic. I will consider them in the order named.

Transaction, Rosenblatt explains, is Dewey's term, a concept he meant to supplant the idea of interaction, which was modeled on the stimulus-response of behavioral psychology. For Dewey the organism in its environment was, like the sign, a three-valued relationship. Nowadays, the notions of recursion and feedback are familiar from information theory and the role it plays in our computer-driven lives, but the complexity of what Rosenblatt, following Gregory Bateson, calls "ecological naturalism" is still not widely recognized. Any and all ideas can be reduced to dyadic terms, flattened out so that whatever generative power which might have been gained is lost; that is to say, transaction can be nothing but interaction if it is entertained in the dyadic perspective, as a matter of I'll-scratch-your-back-if-you'll-scratch-mine.[1] Transaction, as Rosenblatt intends it, means that the relationship between the reader and what is read is not dyadic, like stimulus-response, but is mediated by what he brings to what he reads, by what he presupposes and analyzes and conjectures and concludes about what is being said and what it might mean. *Transaction* is meant to keep the dialectic apparent and lively, but of course the word alone cannot do that: we must form the concept, and to do so we will need concepts to think with, chief among them experience.

Rosenblatt's argument for the primacy of experience is important for us, remembering how this idea has fared in educational philosophy. I would say that underlying her conception of experience is Boas's and Sapir's understanding of language as at once a formal system and a means of cultural and individual expression. Experience, that is to say, is never "merely personal," and its social character is defining. It isn't enough to say "personal experience" any more than it is to say that interpretation is what an interpreter does; *experience* and *person* must both be defined in terms of our social existence. This understanding is best modeled by language seen as a species-specific capacity which can be realized only in the context of our lives as social creatures. Piaget's structuralism hid this truth from view,

though recent study of Vygotsky has helped to reclaim it. But Rosenblatt does not let us forget the dialectic:

> To affirm that the individual consciousness embodies forces that tran-
> scend the biological organism, that there is no sharp division between
> the subjective consciousness and its object does not require dispensing
> with the vital, dynamic, active, empirical self. (*The Reader, the Text, the
> Poem* 172)

The self is, she contends, not a "construct," but neither is it an
autonomous entity. This is consonant with what Peirce meant in
saying that Man is a Sign: he is Thirdness to the facts of the Universe.

Experience is always social and it is active: it is not a collection of
responses to a collection of stimuli. Experience is, for one thing, the
memory of acts and events, represented in images of all sorts. The fact
that Rosenblatt draws upon the Ames perception studies is evidence
that she has seen how "the prime agent of all human perception"—
Coleridge's famous definition of Imagination—is active and creative.
Along with an anthropologically sophisticated understanding of language, there is a theory of imagination which underwrites her reader-
response theory; indeed, her theory could be said to bear about the
same relationship to "affective stylistics" and "subjective criticism" as
Imagination does to Fancy.

In calling the experience of reading a *transaction*, Rosenblatt
is recognizing interpretation as a process of making meaning. It is
a nonlinear, dynamic, dialectical process in which we continually
interpret our interpretations. Response really begins not with the
"response" but with the student's reflection on the response. Her
thoroughly pragmatic sense of what is "valid" in a reading puts the
emphasis on seeing what *difference* taking part of a text *this* way would
make to the rest of it. This critical respect for how the reading of one
line or image or passage will necessarily affect the way we read other
elements of the text is an expression of the same principle which
guides Richards in his insistence on the possibility of distinguishing
"variant readings" from "misreading." Thus, Rosenblatt and Richards
share an understanding of recognizing, identifying, and evaluating
textual constraints on the reader's response: they both follow the
pragmatic maxim. Solipsists should take notice—and those for whom
some vague notion of an "interpretative community" has supplanted
the well-formed concept of *transaction*.

If there is a drawback to the term *transaction*—and I think there
is—it is that some may interpret it as tending to reify the text, to
suggest a power and position equal to that of the reader. Like the
more up-to-date term *negotiate*, it may imply two parties of equal
status. Now it may be that the reader and the writer have this relation-

ship, but the author is not in the picture in reader-response models. To see the transaction as taking place between a gabby reader and a gabby text always reminds me, rather, of the stomach talking to its owner, the thoughtless consumer of pepperoni pizzas in the Alka Selzer ad. The presentation of reader and text as copartners in a transaction may seem to represent a dyadic semiotics; actually, the transaction is between varying interpretations, starts and stops, as they are constrained by an ever-deepening appreciation of the limits of language represented in the text, in dialectic with the experience the reader brings to the reading. Rosenblatt's emphasis on this inter-dependency of openness and selection reminds us that her her-meneutics, like her semiotics, is triadic and pragmatic. Awareness of this can protect us from misconceiving what *transaction* is meant to express.

Just so, in her differentiation of *text* and *poem*, Rosenblatt is mind-ful of what Richards calls "the problem of initial terms." Rather than speaking of a text as "essentially" or "actually" or "really" traces of graphite on processed pulp, or some such circumlocution, Rosenblatt begins with symbols:

> "Text" designates a set or series of signs interpretable as linguistic sym-bols. I use this rather roundabout phrasing to make it clear that the text is not simply the inked marks on the page or even the uttered vibrations in the air. The visual or auditory signs become verbal sym-bols, become words, by virtue of their being potentially recognizable as pointing to something beyond themselves. Thus, in a reading situation "the text" may be thought of as the printed signs in their capacity to serve as symbols. (*The Reader* 12)

And when we recreate the text as poem, those verbal symbols are interpreted, their meanings construed. For this reason, a theory of reading must have a working concept of discourse as well as a philos-ophy of language: words and letters are not the initial terms of dis-course; meanings are.

It has been a chief contribution of hermeneutics to shift the focus of critical theory from abstract definitions of discourse to the nature of the reading process, from rhetoric to interpretation, if you will. Schleiermacher, generally credited by those who chart intellectual currents as the founder of a general theory of hermeneutics, held that we construct the text by means of a "grammatical" approach but that to penetrate to the inner form, we must rely on the "divinatory" power. And he meant nothing mystical: this power is ours by virtue of our common human experience. It seems to me that Rosenblatt is instructive and inspiriting when she is discussing the transactional stance, which entails just such a dialectical method; but when she turns to what purports to be two kinds of reading she is less certain of their relationship.

In the case of this pair, *efferent/aesthetic,* by the time Rosenblatt has explained how both can play a role in reading either literature or mathematical formulas, one might wonder if they are worth keeping. *Efferent* sounds too close to *reading out* which, with *reading in,* constitutes a pernicious dichotomy. The notion that first we neutrally decode "the words on the page" and then we respond is at odds with Rosenblatt's teaching, but the term *efferent* rather distracts us (me?) from her sense that the reader responds from first to last in terms of his experience. For Rosenblatt, the reader responds by means of the meanings which emerge in the process of reading. Taken with *aesthetic, efferent* might suggest, in the absence of a triadic conception of the sign, that meaning making is being deferred. If we remember that *efferent* and *aesthetic* are meant to be taken together, that it is a matter not of sequence but of focus, these terms can serve us in our thinking about the reader's response.

Two other pairs of terms can illuminate Rosenblatt's distinctive pair. One is Wolfgang Iser's *wandering eye/focus.* Mariolina Salvatori has given us an excellent explication of this concept and has noted the pedagogical implications.[2] And I hope someone will investigate Rosenblatt's distinction in the light of C. S. Lewis's between *use* and *receive.*[3] Iser's pair opposes mutually dependent activities; Lewis's are mutually exclusive. We are asked to renounce "use"—reading for message or comfort—and to cultivate instead the habit of receiving what literature has to offer.

One source of confusion is, I think, that Rosenblatt's pair sometimes functions like Iser's and sometimes like Lewis's, but it's what she does with her concepts that counts. Rosenblatt's conception of the aesthetic stance guides her in a brilliant critique of E. D. Hirsch's attempt to deploy Frege's *Sinn* (significance or import) and *Bedeutung* (referent) for purposes which, as she explains, Frege excluded (*The Reader* 111–112). All philosophers must make a stab at differentiating not only what-is-said and what-is-meant but also the modes of representing both what-is-said and what-is-meant. Frege knew that the relationship of these two aspects in works of art is not of the same sort as that relationship in scientific statement. What Richards wrestled with for forty years; what Wittgenstein despaired of figuring out, counseling silence at the end of the *Tractatus;* what Susanne K. Langer labored to develop, a philosophy of presentational form: what others have seen as one of the most challenging philosophical problems of the twentieth century, Hirsch meets by muddling and misapplying terms. Rosenblatt provides as good protection as anyone I have read against such "gangster theories" (Richards' phrase) as are represented by Professor Hirsch's authorial intention, which he identifies with Frege's *Bedeutung*. There are other gangster theories which she can help us defend ourselves against, such as that "structuralist poetics" which sets meaning aside in order to study the codes and conventions that make meaning possible or that deconstruction which Paul de Man proclaims as the mission of literary study in years to come, the collapse of poem into text. Getting rid of the interpreter or destroying what he is meant to interpret are variants of a view of language as a substitute for reality and of literature as only self-referential. As she discusses the actualities of reading, it is clear that Rosenblatt begins, as Vygotsky advises, with "the unit of meaning" and that she suffers from no irrational anxiety about the impossibility of ever knowing what is meant directly, by revelation or no-fault decoding.

Louise Rosenblatt's theory of reading is, like Paulo Freire's pedagogy of knowing and I. A. Richards' philosophy of rhetoric, informed by a trust in what Coleridge called "the all-in-each of human nature." And because of the way she conceives of language and literature, learning to read is the means of learning virtue:

> When we are helping students to better techniques of reading through greater sensitivity to diction, tone, structure, image, symbol, narrative movement, we are also helping them to make the more refined responses that are ultimately the source of human understanding and sensitivity to human values. (*Literature as Exploration* 290)

With Rosenblatt as our guide, we will recognize and celebrate the social contexts of literature, confident that her theory of literature will protect us from "using" it, from teaching for message.

I began by claiming that Rosenblatt is a thoroughgoing pragmatist, and that that is why we have from her such sound guidance for our practice. Her trust in the power of the mind; her commitment to honest and open questioning and discussion; her understanding of the political importance of learning to tolerate not only other people's opinions but ambiguity itself: these are, of course, not exclusively American traits, but when they are found in conjunction with belief in democratic values, we certainly want to claim them as American. Rosenblatt closed one book with John Keats and the other with Walt Whitman—and that makes the symbolic point: her love of beauty is joined by her teacher's passion for literature as exploration, as the best way to open up democratic vistas. In her important essay, "Whitman's Democratic Vistas and the New 'Ethnicity,' " she beautifully shows us how responsive reading—authentic interpretation—reclaims the hermeneutic bond of individual and community, what Schleiermacher saw as the way each person represents humanity in his or her own way. She writes:

Whitman enjoins upon us an active selectivity, a testing, a rejection of all derived from our ancestry that is alien to the special needs
of a free society. . . . Whitman shows us the man and woman accepting themselves in all their uniqueness, honoring their own roots, but
free to reach out in all directions to their fellow humans. ("Whitman's
Democratic Vistas" 199–200)

Louise Rosenblatt makes me proud to be an American.

Notes

1. For Father Ong, transaction is only an ongoing interaction. This profoundly positivist conception trips him into contradiction: "An interpretation," he writes, "is shaped by the text as a given reader interacted with it."
A few sentences later we find him saying that "a text reacts not at all to any
interpretation" ("Beyond Objectivity" The Reader-Writer Transaction as an
Altered State of Consciousness" *The CEA Critic* 40 (1977): 6–13). The second
statement is clearly true, if you take the text out of any dialectical relationship
with emergent discourse, and it negates the first statement, since interaction
surely entails reaction.

2. See "The Pedagogical Implications of Reader-Response Theory," *Reader*
16 (1986): 1–19.

3. See *An Experiment in Criticism* (Cambridge: Cambridge UP, 1961). Here
is one of Lewis's explanations: "A work of (whatever) art can be either
'received' or 'used.' When we receive it we exert our senses and imagination
and various other powers according to a pattern invented by the artist. When
we 'use' it we treat it as an assistance for our own activities. The one, to use
an old-fashioned image, is like being taken for a bicycle ride by a man who may
know roads we have never yet explored. The other is like adding one of those
motor attachments to our own bicycle and then going for one of our familiar
rides. These rides may in themselves be good, bad, or indifferent. . . . 'Using'
is inferior to 'reception' because art, if used rather than received, merely
facilitates, brightens, relieves, or palliates our life, and does not add to it" (88).

Works Cited

Richards, I. A. "Variant Readings and Misreading." *So Much Nearer: Essays
    Towards a World English*. New York: Harcourt, 1960. 183–200.

Rosenblatt, Louise M. *The Reader, the Text, the Poem*. Carbondale, IL: Southern
    Illinois UP, 1978.

———. "Whitman's Democratic Vistas and the New 'Ethnicity.' " *Yale Review*
    67 (1978): 187–204.

Vygotsky, Lev. *Thought and Language*. Trans. Alex Kozulin. Cambridge: MIT P,
    1986.

6

The Lost Reader
of Democracy

John Willinsky

For over half a century, Louise Rosenblatt has celebrated the reader
sitting before the literary text. She has defended the immediate experience of those quiet moments with a book, especially as they might
take place in a classroom, and at the same time she has tried to keep
before us the salutary role that literature can play in a democratic
education. Her work has brought about the accreditation of the reader
as the site of individual meaning and development. It has meant a
viable curricular alternative for the English teacher, one that might be
loosely described as student-centered, and yet that centering has been
carefully situated in the student's ability to realize the aesthetic experience and broadening influence of literature. Her work arose out of the
progressive education movement in the 1930s and eventually developed into a formative influence on contemporary reader-response
theory of the 1970s. It continues to play a significant part in the discourse that surrounds the teaching of English. But over the course of
her career, her theory of literature has undergone its own transaction
with the changing interests of progressive educators and the increasing professionalism of English studies. In considering Rosenblatt's
contribution to the teaching of literature in the schools, I find that she
was increasingly drawn away from her original reconciliation of the
aesthetic and political roles of literary education in favor of a narrower
concentration on the reader's experience with the text.[1]

Perhaps the first consequence of Rosenblatt's original concern with the social and political role of literature was the interest she took in improving the teaching of literature at all levels. I begin with this point because it is not often that a literary scholar turns an eye to literature's place within the sizeable public domain of the schools. Gerald Graff's recent history of English in the university, *Professing Literature: An Institutional History*, provides one instance of what is lost by this oversight. In paying little heed to the schools, he misses the point at which a good deal of the professed ideas about literature are enacted with what is referred to in the sociological literature as a conscripted clientele. When Graff finds English "singularly ineffi- cient" in the politics of "dominant ideology and control" (14), he is simply overlooking the ways in which literature is worked with the young in school. To take one prominent instance, high school English classes give Shakespeare his most widespread hearing, and in the process teachers do more than simply introduce the wonders of the plays to the students in preparation for their university courses. The teachers use the texts to educate and examine the students, to teach them about what counts as official culture, behavior, literacy, and learning. In one sense, then, the literary text in the English class serves as an instrument of ideology and control, but an instrument that is governed by the teachers' understanding of literature and how it should be handled with a class. To her credit, Rosenblatt recognized that literature's lesson is constituted, in part, by the available and accessible theories of literature out of which educators might build their English programs, their ideals and best lessons, if not always their daily practices. She realized that the schools have a profound influence over the place of literature in the culture and that much could be done to improve that understanding of literature and the important ideological part it could play in the development of the individual and the state.

This critical tradition in literary education, which embraces the widespread cultural and moral imperative of literature and its educa- tional function, dates back to Matthew Arnold. As Her Majesty's School Inspector, he was able to secure for literature a central moral place in the emerging public education system of the latter half of the nineteenth century (Willinsky). His efforts to deploy literature as a moral corrective in British schools were furthered in this century by F. R. Leavis and the influential teachers who had been his students. In a similar tradition, Rosenblatt, trained as a literary critic, did not grow deaf to the strains of Shakespeare drifting from high school windows or to the subtle ideological work that goes on in the school: "At no time, of course, has the school been entirely free from the responsibil- ity of influencing character and mental habits" (*Reader* 200). It is a responsibility, she realized and argued, that was ideally suited to literature's calling, and one that should be turned to democracy's purpose. Though she attacks on occasion "the didactic, moralistic concern of the Victorians for the reader" (*Reader* 3), her goals for literary study are no less ethical or functional: "The study of literature can have a very real, and even central, relation to the points of growth in the social and cultural life of a democracy" (*Literature* v). Rosenblatt recognized the important roles schools played in their work with literature, and it was to improve the utilization of literature both aesthetically and politically that she first articulated her new-found promise for literature, a promise that would start the student-reader on the road to being a critical, sensitive individual and citizen. This sense of a moral purpose, of finding both self-development and state improvement through literature, has always been a special part of the English teacher's cultural mission (Mathieson).

However, Rosenblatt was to give it an unmistakably American flavor with a call for a liberal democracy and its eventual stress on an economy of freely engaged transaction with the text. And yet for all of that, when she spoke of literature's ability to "nourish the development of balanced humane personalities" (*Literature* v), it is easy to hear an echo of Arnold's promise that "poetry does undoubtedly tend to form the soul and character" (60). Her work has always reflected an interest in having the reader "participate fully in the poetic experience," a theme she first took up in her doctoral dissertation at the Sorbonne, *L'Idée de l'art pour l'art dans la littérature anglaise pendant la période Victorienne;* yet she has been equally determined to "reconcile two often opposed positions" between "a Keatsian sense of the unique values of art" and "a Shelleyan feeling for its social origins and social impact" (*Reader* xi). In terms of both the unique value and social impact, she understood the potential of the English class and felt a responsibility to ensure its vital place in the larger educational enterprise of a democracy.

Rosenblatt built her theory of literature's aesthetic place out of a pragmatic concern for how the text could work as a progressive force at every level of the educational enterprise, an education to "be judged in terms of its effect on the actual life of the student; the ultimate value of any knowledge depends on its assimilation into the very marrow of personality" (*Literature* 215). To understand the manner in which her work has introduced an appealing and alternative education in literature—one still current in the schools, as I shall demonstrate—is to appreciate what it takes for such progressive alternatives to pervade the schools, and the way in which developments in literary theory can be said to serve public education. To provide this service is also, again as I shall demonstrate, to risk a certain isolation as a scholar, a consequence that Rosenblatt eventually tried to over-come in a book that only served to increase her service to the schools.

Although it is beyond the scope of this paper to determine sequence and cause with any assuredness, it seems fair to say that Rosenblatt played a part in the changing progressive interest in education over a period of four decades. In the course of this complicated process, however, it seems clear to me that of the personal and social aspects of literature which she initially laid out in *Literature as Exploration*, her development of a transactional theory of literature favored the individual's relationship to the text over the social role of literature, or what might be termed a reader's contribution to the democratic state. In this chapter, after reviewing the shift in her position through her two books, I will examine contemporary instances of her work applied to curriculum that demonstrate this shift in her orientation. Throughout her career, her work continued to serve a progressive English program that had grown introverted, if not narcissistic, in its search for more efficient and accurate models in the psychology of learning and self-enhancement. While I would readily admit to an interest in having the political question reinstated in discussions of progressive English teaching, I believe that Rosenblatt's work offers considerable insight into how ideas about literature become embodied in English programs, a dynamic process that reflects equally on the nature of literary theory and public education.

Rosenblatt's first major educational statement, *Literature as Exploration*, was published in 1938. In affirming literature's contribution, she does not simply assume its importance as part of a cultural heritage or a holdover from an organic community long past, as Leavis and Thompson were doing at about the same time with their popular textbook for British schools, *Culture and Environment*. Rosenblatt, instead, sets the stage for a literature that serves not the glories of the past but the practical demands of the present. Her book opens with the pressing needs of the world beyond the school: "In an unsettled world, our schools and colleges are confronted with the demand that they prepare the student directly for living" (3). *Literature as Exploration* was sponsored by the Commission on Human Relations, a group associated with the Progressive Education Association. The association advanced a broadened mandate for American schools, which included introducing into the curriculum new concerns about health and vocation, family and community; it promoted an increased sensitivity to individual differences and represented a vibrant educational force during the first half of this century only to meet its official demise in 1955 (Cremin).

Rosenblatt's book was published during the heyday of the Progressive Education Association. Membership in the association peaked in 1938, and a cover story in *Time* that year confidently reported that "no U. S. school has completely escaped its influence" (Cremin 325). Rosenblatt readily brought the progressive education project to bear in the teaching of literature, a project that educational historian Lawrence Cremin has described as "part of a vast humanitarian effort to apply the promise of American life—the ideal of government by, of, and for the people—to the puzzling new urban-industrial civilization that came into being during the latter half of the nineteenth century" (vii). In *Literature as Exploration*, Rosenblatt summarizes the task of a progressive literary education "in our present era of social change" in broad and ambitious terms:

1. To supply youth with the tools and knowledge necessary for a scientifically objective, critical appraisal of accepted opinion . . .

2. To . . . predispose the individual toward working out a basis for a more fruitful living. (*Literature* 212)

Rosenblatt's contribution to the Progressive Education Association was to specify how literature could facilitate the achievement of what might be seen as broadly liberal goals in the exploration of human relations as literature serves the individual in advancing the democratic state. It must have seemed that a well-armed reader intent on working toward a better life was an ideal democrat in the voting booth or an elected position. Rosenblatt imagined literature serving these political goals in conjunction with the promising new work in the sciences both technological and human.

Literature as Exploration is striking in its optimism. Rosenblatt comes across as more than a little sanguine about the powers of the scientific spirit, and she suggests that the literature teacher would do well to embrace it. Quick to attack what she saw as a romantic opposition to the new science, she extols its virtues in tones that now seem as dated as cars finned like jet airplanes: "More and more evidence is accruing to demonstrate that science, properly exploited, might eventually liberate the whole mass of our people from the drudgery of mere money-getting for physical survival, so that they would have the leisure and the energy for the rich imaginative life that literature and the arts offer" (157). It has turned out somewhat otherwise with science and the ensuing rich imaginative life; but then, too, Rosenblatt's initial interest in liberating "the whole mass of our people" might be said to have gradually narrowed into an effort to reduce the drudgery people experienced with the literary text in English classes.

In the 1930s, her utopian vision also drew on the young and positivist growth areas of sociology, psychology, and anthropology; the human sciences appeared to be another essential element in the promise of "fruitful living": "The social sciences, then, are slowly building up a body of knowledge concerning important factors in the development of human personality and in the patterning of human society" (192). Rosenblatt had done post-graduate studies with Franz Boas and Ruth Benedict at Columbia University and took the time in *Literature as Exploration* to bring the "particularly useful" insights from anthropology and related fields to the literature teacher. She carefully outlines "some of the basic concepts the teacher of literature should draw from the social sciences" (168) and reminds the teacher of educational responsibilities that go well beyond the teaching of the literary text. As part of the progressive education mandate, she imagined an integrated curriculum with literature as a vital component of what was broadly conceived of as a social studies program. The sense of a common project and responsibility in which literature had its unique role to play gave this program its messianic drive, its strength as a promising curriculum for progressive schools.

In balancing this program among the sciences and the literary arts, she often let the former serve as background, by describing, for example, the cultural influences on personality, after which she would give the more active pedagogical role to literature. It alone offered the most engaging manner of broadening the experience and enriching the personality of the young: "Books are a means of getting outside the particular limited cultural group into which the individual was born" (228). Yet literature's service to the development of the whole and healthy child is a means of entry, of getting the child more fully into this burgeoning American society. At one point on this theme, she momentarily loses the balance she normally struck between the individual's integrity and the state: "Literature can play an important part in the process through which the individual becomes assimilated into the cultural pattern" (222). Whatever the truth to this supposition, it was frankly addressed to the political function of education, if only to offer each student a literary plunge into the great melting pot through their progressive English class. This frankness about the politics of English teaching, however, was to become less fashionable among progressive educators and literary theorists as both fields developed a greater interest in a form of proficient specialization.

Although I have been emphasizing how widely Rosenblatt ranges in this work from purely literary concerns, I would also note that a feature of her work at this time was that at the very point where she seems to roam too far, too naively, into the powers of either science or literature, she is careful to qualify her work. She remains sensitive to the dangers of the literary text getting lost in this collaboration with the masterly social sciences. It was clear to her that while reading had its place with the social and psychological services rendered to the citizenry of this democracy, it also engaged the reader in a private and aesthetic experience of the text: "The reading of any work of literature is, of necessity, an individual and unique occurrence involving the mind and emotions of some particular reader" (32).

It might be said that the democratic role that she first imagined for literature hinged on a respect for the integrity of the individual's response to the text, combined with a collective responsibility to pursue, through science, a more fruitful life for all. In advising teachers of literature's place in the curriculum, Rosenblatt drew on the social and applied sciences, as well as literature, to equip and thus further enfranchise the student readers while offering them incorporation into the larger culture. In a common striking of parallels, she saw the educational development of the student's personality as concurrent with the enhancement of the political state. In looking back at this perspective, one can see that it was motivated by an interest that went far beyond an interest in developing a (literary) authority for the teaching of English. Though we may doubt whether the teacher of literature can successfully juggle so many interests, Rosenblatt does her best to find the encouraging points of union: "The enhancement of these human values will therefore depend upon the intensification and enrichment of the individual's esthetic experience" (53). The literary text was the very instrument both to inform and sensitize the student; it would hone the critical tools necessary for development of the student within the democratic state.

Forty years and many articles after her initial statement "addressed primarily to teachers of literature in high schools and colleges" (*Literature* xi), Rosenblatt put aside pedagogical concerns in her second major statement, *The Reader, the Text, the Poem: The Transactional Theory of Literary Work*, which was published in 1978. In this work, she attempts to step over the educational and political mandate she had once embraced in favor of the seeming maturity of literature read outside of school which so lends itself to literature in theory: "Eschewing further educational themes, I concentrate on presenting a matured and more fully developed theory of the literary work of art and the implications of criticism" (*Reader* xii). By the time of *The Reader, the Text, the Poem*, Rosenblatt's primary focus had shifted from the role of literature as part of a broadly conceived social studies program to one more purely literary; her faith in the social sciences appears to have waned. On the other hand, the discipline of her doctorate, literary criticism, had blossomed into a professional undertaking, which had in a sense left her behind. Her touchstone in this second book shifts from the scientist's hypothesis testing, the anthropologist's comparative cultural studies, and Dewey's democratic experimentalism to the wordy and esoteric labors of the literary critic, to the works of Empson, Hirsch, and Barthes.

In this book, the reading of a poem is above all else a private and a literary event. Rosenblatt not only sets aside her earlier stress on the social sciences, but she also discards the *vicarious* powers of literature through which a work could bring readers the experiences of their fellow citizens in a sympathetic framework, making it the very tool of a diverse democracy. Her debt to Dewey also moves from his attempts at reconciling the aesthetic and social to his formulation of the *transactional*, which in her terms indicates "an ongoing process, in which the elements or factors are, one might say, aspects of a total situation, each conditioned by and conditioning the other" (17). Yet this concentration on the reader's transaction with the text meant a certain narrowing of her original scope—"the text becomes the element of the environment to which the individual responds" (18)—and the social function of literature becomes somewhat more introverted: "Literary texts provide us with a widely broadened 'other' through which to define ourselves and our world" (*Reader* 145). Her circle of interest at many times in the book, though by no means all, closes in on the reader and the text, as the title of the book suggests (in contrast to the outward-looking *Literature as Exploration*). Even as it closes in on the literary event, it begins to reach into the curriculum of English teaching with a new forcefulness.

One lesson that becomes apparent from this and other instances of the transfer from literary theory to public education is the particular efficacy of terminology and taxonomy. In order to advance their program, progressive educators require fresh distinctions around which to rally their attack on regressive traditions in the schools. Rosenblatt, however, approached the task apologetically, stressing the fact that she requires only a modest set of three new coinages—"it is the only jargon I think I've indulged in" ("Interview" 5). Her transactional theory of the literary work was based on the distinctions that could be made between an *aesthetic* and *efferent* reading of a text. As is now well known to English teachers, the aesthetic reading was distinguished from the efferent one by its concentration on the "experience" that is being lived through with the text, rather than in what can be "carried away" in an efferent reading (*Reader* 24–25).

Although Rosenblatt eschews educational intent in this book, I would argue that the aesthetic/efferent distinction she proposes therein works most effectively in a pedagogical setting. It has become part of the rhetoric of the progressive educator's paradigm struggle. Outside of the context of the English classroom, the efficacy of the terms remains questionable and in a way appear to turn against Rosenblatt's own work. The terms are often employed to attack a pedagogical tradition that was satisfied to teach literature by asking students twenty questions about the poem's form and content. Such an approach was clearly attempting to teach literature efferently, with an eye to what students could cart away from the work. What was missing, the use of the two categories made clear, was the opportunity for students to experience the text in an aesthetic manner, an experience that was, after all, what art was all about and that might in the context of the classroom be profitably shared, refined, cultivated, examined.

In considering the terms outside of this pedagogical context, the first difficulty is that the aesthetic and efferent reading seem too much like exclusive categories, an idea that Rosenblatt reinforces on occasion—"the text may be read either efferently or aesthetically" (*Reader* (25). The very definition through opposition seems to discourage the sense of combination or oscillation that we might suspect is closer to our own varied experiences in reading any given text. Even when she sets two terms on a continuum, the tendency is to place the entire "reading act" at a given point, even if the choice is left up to the reader ("Viewpoints" 101): "It is the reader who must adopt predominantly one or another model of activity during the transaction with the text" ("Aesthetic" 20). But then, too, consider whether between this "experiencing" and "carrying" of texts, there is sufficient space provided for *bringing* a critical eye to the text or *giving* it a close scrutiny. Which is to say that, in terms of Rosenblatt's earlier goals, this theory of reading and literature does not give proper status to the sort of "critical appraisal of accepted opinion" that she had held as the principal function of education in her earlier book (*Literature* 212).

A second point to be made on the importance of the educational context to *The Reader, the Text, the Poem* is Rosenblatt's professed interest in making the literary work "part of the fabric of individual lives" (143). It is a thread running back to *Literature as Exploration*, in which literature was to be integrated into a broadly conceived program given to developing the person and the state. However, in this later version a certain subject specialization has settled over the theme, which limits the reach of this fabric. She has decided, for example, that in *The Reader*, "the poem" will serve as a stand-in for all literary texts. The poem provides a convenient text for analysis and criticism, but it is not a very representative one of the general literary activity of the populace. Not without a touch of irony, then, does she attempt to set aside the chalk and lectern; it is a time when the reading of poetry and the writing of criticism have never been more institutionally bound and today's poetry readers must seem a very slight population, apart from students, teachers, and other writers.

While I seem to fault her for forsaking the original role that she created for literature in the fabric of individual lives, I have come to recognize that certain personal and professional elements may have

directed her shift of attention. The point worth noting is that these
ideas about literature and curriculum are located in the lives and
careers of individuals. Rosenblatt's pursuit of a "more fully developed
theory" within the specialized realm of literary theory represents
another important element in considering the movement of ideas
about literature as they wend their way into the teaching of English in
the schools. Her drive to push her work beyond education to literary
theory can be seen as a final effort to escape the element of intellectual
isolation that can haunt those who work in schools and schools of
education. In the fashion of these postmodern times, she would situate the true claim of her work as a theory competing with textual
theories. Rosenblatt had originally fought against this seeming isolation of literature from the political agenda for the schools. But that has
remained a minority position and she may well have felt her own
sense of isolation in the academic community. She has given indications in her later work that she suffered an undue neglect in a manner
related to questions of gender and education in our society ("The
Transactional Theory" 33–34). David Bleich has speculated that "for
reasons not altogether clear—perhaps having to do with her being a
woman in a School of Education—her work did not (or was not permitted to) enter the continuing critical exchange in academic literary
communities" ("Intersubjective" 402).

This personal issue, within what might be termed another aspect
of "reception theory," plays an important part, to my mind, in understanding the relationship between the literary scholar and the public
school. When she was first teaching English literature at Barnard
College, she had dared to take up the social cause and conscience
of education in a democracy, only to find herself toward the end of
a distinguished career in the School of Education at New York University, writing a book intended, one might say, to re-insert herself into the academy of literary theory, into the mainstream of the
profession. The opening line of her preface to *Literature as Exploration*
had been a prophetic one: "Many teachers of literature feel themselves to be somehow outside the sphere of present-day intellectual
ferment" (v).

Elizabeth Flynn has written sympathetically of Rosenblatt's place
within reader-response criticism, treating her orientation as progres-
sively feminist from its early concerns with the emancipated woman
in literature to the later interest in the woman's voice as writer and
critic (23). Yet Flynn notes that the "important contribution" of her
work had been ignored by this field of criticism until the 1970s, and
only then footnoted more often than anthologized (20). Bleich, for
one, has tried to make good this lapse in the 1980s by opening a piece
on reader-response with "this path for criticism was introduced into

contemporary thought in 1938 by Louise Rosenblatt when she proposed, in the idiom of John Dewey, that contributions to reading
experience must be coming from both the text and the reader"
("Intersubjective" 401). The fact is that in 1938, Rosenblatt was using
her own language to speak of the literary experience, and that her
employment of Dewey's term "transaction," which he developed in a
1949 book with Arthur Bentley, came in her later development of the
relationship between reader and text.

In addressing the oversight of Rosenblatt's contribution on the
part of these communities, Bleich offers that her work "was soon lost
in the onrush of formalist exegetical criticism which emphasized the
objectivity of literary knowledge" ("The Identity" 254). By an interesting coincidence, *Literature as Exploration* was published the same year
as Brooks and Warren's *Understanding Poetry*, a book which effectively
launched New Criticism. Rosenblatt was to later treat New Criticism
as a mistaken response to I. A. Richards's influential work. For her
part, she had taken Richards's psychological interest in the process of
reading as the basis of what was to become reader-response theory.
Yet New Criticism was to become the effective site of something more
than a critical method for reading literary texts. As Graff makes clear
in his history of the discipline, New Criticism was part of the English
professoriate's search for a distinct identity and projection as a profession, which is what Bleich's reference to "onrush" was all about.

Whether reader-response critics such as Flynn or Bleich have succeeded in rectifying the earlier oversight, they cover over her shift in
interests by concentrating on their own interests. In spite of their call
for belated recognition for Rosenblatt's work, they make it clear that
the breadth of her concerns, as they originally spanned the individual
and the state, have selectively found their way into educational practice and lore. This shift occurred over a period marked by the success
of the New Critics, who had followed their own form of the scientific
and professional spirit of the times, a spirit distinguished from Rosenblatt's expansive progressivism by a skill-centered specialization. The
distinction is helpfully made by John Fekete's rather harsh characterization of New Criticism, in the form John Crowe Ransom was to give
it, as that which "abdicates the social critique, forgets the 'anaesthesia'
of the scientific machine efficiency, and reduces a profound problematic to the typically modern fetish of a language abstracted from material reality" (90). Although New Criticism's lack of a social critique has
been challenged by Mark Walhout's recent suggestion that it, in
fact, embodied a cold-war response to liberalism, Fekete's attack has a
certain face validity to it, and for my purposes is applicable to Rosenblatt's later work even as it repeatedly took on "the New Critics' neglect
of the reader" ("Viewpoints" 103). Fekete's criticism of New Criticism,

with its charges of "abdication," "forgetfulness," and "abstraction,"
describe the educational mood which Rosenblatt increasingly had to
cater to in the construction of a literary curriculum for an individualism of self-enhancement.

While I have stressed up to this point the differences between the
orientations of Rosenblatt's 1938 and 1978 books, I would not misrep-
resent the continuities that certainly exist between the works. For
example, the chapter in the earlier book entitled "The Literary Experience" concentrates on the "fruitful interrelationship between the individual book or poem or play and the individual student," which she
compares to "the interaction of two complex chemical compounds"
(32–34); the direction of this reaction is toward both "the student's
appreciation and enjoyment of literature" and "a parallel development of his emotional nature and his understanding of life" (64). The
seeds of the later transactional theory had taken root. Similarly, in the
later book, Rosenblatt addresses the place of literature in the democratic state. Yet politics takes on a more marginal role, turning up in
the preface and in the final chapter of the book. She closes this work
on her transactional theory of literature with Walt Whitman's "vision
of a great literature for a truly democratic society," which required
strong readers: "Not the book needs so much to be the complete
thing, but the reader of the book does" (175). My point remains that
this vision suffered a certain tunneling, as Rosenblatt pursued the
completeness of what the reader "is living through during the reading
event" ("Aesthetic," original emphasis, 22), rather than developing
the broader critical mandate that she had originally pursued.

A second point I would add to this consideration of intellectual
shift in her work is that although literature's political role was to slip
from the progressive education agenda set by Rosenblatt, the topic is
far from moribund or resolved in literary and educational circles. It is
not that she had found and then abandoned the answers to pressing
questions of equality in a democracy through the teaching of literature. But she did recognize the issue as a fair question for English
teachers. However naively Rosenblatt championed the scientific spirit
and literature's promising role in more fruitful and democratic life, she
had pressed ahead with the troubling issues of a literary education
within the ideological realm of public education. Nor has there been
a complete lack of interest in these issues, since the days of her early
politically sensitive work. English's ideological role in the educational
marketplace has had its interested inquirers, as the work of, among
others, Judith Fetterley, Richard Ohmann, Edward Said, and Elaine
Showalter might indicate. But in Rosenblatt's case the concern with
the social impact of literature was met with polite silence by the
majority of progressive educators as increasing interest was shown in

her ability to celebrate the individual reader's response to the isolated text. Yet, the minority interest in her earlier work has put *Literature as Exploration* through four editions, and she has held to the continuing relevance of the book—"As the fourth edition goes to press," Rosenblatt wrote in 1983, "the concerns of the book are more urgent than ever." In this way, she has been able to keep alive the full spectrum of her work, even if all elements have not been developed equally.

Yet had she sought to develop this element of literature's political role, rather than the nature of its psychology, she might have found pockets of supporting critical interest that would have welcomed her contribution. Among the New Critics, Robert Penn Warren continued throughout his life to declaim the critical democratic function of the literary text: "Our poetry, in fulfilling its function of bringing us face to face with our nature and our fate, has told us, directly or indirectly, consciously or unconsciously, that we are driving toward the destruction of the very assumptions on which our nation is presumably founded" (31). Equally so, Henry Giroux's Marxist criticism of education echoes Dewey's call for a critical pedagogy with results that sound like early Rosenblatt as Giroux admonishes, "We must prevent democracy from retreating to the periphery of public life" (17). Finally, in seeking instances of this continuing political concern with literature, I was surprised to find Paulo Freire and Donaldo Macedo innocently citing Rosenblatt as a "seeming liberal approach to literacy [which] fails to make problematic class conflict, gender, or racial inequalities" (149). The fact is that, while she did celebrate the aesthetic moment, she also dealt with those issues in her early work and more importantly, like Freire, she demonstrated how the power of the word was a political force, which began in the reader's experience in language and the world. One need not subscribe to Rosenblatt's original sense of literature's vicarious function in a democracy, which is clearly more than "seeming" liberal, to note that her original work on the politics of literature was a promising starting point and worthy of development.

To give examples of how this shift in Rosenblatt's work has affected the curriculum of the schools, I thought to turn to the testimonial of a teacher employing her work, an authority in a position to assess its impact on the field, and, finally, an official curriculum document that incorporates her work into policy statements. Among these instances, there is a certain imperfection in the adaptation of her work, which is to be expected, and there is also the selective use made of it, which is also hardly surprising. Yet the aspects selected tend to reinforce my concern that her work has come to stand for reading as an isolated experience of the reader alone with the text, and that, in turn, the book is not part of the political and cultural fabric, which had been Rosenblatt's starting point.

My example from the classroom comes from the *Journal of Reading*. In 1982, Miriam Chaplin published a piece entitled "Rosenblatt Revisited" in which she described how her courses in developmental reading and reading methods at the college level have been guided by a transactional theory of reading. Chaplin has found that Rosenblatt's analysis can be applied to any course to encourage a "move from efferent to aesthetic transactions," recalling to mind how the categories function as a critical tool in reshaping curriculum. She concludes that "the personal response, so necessary in literary reading, is equally important in efferent reading" (154). In Chaplin's evocation of a transactional theory in what she terms a "skills instruction" setting, we see the final traces of Rosenblatt's concerns with a politics of reading disappear in this process of intellectual transfer; the personal elements that do remain are absorbed into a scheme of personal development that focuses on greater cognitive efficiency. It hardly needs adding that Rosenblatt had always held out something more for the reader.

Chaplin's selective paring down of Rosenblatt to fit her program forms a common pattern. When James Squire, former president of the National Council of Teachers of English, decided on the "Ten Great Ideas in the Teaching of English During the Past Half-Century," he placed Rosenblatt's contribution second on his list. His description of that contribution centers on the transactional theory, although he ends up giving her work a New Critics' exclusiveness of focus: "The teaching of literature must focus on the transaction between reader and the literary work, not on the work itself, the history of the work, the social milieu from which it sprang nor the biography of the author" (10). She is also credited with drawing our attention to the complexities of responding to literature and fostering a good deal of research in this area. Yet in so setting aside her once and great concern with literature's role in the democratic state, the very thing which she had first taken issue with in fashioning a new approach to literature— "art for art's sake"—has become, with only a slight twist, her most important accomplishment in shaping the teaching of literature.

The final instance is from my own educational jurisdiction of Alberta; the Department of Education has issued a new *Junior High School Language Arts Curriculum Guide*, which pays a certain tribute to Rosenblatt's efforts. Her place is firmly entrenched in the section entitled "Reading/Literature" in which the *Guide* explores the differences between "efferent and aesthetic reading." However, the distinction is applied in what seems to be a rather crude manner. The *Guide* stresses that "in junior high there needs to be a greater emphasis upon reading literature aesthetically, since lifelong reading is an objective of the Alberta language arts curriculum, and most lifelong readers read aesthetically" (42). (The point is certainly debatable, given the repeated best-seller status of such genres as the how-to books—a success dating back at least to Caxton's *The Arte and Crafte to Knowe Well to Dye*—but the policy is also notable for the way it implies that the goal of reading is simply a lot more reading.) The *Guide* goes on to state that to "understand and appreciate imagery or figurative language in a passage is part of an efferent analysis" (42), which is not only misleading but carries with it the implication that such "appreciation" is not the sort of thing that lifelong aesthetic readers do. Rosenblatt has herself had occasion to object to the blurring of her terms in educational settings ("Viewpoints"), and I think that the nuances are obscured because the purpose here is not so much to clarify the literary experiences of students but to further pedagogical ends with teachers. The province's curriculum committee appears to employ Rosenblatt's distinctions to steer teachers away from a reading skill and drill approach to literature, which goes after the *facts* that a poem teaches, as Rosenblatt has put it with some indignation ("What Facts").

The *Guide* does employ parts of Rosenblatt's earlier position in making broad claims for literature, although these lack the pedagogical focus that the transactional theory provided: "Vicariously and artistically, it extends and illuminates students' ideas and experiences" and it encourages students "to develop a sense of their own values and a sense of tolerance and understanding of others" (42–43). Finally, it returns with greater precision to Rosenblatt's contribution to affirm the special relationship that should be struck in the classroom between the student and the page: "Personal response is an account of the transaction that occurs between the reader and the text as meaning evolves" (43). Here we have the idealization of the reading process contained in Rosenblatt's work, which imagines, to borrow the appropriate economic model, an unrestrained transaction between equals without acknowledging the considerable market forces exercised by the English classroom in determining value and meaning.

In this way, the literary theorist can be thought to reach the classroom and affect the ways in which literature is worked by students and teachers. The theorist does so by generating a language and conceptual framework for talking about literature that offers educators, one might say, a way of transacting with their profession as its meaning evolves. For English teachers this is never a purely literary exercise, but neither is it completely removed from their own feeling for the work of literature as an important cultural and moral form. There is something in Rosenblatt's transactional theory of literature that corresponds to these teachers' sense of reading. While I have pointed to certain limits to this theory, I also think it fair to say that it has contributed to a less authoritarian handling of the texts and students, which offers them considerably more room to find their own way into literature, as well as into the program and norms that the school fosters.

But in comparison with the original agenda set for literature by Rosenblatt, the scope of this transformed transaction remains limited to the space between reader and page. The development of a larger literary transaction with the world of authority and meaning has not been pursued. It is possible that in this I hope for too much from literature and the English teacher; it does seem to me that Rosenblatt has at times given literature a certain overstated claim: "Literature can compensate, thus, for the limitations of time and place and class and nation; can compensate, too, perhaps, for the limitations and sorrows of the human condition" ("A Way" 169). It may seem enough for educators to seek a limited, if quiet, transaction between student and text. Certainly, the larger questions of class and sorrow can seem unduly taxing for an English teacher facing them without considerable support. But the key here is the provision of support which entails the imaginative exploration of the possibilities by those who are working with literature and education. In this case, literature's relationship to these larger concerns has failed to receive from Rosenblatt the same degree of energy, vision, and theoretical development that marked her later work on the transactional theory of literature.

In bringing about a transfer from literary theory to public education, it is the transactional theory of the literary work that has successfully, if not always accurately, entered the language of literature teaching. Through the development of this concept Rosenblatt was able to offer a new degree of enfranchisement for the student as a reader capable of participating in the literary experience, even if the important role this might play in a democratic society was not to be fully realized or explored. Yet I hesitate in making such a pronouncement; judgments of such seeming finality can often be premature. One encouraging sign has been the formation in 1987 of the English Coalition, a collaborative effort by school and university English teachers in the interest of working toward a program of common purpose in the teaching of language and literature (Lloyd-Jones and Lunsford). I take special comfort in their official slogan, "Democracy through Language," as it offers a certain hope that the balance of Rosenblatt's original position may have begun to find its time again, and that we might continue to "develop curriculums based on the vital role of literature in the lives of individual students and in the development of a democratic society" ("Pattern" 1012).

Notes

1. Although my interest in this chapter is in the development of Rosenblatt's ideas for progressive education, there is more involved in the implementation of her work than writing essays and books. She assisted in the transfer of her ideas into the classroom through an active "service" role as well. Besides her involvement with the Commission on Human Relations which resulted in *Literature as Exploration*, she was part of the three-person drafting team for the Joint Committee of Twenty-Four of the MLA, which formulated a statement on literary aims (Applebee 136 n45). Rosenblatt also advised the Commission on Secondary School Curriculum, which issued the report *Language in General Education* in 1940 (Applebee 181 n46). In 1946, she edited a special issue of *English Journal* devoted to encouraging racial and religious tolerance through the study of English (Applebee 179 n26). In 1980, she was still seeking out new educational paths as she addressed "how recent findings about children's acquisition of language support" the transactional theory of reading and "some of the implications for the teaching of reading, with emphasis on the treatment of literature in the early years" ("What Facts" 386).

Works Cited

Alberta, Canada. Dept. of Education. *Junior High Language Arts Curriculum Guide*. Edmonton, Alberta: Alberta Education, 1987.

Applebee, Arthur N. *Tradition and Reform in the Teaching of English: A History*. Urbana, Ill.: National Council of Teachers of English, 1974.

Arnold, Matthew. *Reports on Elementary School, 1852–1882*. London: HMSO, 1908.

Bleich, David. "The Identity of Pedagogy and Research in the Study of Response to Literature." *Researching Response to Literature and the Teaching of Literature: Points of Departure*. Ed. Charles R. Cooper. Norwood, N.J.: Ablex, 1985. 253–72.

———. "Intersubjective Reading." *New Literary History* 17.3 (1986): 401–21.

Chaplin, Miriam T. "Rosenblatt Revisited: The Transaction Between Reader and Text." *Journal of Reading* 26.2 (1982): 150–54.

Cremin, Lawrence A. *The Transformation of the School: Progressivism in American Education, 1876–1957*. New York: Vintage, 1961.

Fekete, John. *The Critical Twilight: Explorations in the Ideology of Anglo-American Literary Theory from Eliot to McLuhan*. London: Routledge and Kegan Paul, 1977.

Fetterley, Judith. *The Resisting Reader: A Feminist Approach to American Fiction*. Bloomington, Ind.: Indiana UP, 1978.

Flynn, Elizabeth A. "Women as Reader-Response Critics." *New Orleans Review* 10 (1983): 20–25.

Freire, Paulo, and Donaldo Macedo. *Literacy: Reading the Word and the World.* South Haley, Mass.: Bergin and Garvey, 1987.

Giroux, Henry. "Liberal Arts, Public Philosophy, and the Politics of Civic Courage." *Curriculum Inquiry* 17 (1987): 335.

Graff, Gerald. *Professing Literature: An Institutional History.* Chicago: U of Chicago P, 1987.

Leavis, F. R., and Denys Thompson. *Culture and Environment: The Training of Critical Awareness.* London: Chatto and Windus, 1935.

Lloyd-Jones, Richard, and Andrea Lunsford, eds. *The English Coalition: Democracy Through Language.* Urbana, Ill.: National Council of Teachers of English, 1989.

Mathieson, Heather. *The Preachers of Culture: A Study of English and Its Teachers.* London: Methuen, 1975.

Ohmann, Richard. *English in America: A Radical Look at the Profession.* New York: Oxford UP, 1976.

Rosenblatt, Louise M. *L'Idée de l'art pour l'art dans la littérature anglaise pendant la période victorienne.* Paris: Champion, 1931. New York: AMS Press, 1976.

———. "Interview with Louise Rosenblatt: The Reader's Contribution in the Literary Experience." *English Quarterly* 14 (1981): 3–12.

———. *Literature as Exploration.* For the Commission of Human Relations. New York: Appleton-Century, 1938.

———. "On the Aesthetic as the Basic Model of the Reading Process." *Bucknell Review* 26.1 (1981): 17–32.

———. "Pattern and Process—A Polemic." *English Journal* 58.7 (1969): 1005–12.

———. *The Reader, the Text, the Poem: The Transactional Theory of the Literary Work.* Carbondale, Ill.: Southern Illinois UP, 1978.

———. "The Transactional Theory of the Literary Work: Implications for Research." *Researching Response to Literature and the Teaching of Literature: Points of Departure.* Ed. Charles R. Cooper. Norwood, N.J.: Ablex, 1985. 33–53.

———. "Viewpoints: Transaction Versus Interaction—A Terminological Rescue Operation." *Research in the Teaching of English* 19.1 (1985): 96–107.

———. "A Way of Happening." *Challenge and Change in the Teaching of English.* Ed. Arthur Daigon and Ronald Carter. Boston: Allyn and Bacon, 1977. 155–69.

———. " 'What Facts Does This Poem Teach You?' " *Language Arts* 57.4 (1980): 386–94.

Said, Edward W. *The World, the Text, and the Critic.* Cambridge, Mass.: Harvard UP, 1983.

Showalter, Elaine. "Women and the Literary Curriculum." *College English* 32.8 (1971): 855–63.

Squire, James. "The Ten Great Ideas in the Teaching of English During the Past Half Century." *Teacher as Learner.* Ed. Merron Chorny. Calgary, Alberta: Language in the Classroom Project, 1985. 19–32.

Walhout, Mark. "The New Criticism and the Crisis of American Liberalism: The Poetics of the Cold War." *College English* 49.8 (1987): 861–71.

Warren, Robert Penn. *Democracy and Poetry.* Cambridge, Mass.: Harvard UP, 1975.

Willinsky, John. Recalling the Moral Force of Literature in Education. *Journal of Educational Thought* 22.2 (1988): 118–32.

7

Modes of Reading, and
Modes of Reading Swift

Russell A. Hunt

Over the past few years it has become clear to me that I don't know nearly as much about reading as I once did. For instance, ten years ago I was sure I knew what one did with a passage like the one I'm going to quote here. In fact, what I did know was what one was *supposed* to do with it, and it was fairly direct (if not exactly uncomplicated): one was to find out what its *real* meaning was. I now think, however, that the act of reading is a lot more complicated than that model allowed for, perhaps especially when you're dealing with a text that's as rich and rewarding and endlessly engaging as the one I'm going to cite here (or, perhaps, as rich as most of the texts we've all agreed to call "classics" of literature). Thus I'm no longer nearly so sure I know the appropriate way to deal with this text.

These days, I can think of at least four quite different ways in which one might read it. It's an excerpt from a book published anonymously in London in the year 1726. In it, a world traveler who identifies himself as one Lemuel Gulliver describes a custom he's observed in one country he visited. He calls the participants "Rope-Dancers":

> This Diversion is only practised by those Persons who are Candidates for great Employments, and high Favour, at Court. They are trained in this Art from their Youth, and are not always of noble Birth, or liberal Education. When a great Office is vacant either by Death or Disgrace (which often happens), five or six of those Candidates petition the Emperor to entertain his Majesty and the Court with a Dance on the

Rope, and whoever jumps the highest without falling, succeeds in the
Office. Very often the chief Ministers themselves are commanded to
shew their Skill, and to convince the Emperor that they have not lost
their Faculty. *Flimnap*, the Treasurer, is allowed to cut a Caper on the
strait Rope, at least an inch higher than any other Lord in the whole
Empire. I have seen him do the Summerset several times together
upon a Trencher fixed on the Rope, which is no thicker than a common Packthread in *England*. My friend *Reldresal*, principal Secretary for
private Affairs, is, in my opinion, if I am not partial, the second after
the Treasurer; the rest of the great Officers are much upon a Par.
(Davis 39)

In an article in *College English* in 1987, William Dowling, a re-
spected scholar of eighteenth-century literature, pointed out that
when he studied Swift in university, this—in part—is what was
offered by the notes on that passage in the text he used (it was also the
one I used when I studied Swift as an undergraduate):

> Flimnap represents the famous Whig statesman, Sir Robert Wal-
> pole, head of the government from 1715 to 1717 and from 1721 to 1742.
> His political dexterity is here satirized. Swift disliked him both as a
> man and a politician. . . . Reldresal [is] possibly Lord Carteret, Secre-
> tary of State in 1721 and later Lord-Lieutenant of Ireland; . . . Also
> suggested as Reldresal: Lord Townshend, Secretary of State and a chief
> ally of Walpole. (Landa 504)

Now, Dowling can't for the life of him understand—nor can I—how
we ever came to like the eighteenth century and its literature in the
face of the assumptions about reading that seem to be implicit in that
note. As Dowling phrases it, "The most unrepentant biographical-
historical critic who ever lived might see, one supposes, the sense in
which this sort of thing spells death in the classroom" (526). It is clear,
though, that Louis Landa, who wrote the notes to that edition,
believed—and we must agree that the reasons he believed it were not
trivial ones—that it was important for students to follow the complex
political and social allegory of Gulliver's visit to Lilliput.

Still, it is apparent that that note invites you to read as though the
text were primarily a source of information about the eighteenth century, an example of literary history, or evidence about the author's
life. Looking at Gulliver in Lilliput in such a way you are likely to find
interpretations like this appropriate: Gulliver represents Lord Bolingbroke, "tied down" (politically immobilized) by a legion of (morally or
intellectually) tiny bureaucrats and packthread laws. Lilliput is England, and Blefescu, across the channel, is France. The Emperor of
Lilliput is George I. (One of the problems with this sort of allegorizing
is exemplified by Arthur Case's classic footnote: "The Emperor represents George I, although much of the description of his physical and

mental characteristics is inconsistent with the facts" [14–15]. Any student must wonder, as I did, if the description were so inconsistent with "the facts," how anyone ever recognized the allegory.)

It was, of course, true that most teachers agreed with Landa that knowing about all those obscure details of the history of English parliamentary politics was justified because it helped us enjoy Swift. And as it turned out, Dowling and I, and a few other people, must have enjoyed him: we apparently did, in fact, go on to read lots of other eighteenth-century texts, and build up our knowledge of the background, and sometimes even became experts on the political allegory of *Gulliver's Travels* and professors of eighteenth-century literature. Most people, though, responded exactly as you might expect. Dowling phrases it this way: "The dense circumstantiality of so much eighteenth-century poetry and prose, the relentless allusion to people and places and acts of Parliament one never heard of, puts off the inquiring undergraduate student" (524). And, even for those of us whom it didn't put off, it certainly tended to render Swift a writer whose concerns seemed far distant from our own.

One important problem with that sort of focus on information is the way in which it affected how I and other students actually read and responded to Swift and other writers. At the time, of course, none of us knew that Louise Rosenblatt, in 1938, in *Literature as Exploration*—a book hardly anyone in traditional university English studies was to notice until the seventies (cf. Suleiman and Crosman, and Clifford)—had distinguished between two kinds of reading one might do with literary texts. She called one of them *efferent*—meaning that you wanted to take something away from the reading with you to remember—and the other *aesthetic*—meaning that you wanted to live through an experience with the text. That distinction—and even more basically, the important idea that reading might not be a unitary, unproblematic phenomenon, but different things entirely in different situations—allows me now to think more clearly about the reading I was doing then. It was *possible* to read the Flimnap and Reldresal passage aesthetically with Landa's footnote staring you in the face, but it wasn't easy. And since eighteenth-century literature was so circumstantial anyway, and thus more difficult to begin with, it was pretty easy to lose sight of what Rosenblatt called the aesthetic, the "lived-through experience," and just find a way to rejoice efferently in the biographical, historical, and political details. (Or, of course, to give up on Swift altogether, which is what most people did.)

What I now suspect was particularly important about reading in this way was that it was a distancing procedure. Once I had mastered it, I could read Swift without being directly involved at all; I could admire his skill, even gasp at his rhetorical brilliance, and still hold myself quite aloof from the implications of his ideas. Thus I never understood at all why so many nineteenth-century literary figures— the most well known was William Makepeace Thackeray—were so outraged, even angry, at Swift for being cynical and occasionally obscene and outrageously skeptical about human dignity. I thought of myself and my colleagues as pretty enlightened and tolerant to be able to read Swift with a cool appreciation of his brilliance.

All this was a long time ago, and in another country. Though many of us graduate students weren't exactly aware of it then, a revolution was not only underway, but had in most circles long before been won (and in fact the new regime was already under counterattack). Among people who argued and cared about literary theory and criticism, the critical approach that had come to be called New Criticism had long before swept the field, and the fruits of that revolution were already apparent in many classrooms. (It is not entirely irrelevant, by the way, that the dominance of the New Critical defense of literature as something approaching an "objective science" was one of the main reasons so few people knew of the existence of *Literature as Exploration.*) Among lots of other changes, the New Critics offered us a new way to read *Gulliver*.

It's no simple matter to describe exactly the difference New Criticism made to the classrooms of the late fifties and early sixties. It's difficult partly because so much of what it proposed became so widely accepted that soon we didn't know we believed it any more: it became almost immediately the new common sense. Dowling presents an excellent description of the impact of New Criticism on the way he (and I) taught Swift and the other eighteenth-century writers. At the same time it suggests something more general about what the New Criticism was.

> What New Criticism said, in a word, was that this episode wasn't about Robert Walpole, head of the government from 1721 to 1742: it was about politicians, who are still there, walking tightropes, in this morning's *New York Times*. Flimnap was a politician, but he was not Walpole; he was, as Fielding says about the lawyer in *Joseph Andrews*, someone who has been alive these four thousand years. (526)

Though New Criticism said, of course, quite a lot more than that, what is relevant here is the way it convinced us all that the historical origins of a work of literature, or what you might find out about what its author thought he meant to do in it or through it, or with it, couldn't tell you what the work actually *did:* only the work could tell you that. The result of believing that was that all the work those generations of scholars had done in identifying Flimnap, and Reldresal—and even the cushion that Gulliver says once kept Flimnap from breaking his neck (Queen Caroline)—was rendered, apparently, irrelevant to the classroom. What mattered now was what the work meant, said, and did, in and of itself. This led us toward designating as our central critical and pedagogical activity what we called then— what we still call—"close reading of the text." Rather than trying to look through the text to what might lie behind it—what it might tell you about Swift's political opinions, or the character of the age he lived in, or even about Swift's psychological adjustment or lack of it—we were to look at "the text itself."

This had some good effects and some bad ones. At the time, most of us who were teaching undergraduate courses in eighteenth-century literature thought the results were pretty much all to the good. Now, we thought, we could ask our students to read *Gulliver* in the faith that the text would make everything clear if only we all just read it hard enough—we wouldn't have to go through that long, distracting, boring period of preparation, of filling in historical and social background, before our students would be "ready" to read Swift. If you read the Flimnap and Reldresal passage carefully and closely enough, we said, it just sort of "automatically" became a comment on politicians in general. What else could it possibly mean?

Another effect of buying into New Criticism was that we focused our attention on different kinds of passages (and, in fact, often even on different works altogether—as, for instance, Donne's poetry replaced Milton's as the central work of the seventeenth century). In the case of *Gulliver*, for example, different events and passages became central. Klaus Zöllner has shown how the choices of passages that scholars quoted from Gulliver to prove their various contentions changed over the course of this period—how, for instance, passages concerned with *text* gradually replaced passages concerned with *philosophy*. For us as teachers, the Flimnap and Reldresal passages became more like background, and they were replaced in the center of our lens by passages like the wonderful, ironic attack on war, when Gulliver explains to the poor, dumb king of Brobdingnag why he ought to be happy to have the secret of gunpowder. Poor Gulliver doesn't understand the king's appalled response.

> The King was struck with Horror at the Description I had given of those terrible Engines and the Proposal I had made. He was amazed how so impotent and groveling an Insect as I (these were his Expressions) could entertain such inhuman Ideas, and in so familiar a Manner as to appear wholly unmoved at all the Scenes of Blood and Desolation, which I had painted . . .
>
> A strange Effect of *narrow Principles* and *short Views!* that a Prince possessed of every Quality which produces Veneration, Love and Esteem; of strong Parts, great Wisdom and profound Learning, endued

with admirable Talents for Government, and almost adored by his Subjects, should from a *nice unnecessary Scruple,* whereof in *Europe* we can
have no Conception, let slip an Opportunity put into his Hands, that
would have made him absolute Master of the Lives, the Liberties, and
the Fortunes of his People. Neither do I say this with the least Intention to detract from the many Virtues of that excellent King, whose
character I am sensible will on this Account be very much lessened in
the Opinion of an *English* Reader. (Davis 134–35)

What New Criticism did with a passage like that, of course, was
to direct our attention to its exquisite and elegant irony—to the facts,
for instance, that Gulliver had just previously betrayed himself to the
king as a member of what the king now called "the most pernicious
Race of little odious Vermin that Nature ever suffered to crawl upon
the Surface of the Earth" (Davis 132), and that Gulliver himself clearly
has not the least idea why the king is beloved by his people, or what
makes him an excellent king. Teaching this, then, we didn't have to
bother with the historical background—the fact, for example, that
gunpowder had been a common example of the evils of technology in
the arguments between traditionalists and progressives ("Ancients"
and "Moderns"), arguments that Swift had been engaged in most of
his adult life. We could skip all that background and get right to the
literature. Dowling says this "appeared to scholars and teachers of my
generation as a kind of classroom salvation" (525).

But, as it turned out, we weren't to be so readily saved. I now
think we were deluding ourselves. That we weren't conscious of all
our historical and social background didn't mean it wasn't conditioning and determining how (and what) we read. It *did,* however, mean
that when we told students that it was "just them and the text," when
we assured them that if they just read closely enough they'd get it,
what we really did was to make it seem like magic to most of them. We
made reading seem, even more than it had, something that only the
really brilliant, the inexplicably initiated, could do. The students simply didn't have access to the contextual information we were tacitly
bringing to bear on our reading—and, moreover, didn't have any way
to know that that was the problem. So, just as the students of a
previous generation had done, they relied on us to tell them what the
text said—and, now, even to tell them what it did. The New Criticism,
even though it was embraced by many of us in the sixties as a method
of liberating students from the domination of specialized knowledge,
a way to free literature from its bondage as the private possession of
a small, initiated group of highly trained specialists, didn't ultimately
do that at all. What it did was to change the nature of the required
training and give authority to a new group of initiated and sophisticated specialists: ourselves.

Again, let me come back to reading Swift here to make a little clearer what I mean. What happened was that a new way to read the book was substituted for the old one. The new one asked us to be aware of irony and paradox and ambiguity rather than to know or learn about historical background, and it thus asked a reader to make a quite different set of connections among elements of the text. Instead of asking students to connect Flimnap with Jonathan Swift's specific political and social context—with Robert Walpole—we asked them to connect him with the narrator's and the ironist's views, with Reldresal and the king and with other elements within the book. (At the same time, it was at least in part the specialist knowledge of Walpole and of Swift's social context that made it possible for us to see what kinds of connections were likely to be fruitful, although most of us were not aware of it.)

As a teacher, I found this New Critical stance a lot more comfortable, but I have never seen any convincing evidence that my students thought it was such a wonderful advance, or that they were more likely to leave my classes convinced that Swift and the other eighteenth-century writers spoke to them as well as to the ages. I thought they enjoyed the classes a little more, but they didn't seem to enjoy Swift more. I met, ten years later, one of the brightest students I'd had in the mid-sixties, and he told me that he'd really liked the classes and the discussions of politics and morality, but he'd hated Swift and Johnson then, hadn't looked at them since, and couldn't remember anything they'd written. If I'd known of it, of course, *Literature as Exploration* might have suggested a good deal of what was wrong— but of course I did not.

Another way to say this, perhaps, is that the New Critical assault had not really touched at all the citadel of the old historicism, the ability of the reader coolly and judiciously to distance herself from the text. Our distancing strategies were different, but their effect was the same: I still didn't understand why Thackeray could have been so angry.

There were a lot of other reasons why we all began to question our New Critical principles in the later sixties and seventies, and many of them didn't seem to have much to do with teaching or with Swift.

One, for example, had to do with the growing interest in different kinds of texts from those—predominantly, lyric poems of the seventeenth or twentieth century—with which New Criticism had seemed to work reasonably well. For longer narratives, for long poems, for the novel, for texts like *Gulliver*—which, when you come right down to it, doesn't have a lot of internal coherence—New Criticism didn't really get us much of anywhere. After all, Flimnap and Reldresal and the rope dancing only appear once in the text: even the notion of parlia-

mentary democracy is a preoccupation that really only occurs in Book
One, and I (and many readers) have a very difficult time connecting
it with the rest of *Gulliver*. It's the same with the King of Brobdingnag
and the gunpowder: Swift's skepticism about technology does come
up elsewhere, but you'd hardly call it the controlling theme of the
book—unless, of course, you were writing an article and trying to gain
tenure or promotion.

But another problem was more generally important: New Criticism had called on us to disconnect writings from their authors (we
weren't to ask what the author intended, or said he intended: this was
Wimsatt and Beardsley's "intentional fallacy") and from their readers
(we weren't to be concerned with how real readers now actually
reacted: this was their "affective fallacy"). The text was all there was,
and it was our job to see the real nature of each text in and of itself, to
see how it attained its own unity and coherence and balance. This New
Critical disconnection of the text from writer and reader—as Frank
Lentricchia and Terry Eagleton, among many others, have pointed
out—rendered literature ideologically and practically innocuous,
made it seem to have little or nothing to do with real history or the real
world.

As Dowling phrases it, "The same New Critical magic that made
Dryden's and Pope's poetry [and Swift's prose] universal also rendered
it in a curious sense bodiless, robbed it of the rootedness in human
history that allows it to speak *about* history in a way no literature more
openly engaged with cosmic or universal issues can do" (527). In other
words, if Swift was really about politics as an abstract idea, he somehow didn't seem nearly as interesting as he would have seemed to
someone—a contemporary, perhaps, or a carefully and fully informed
and educated modern reader—who knew and cared about Walpole
and parliamentary history. He wasn't really the same Swift any more.
No wonder my student hadn't been as turned on by Swift and Johnson
and Pope as I was: he hadn't read the same writers. He'd read writers
who were going the long way round to make abstract points about
politics in general—points we could have made just as well by
ourselves, with current examples. Surely it would be more powerful,
if you wanted to make an abstract political point, to use the examples
of deputy ministers in the reader's own capital city leaping up and
down from their tightropes for their jobs after an election.

It should hardly be a surprise, then, that many teachers of eighteenth-century literature (among others) began to look for new ways
to help other people share their conviction that writers like Swift were
worth spending some time with.

In recent years, one of the most important of those new ways has
arisen out of a critical movement which has come to be called the New

Historicism. For some people, this has meant going back to talking about Walpole and Bolingbroke and Queen Caroline, but for others it has offered what seems a new way to reconnect Swift's work with his—and our—real concerns. The new reading that such an approach would recommend asks different questions of the text. It doesn't ask the traditional historical questions: "What do we need to know to understand this text?" or "What does this text tell us about the age?"—the ones Rosenblatt made fun of in her article title: "What Facts Does This Poem Teach You?" Nor does it ask the New Critical questions: "What *is* this text, in and of itself? How does it work and what holds it together?" The question it asks is something more like this: "What was Swift actually *getting at*"? If, in other words, we see Swift in his historical context, can we understand what he was actually using Flimnap and Reldresal and the King of Brobdingnag *for?*

As I rethought my own teaching and understanding of Swift under the impetus of this set of ideas, a number of things seemed more important to me than they had before. One of them, for example, was the fact that Swift was an Irishman. I'd known that before, of course, but it hadn't seemed very significant. Most of Swift's major works were really written in English contexts, so they didn't tell you much about Ireland, nor did you need to know much about Ireland to identify Flimnap. And if *Gulliver* was really about abstract ideas, and if Swift's intentions were irrelevant to a reading of the text, it didn't much matter what nationality Swift was.

But, in fact, it now began to seem to me that it did make a difference. Describing that difference may illustrate some of the ways in which this new approach might make "what we do with Swift" different. Let me try to explain how much difference it made to me to read Swift in this new way.

If you ask most people where Swift was born, or grew up, or where he wrote *Gulliver*, they'd probably answer, "England, of course." But, of course, it's not so. Swift was born in Ireland, spent virtually all his life there, wrote most of his masterpieces there, and died in Dublin a national hero.

To call Swift English and teach his works as masterpieces of English literature makes about as much sense as calling Nathaniel Hawthorne English because he lived for some time in London, or Joyce Carol Oates Canadian because she taught at the University of Windsor. But with the sort of natural, effortless imperialism whereby England in the nineteenth century always assumed that anything fine must really be English at bottom, Swift simply got appropriated. He's been taken over so thoroughly that textbooks that include his works rarely make much of the fact that Swift's birth and upbringing made him something quite different from a typical Englishman of the eighteenth century—or of any time, for that matter. They don't often suggest that he might have become the greatest satirist ever to write the English language precisely because he spent his childhood in a society alienated from and colonized by England, surrounded by Irish attitudes toward life, humor, and language. They don't give you much reason to guess that a great deal of the power of his satire might come from the same springs that produced Oliver Goldsmith and George Bernard Shaw, Oscar Wilde and James Joyce and Samuel Beckett, Sean O'Casey and Brendan Behan and Flann O'Brien.

It was under the influence of such a New Historicist viewpoint that I began to understand the peculiarity of Swift's position, and that of many Irish writers. He'd been raised an Anglican in a Catholic country; he was a member of an economically privileged colonial ruling class who, almost within living memory, had been imposed on Irish society from outside, by military conquest; he'd lived in a middle-class enclave surrounded by the most abject kind of poverty, the kind we might see now only in a particularly disadvantaged third-world country. These things affected Swift and everything he wrote in profound ways.

Among other things, knowing this helped me feel the depth of Swift's contempt for that political rope dancing, or why he might have thought of having the pompous little Englishman, Gulliver, offer the King of Brobdingnag the gunpowder that would have made him absolute master of the lives, the liberties, and the fortunes of his people.

Now there may not seem to be much difference between reading Swift as an eighteenth-century Irishman and reading him as an eighteenth-century Englishman, at least in terms of the reading itself. In my view, though, the difference seemed dramatic. When the New Critics argued against the old historical approaches to literature, they did so on the grounds—I thought they were correct then, and I think so still—that such approaches tended to make literature into a kind of inferior history, and tended to lose track of what makes literature itself important. In their view, what made literature so important was its form, its internal perfection, its status as a timeless achievement of permanent beauty.

I'd suggest that such a New Historicist reading of *Gulliver*—which asks, among other things, who its author was and whom he was writing to—takes still another view of what makes literature so special. I think it's saying that what makes literature worth paying attention to is that it is through literature that human beings have used the power of written language to speak to other human beings about things that genuinely mattered, to writers and to readers, and that by overhearing those frozen conversations, by thawing and participating in them, we can come to understand them, both the readers and the writers, and become ourselves better participants in that long-standing conversation—which is, after all, our civilization.

To read Swift as the Irish outsider this new perspective made him seem, passionately attacking attitudes and practices whose consequences he knew and had witnessed and suffered, is, it seems to me, to participate in that conversation in a way that using him as a door to history, or as an example of delicate and perfect ironic patterns, could never do. It is to call for this kind of historically coherent understanding of the context in which Swift (and other writers) wrote that Dowling wrote the article I began by quoting.

But such a New Historicist approach is only a third way of reading Swift. I said at the beginning that I knew of at least four.

My last kind of reading really depends on, or arises out of, this attempt to see Swift as a real figure, acting in a real historical situation. My involvement in empirical research on reading over the past few years has made me think that there is a kind or mode of reading, regularly used by people who are attempting to engage themselves with texts like *Gulliver*, that has not been much considered by literary theorists or played much role in pedagogical thinking or practice.

As I have already noted, the very idea that there may be quite different kinds of reading, and that some are promoted by educational institutions and others ignored or marginalized, is one we owe primarily to Rosenblatt's illuminating and important distinction between *efferent* and *aesthetic* reading (see especially *The Reader, the Text, the Poem*).

As we have tried to think through the implications of this insight, my colleagues in reading research and I have come to think that you can—and that many people do—also read in another way, one that looks like something a little different again from either of the kinds that Rosenblatt described, although it is entirely consistent with her argument that what is central is the idea of reading as a "transaction." (See below for a discussion of the importance of this concept.) You can, it seems to us, read as though your central purpose were to "make contact" with another human being (Vipond and Hunt, "Point-Driven Understanding" and "Shunting Information"). This may, in fact (as Rosenblatt has suggested in a personal communication of 1985) be a subcategory of *aesthetic* reading; we believe, however, it's important to distinguish it from the larger category, which includes reading for the vicarious experience afforded by the text, but without attention to author, purpose, or significance—ignoring, that is, what one might call the status of the language as social discourse.

In a casual conversation, the sort of contact we're talking about is made through the sharing or exchange of "evaluations," as they are defined in sociolinguistic analyses of conversational storytelling by, for example, William Labov or Livia Polanyi. Evaluations, which can be conveyed either directly (a narrator might overtly comment, "I was never so scared in my life") or indirectly (for instance, by a striking metaphor or unexpected detail or other "departure from the local norm of the text"), seem to invite the reader to share fundamental values with the narrator, and thus allow for the narrative to be understood in such a way that it seems meaningful, significant, potentially relevant to the hearer's immediate social context.

Although all the participants in such a conversation might not agree on any given formulation of what "the point" of a successful story might be, or on what the motives or character of the teller were, they would agree that it wasn't "pointless" (this is what it means to say it was "successful"). The auditors wouldn't, in Labov's terms, be tempted to ask the teller, "So what? Why did you tell us that story?" It's important to stress that "points" aren't exactly equivalent to "meanings" or "gists" or even "purposes." Nor are they something that can be found "in" stories. They are a function of the story's relationship to its social situation, and they are much more accurately described as a social consensus about relevance than as any set of textual features. A story in one situation might afford the creation of a quite different set of "points" than in another, and in the same situation might seem to be making different points to different readers. Often, as Polanyi has pointed out, the construction of a point or points for a story can become a social process in its own right.

Some of the readers we have studied seem to be reading in a way that is closely analogous to this way of listening; for instance, they are particularly likely to notice opportunities to construct evaluations (Hunt and Vipond, "Evaluations"). They are also more likely to make connections between their experience of reading and their own immediate situations, or to take into account peripheral information about the physical presentation of the text (Vipond, Hunt, Jewett, and Reither). Whether a reader reads in this way (or focuses mainly on acquiring information from text, or on immersion in a vicarious fictional experience), is influenced by the reader's own experience, preferences, and expectations; by what sorts of reading the text seems to the reader to afford; and by the situation in which the reading occurs (see Hunt and Vipond, "Crash-Testing," and Vipond and Hunt, "Literary Processing").

In other words, reading is a *transaction*. Used in this way, the term is, of course, Rosenblatt's ("Towards a Transactional Theory," "Transaction Versus Interaction," "Writing and Reading"; see also Vipond and Hunt, "Literary Processing"), and was originally drawn from Dewey and Bentley. To consider an event a transaction is to make no rigid separation of *object* (text) from *subject* (reader), but to see that the two together, each participating and each being affected, produce—or, rather, are—an "event" (a poem). Perhaps even more important, the transaction—as Dewey and Bentley particularly insisted—does not take place in a vacuum, in some grey, bracketed-out experimental space, but rather in the world, and thus in the case of reading must be seen as integrally involved with the immediate social experience of readers and writers—indeed, cannot be understood without taking that situation into account. Dewey and Bentley argued in 1949 that it was already becoming clear that we cannot understand even the most classically mechanical physical processes if we abstract the process from the observer and the specific situation in which it occurs, or if we try to understand the objects as they are "in themselves," outside the transaction or the situation in some unimaginable isolation. In just this way, Rosenblatt makes clear that the richer, more complex phenomenon of reading cannot be understood except as a contextualized whole. Our research has supported and perhaps extended this view.

In general, we have found that the readers who seem most engaged in, and who feel most satisfied with, their readings (of these texts, in these situations) appear to act as though the purpose predominating in their reading were to make social contact, by sharing evaluations, with a narrator or author who is assumed to be somehow "behind" or "implicit in" the text. Using Bakhtin's terminology, one might say that they are taking the text as an "utterance," with all the rich dialogic connections with preceding and succeeding and concurrent utterances that that implies. It is of course true that traditional literary theories—e.g., Wimsatt and Beardsley—suggest that readers should not be doing that (or, alternatively, that they should be attempting to ascertain exactly what the historical author intended, as argued by E. D. Hirsch). Still, our observation suggests that many readers—often those who apparently feel most comfortable in dealing with "literary" texts—do it anyway (and on the other hand show little interest in investigating the opinions or aims of the historical author).

All this work leads me back to some speculations on the reading of *Gulliver's Travels*. What might it mean to "make social contact" with the implicit author of *Gulliver's Travels*? In what ways might a reader connect *Gulliver* with the immediate social context of her reading, and with the larger society in which the reading occurs? It is tempting to suggest that such "literary" contact is exactly similar to the sorts of contact we make in conversation, but that it can potentially run much deeper and entail more complicated kinds of sharing of more sophisticated evaluations—and with people like the author of *Gulliver's Travels*.

It may be important to remember here that we do not normally participate in conversations in order to produce new interpretations—

or to voice, like Randall Jarrell's mockingbird (see also Hunt, "Lots of Holes"), condescending and "helpful" approval of the contributions of others. Nor is it usual to "respond" to conversational story or statement by voicing, to a third party, an interpretation or explanatory restatement of what has been said. If someone in a conversation had "made social contact" (or failed to make it) with the author of *Gulliver's Travels,* she would probably not turn to explain to someone else what he had said or to expatiate on its brilliance—or, if she did, such an act would constitute changing the subject and potentially derailing the conversation. (On the other hand, it might, of course, become necessary to "negotiate" an appropriate social relevance among those readers present, the way the group in Polanyi ["So What's the Point?"] describes negotiating "a point" to help their friend save her story about "fainting on the subway.")

What we normally do, when a story or piece of discourse—a conversational turn, an utterance—is successful, is to express our response (e.g., by laughing) or to tell a new story that responds to the original, elaborates on it or connects with it in some way, to retell the story in a new context. Or perhaps we adopt the story's metaphors and terms to deal with our own later experiences. In general, we *use* what the story has given us. Emerson points out that Bakhtin has made the powerful argument that it is only by assimilating the words of others—"retelling"—that we can orginate anything, and that it is this struggle between the language of others and our need to internalize it that we "recognize as intellectual and moral growth" (31). (It is, of course, also true that we may, especially if we're professional critics, try to account for the success of the story to ourselves and to others. But we can't do that until it's *had* that success.)

I would suggest that it is in order to do that sort of thing, in order to participate in such dialogue, that we read writers like Jonathan Swift. I read Swift, as I converse with a friend who's important to me, in order that he might change my life, and in order, perhaps, to internalize his story and retell it to someone else (literature teaching is one important way in which this is done). If he tries to change my life in unacceptable ways it's okay for me to be angry. Reading Swift in such a way makes him matter. It's this that makes it potentially important to know about Swift's Irish context, but the only reason that's valuable to know about is if I think Swift has the potential to change my thinking, my relationship to the world around me and other people: to change what I *do.*

Now, there can be many Jonathan Swifts, just as there are many individuals in each of the people we converse with every day. My Jonathan Swift, this year, in the current situation of my own life, happens to be a passionate Irishman, who has things to say to me

about the current troubles in Ulster and the Irish heritage of eastern
Canada, where I now live. A few years ago, however, he was a
skeptical Anglican rationalist, who spoke to me about my interests in
the history of the Church of England and my wife's involvement in the
Canadian Anglican church. Before that, he was a profoundly committed political and social conservative and journalist, with whom I
argued about the political convictions with which I was struggling,
and about which I was writing. At the very beginning, he was a
childlike fantasist who (as Dr. Johnson put it) "thought of big men and
little men," and spoke to my fascination with science fiction and
various kinds of logical extrapolation.

In each case, though, the basis of my engagement—whether I was
aware of it or not—was my reading Swift as though he were talking to
me, as though he were trying to change my mind and my soul—and
I think sometimes, in spite of my training, he succeeded. He has also
(more often recently) succeeded in making me angry. (I now think
I understand why Thackeray could have been so indignant at Swift.
He misunderstood, I think, but he and I would have agreed about
one thing: Swift is for us worth caring about, worth engaging
ourselves with, worth making contact with. He can make us angry,
with reason.)

What all this means, I think, is that people who engage themselves with him and enjoy his work don't normally read Swift in order
to produce "the truth" about his meaning, just as we don't do that
with conversations. We strive for what will work for us, what we can
use, about conversations and about texts, as C. S. Peirce suggested we
do about the world. (The question whether there is "a truth" about a
text—like the question about truth in general, as Richard Rorty
observes—is not a question about which you'd expect to find many
interesting opinions. The important and interesting question is what
we can do with it.)

Thus, my discovery of Swift's Irishness isn't very important in
itself. For one thing, it hardly counts, in the larger arena, as a discovery at all; it's far from news to most scholars of eighteenth-century
literature. One might "discover," in this sense, lots of things about the
author of *Gulliver's Travels* that might make him seem more clearly an
engaged, committed, living human intelligence, and one with whom
one might engage oneself—the Irish Swift happens to be the one I
currently create. It's that process of creating and recreating and engaging with one's own Swift in one's own world that is central—and it is
not a process for which there's much provision in most university
English classes. If we believe with Rosenblatt that the best reading is
the most richly transactional, we must ask ourselves how we can
create classroom contexts in which such transactions are supported

and promoted. It seems to me that they are just as unlikely to be effectively supported by situations in which we focus entirely on meaning (even when we define that meaning as the responsibility of the reader rather than the property of the writer) as they ever were by the situations in which it was our aim to read "through" the text to the historical or biographical information lurking behind it.

It's important to insist, too, that it's a matter of *creating situations* rather than of explaining things discursively. The classroom situation that already exists, what we might call the "default context," is one in which, as Derek Edwards and Neil Mercer make clear, discourse is inevitably centered on the teacher and transactions are mediated by that fact. Anne Freadman has observed that the situation of a class in French means that it is virtually impossible for a text to be seen as anything more than "an example of French"; similarly, it seems to me, literature classes render texts "examples of literature." To change this we must change the situation, not merely tell people how they ought to be reading. The processes by which people make connections with texts—make them into utterances in an authentic dialogue—are not so easily or consciously invoked or altered.

What, then, are my alternatives? More generally, what are the alternatives of any literature teacher? Is there a way to teach literature that promotes the kind of reading (of Swift and of other texts) that I'm arguing is appropriate, that does not compel readers to break off the potential conversation, or to change the subject? In fact, some practical alternatives are being developed to the standard classroom pattern, the pattern whereby a fixed text is assigned, read by a group, and discussed with the aim of arriving at a consensus (usually, tacitly or overtly, the "right" consensus) about its meaning. Such alternatives are appearing in locations as disparate as South Australia (Homer, Cook, and Nixon); England (Miall); and in Canada at McGill (Dias) and my own university.

To illustrate concretely one way in which the situation might be changed, let me describe briefly how my classes in eighteenth-century literature have been dealing with Swift over the past few years. The basic pedagogical strategy, which is being worked out in collaboration with a number of colleagues in English and other disciplines, is called "collaborative investigation," and full descriptions of its rationale and procedure in this and other disciplines are available elsewhere (see, for instance, Hunt "A Decade of Change," "A Boy Named Shawn"; Hunt, Parkhill, Reither, and Vipond; Parkhill; Reither "Writing and Knowing," "Writing Student as Researcher"; Reither and Vipond). Its basic purpose is to give students the opportunity and the responsibility to create for themselves, and to share with others, the knowledge and understanding that more traditional courses attempt to transmit.

(I should make clear that this particular description is based on a two-term course in Restoration and Eighteenth-Century Literature for undergraduate students specializing in English, and usually three weeks can be spent on Swift; parallel strategies can be used at other levels and in other disciplines. I assume here, simply for purposes of making the description concrete, a class of twenty-four; similarly, details can be altered for more or fewer students.) One result of implementing this strategy in a literature class is to give a new social status to texts and to widen the range of possible student activities in connection with them.

In such a class, when we approach Swift, there are a series of assignments, which students usually undertake in ad hoc groups, changed for each new task. The first sends eight groups of three to the library (usually to work during a scheduled class meeting time) to bring back written recommendations for the rest of the class about what works of Swift should be read, and why. As sources (the course has no uniform text or anthology) they use literary histories, textbook anthologies, critical and text editions of Swift, critical and historical work on Swift and the period, general literary references, and so forth. Each group prepares a list and some preliminary written arguments explaining why they believe each work is important. Before class seven photocopies of each report are prepared, and during class each is read and considered by a newly formed group of four students. Each group comes up with a consensus about works that should be read. A representative of each group then puts its list on the blackboard, and the class as a whole decides on a final list.

The class then divides up this list of works into eight workable categories or sets of texts, which might range from a selection of poems to *The Battle of the Books*, from a selection of *Examiner* essays to the Drapier's letters, from *A Digression on Madness* to *Gulliver*. A new set of groups is formed (again randomly) to prepare full reports and to recommend whether their texts, or some portion of them, should be read by the whole class. At the end of the class session these groups decide which sets they wish to report on, and, in a sort of auction, as each group announces its decision the item is crossed off the final list.

Over the next week, groups meet to prepare reports on their individual texts. These reports have typically included descriptions of the work, summaries, quotations of representative passages, and varying amounts of critical, bibliographical, or biographical background material. Reports are limited in length—a practical limit is what can be photocopied on two or three sheets of paper (eight to twelve pages, if the photocopier uses half-size reduction and if the copy is printed on both sides of the page). These reports are prepared over a week in which there are no class meetings (I am in the library for consultation during scheduled class meeting times), and then photocopied and distributed through a "mailbox system"—usually a set of large envelopes attached to the wall outside my office or the classroom—which allows the reports to be exchanged and read before class.

During that next class, working in new groups, the class decides on which (or which parts) of the works the whole class should read, and which should be the subject of expanded and edited reports, to be included in a permanent "course textbook," photocopied and bound at the end of the term. Groups that recommended the texts the whole class decides to read are assigned the job of making texts available (putting them on reserve in the library, photocopying them, etc.); those that recommended the ones accepted for inclusion in the course book are given the task of editing the final reports.

Finally, class time is set aside for discussion of some of the works to be read by everyone. One common way of conducting such a discussion is for each member of the class to write a page or two of immediate response, as soon as the reading is completed (or even to keep a "reading journal" of in-process responses). This impromptu, unrevised (and often anonymous) writing is brought to class and the class begins with everyone reading the writing of at least five or six other people. As they read, they respond to each piece of writing with marks in the margin next to passages that seem to them striking or interesting, and sometimes with accumulating graffiti (those of us developing this teaching strategy call this impromptu transactional writing "inkshedding"). Often the pieces are collected and passages with the most marginal marks transcribed on a word processor, printed, duplicated, and distributed at a later class session. Occasionally the class is continued with a further cycle of writing, reading, editing, and commenting; on other occasions oral discussion ensues. Occasionally, the "inksheddings" are edited for preservation in the "course textbook"; more usually, they are discarded once everyone has read them.

At least some of the potential general advantages of learning in such a way—which, I think, go well beyond the usual scope of a course in literature and literary history—should be clear from this very cursory description. Here, I want to focus on the ways in which such a strategy is consistent with what I am arguing about the nature of reading. Students in such a situation are not reading in order to form interpretations that they can write down for evaluation by an authority whom (rightly or wrongly) they assume already knows anything they might say. They are reading in order to describe texts to people who need descriptions, to persuade others to read them, to share what they read with their peers—to assimilate the words of others and appropriate them to their own uses, as Bakhtin might say, generating texts that are in a dialogic relationship with each other. Their success or failure in this reading (and writing) is not a matter of judgment by an outside authority, but an immediately and socially perceptible consequence: either others are persuaded by their arguments to read the text or not; others read their description of the text with interest or they don't; others are affected and respond or they aren't and don't.

What is most important for my argument here is the way in which the situation I am describing enables written texts to be taken as utterances, to serve as a basis for dialogue, to become a medium for social transactions among their readers. Because the students are involved in connecting texts to both historical and immediate social contexts for the readings, it becomes more likely that they will recognize the potential of the texts to make a difference to their own lives. Because they are so often engaged in exchanging the texts with, and recommending them to, each other, they are more likely to create relationships between the text and their own practical and immediate concerns. In other words, the situation is one that, more than a conventional interpretation- and teacher-centered course, affords the kind of reading I have been describing. Students are more likely to respond to anomalies, to "departures from the local norm of the text," by attempting to construct evaluations and less likely to dismiss them as meaningless "noise."

A good example, and one that is of course particularly appropriate to the reading of Swift, is the long-standing pedagogic problem of irony. That students so often "miss the point" of metaphoric or (especially) ironic passages is a problem often addressed as though it were a matter of acquiring information, but, as Chamberlain points out, it is much more a matter of attitudes or stances toward texts than of availability of information. Indeed, there is evidence that whether a reader brings any particular information to bear on a text is in large part a matter of such attitudes, and, in turn, of the situation in which the reading occurs (Hunt "Pragmatic Aspects"). A situation that affords the construction of evaluations is almost by definition one in which rhetorical devices like irony and metaphor—the "literary" embodiments of evaluations—are likely to find readers appropriately engaged.

Thus, in such a situation, a reader is more likely to respond to the passages about gunpowder or rope jumping in all the four ways I have described: not only as a window on eighteenth-century politics and history, or an example of brilliant ironic text construction, or even a voice speaking out of a personal context of real social suffering and conflict—but also to engage in dialogue with it, to take it into her own language and society, to respond as though it embodied a voice speaking directly to her. The reader may, that is, take the text as an utterance—or, to use Rosenblatt's terminology, engage in the kind of transaction with it that is, after all, the whole point of literature.

Works Cited

Bakhtin, M[ikhail] M[ikhailovich]. *Speech Genres and Other Late Essays.* Trans. Vern W. McGee. Ed. Caryl Emerson and Michael Holquist. Austin: U of Texas P, 1986.

Case, Arthur E., ed. *Gulliver's Travels.* By Jonathan Swift. New York: Ronald Press, 1938.

Chamberlain, Lori. "Bombs and Other Exciting Devices, Or The Problem of Teaching Irony." *College English* 51.1 (January 1989): 29–40.

Clifford, John. "Introduction: On First Reading Rosenblatt." *Reader* 20 (Fall 1988): 1–6.

Davis, Herbert, ed. *Gulliver's Travels.* By Jonathan Swift. Vol. 9 of *The Prose Works of Jonathan Swift.* Oxford: Basil Blackwell, 1965.

Dewey, John, and Arthur F. Bentley. *Knowing and the Known.* Boston: Beacon P, 1949.

Dias, Patrick X. *Making Sense of Poetry: Patterns in the Process.* Ottawa: Canadian Council of Teachers of English, 1987.

Dowling, William. "Teaching Eighteenth-Century Literature in the Pockockian Moment (or, Flimnap on the Tightrope, Kramnick to the Rescue)." *College English* 49.5 (September 1987): 523–32.

Eagleton, Terry. *Literary Theory: An Introduction.* Oxford: Blackwell; Minneapolis: U of Minnesota P, 1983.

Edwards, Derek, and Neil Mercer. *Common Knowledge: The Development of Understanding in the Classroom.* London: Methuen, 1987.

Emerson, Caryl. "The Outer Word and Inner Speech: Bakhtin, Vygotsky, and the Internalization of Language." *Critical Inquiry* 10.2 (December, 1983): 245–64. Rpt in *Bakhtin: Essays and Dialogues on His Work.* Ed. Gary Saul Morson. Chicago: U of Chicago P, 1986. 21–40.

Freadman, Anne. "On Genre." *Typereader: The Journal of the Centre for Studies in Literary Education* 1 (November 1988): 3–9.

Lentricchia, Frank. *After the New Criticism.* Chicago: U of Chicago P, 1980.

Hirsch, E. D., Jr. *Validity in Interpretation.* New Haven: Yale UP, 1967.

Homer, David, Jackie Cook, and Helen Nixon. *Reconstructing English: A Course for English Teachers.* Salisbury: South Australian College of Advanced Education, 1989.

Hunt, Russell A. "A Boy Named Shawn, a Horse Named Hans: Responding to Writing by the Herr von Osten Model." *Writing and Response: Theory,*

Practice, and Research. Ed. Chris M. Anson. Champaign-Urbana: National Council of Teachers of English, 1989. 80–100.

———. " 'Could You Put in Lots of Holes?' Modes of Response to Writing." *Language Arts* 64:2 (February 1987): 229–32.

———. "A Decade of Change: A Correspondence on Theory and Teaching." *Reading-Canada-Lecture* 5:3 (Fall 1987): 148–153.

———. *Pragmatic Aspects of Literary Reading*. LUMIS-Schriften 19. Siegen, West Germany: Siegen University Institute for Empirical Literature and Media Research, 1988.

Hunt, Russell A., Thomas Parkhill, James A. Reither, and Douglas Vipond. "Writing Under the Curriculum: Learning to Write by Using Writing to Teach." Panel presentation. Conference on College Composition and Communication. St. Louis, Missouri, March 1988.

Hunt, Russell A., and Douglas Vipond. "Aesthetic Reading: Some Strategies for Research." *English Quarterly* 20 (1987): 178–83.

———. "Crash-Testing a Transactional Model of Literary Reading." *Reader: Essays in Reader-Oriented Theory, Criticism and Pedagogy* 14 (1985): 23–29.

———. "Evaluations in Literary Reading." *TEXT* 6 (1986): 53–71.

Jarrell, Randall. *The Bat-Poet*. Illustrated by Maurice Sendak. New York: Macmillan, 1963.

Labov, William. "The Transformation of Experience in Narrative Syntax." *Language in the Inner City: Studies in the Black English Vernacular*. Philadelphia: U of Pennsylvania P, 1972. 354–96.

Landa, Louis A., ed. *Gulliver's Travels, And Other Writings*. By Jonathan Swift. New York: Houghton Mifflin, 1960.

Miall, David S. "Welcome the Crisis! Rethinking Learning Methods in English Studies." *Studies in Higher Education* 14.1 (1989): 69–81.

Parkhill, Thom. "Inkshedding in Religion Studies: Underwriting Collaboration." *Inkshed* 7.4 (September 1988): 1–4.

Peirce, Charles S. *Philosophical Writings of Peirce*. Ed. Justus Buchler. New York: Dover, 1955.

Polanyi, Livia. "So What's the Point?" *Semiotica* 25: 3/4 (1979): 207–41.

———. *Telling the American Story: A Structural and Cultural Analysis of Conversational Storytelling*. Norwood, N.J.: Ablex, 1985.

Reither, James A. "Writing and Knowing: Toward Redefining the Writing Process." *College English* 47:6 (Oct. 1985): 620–28. Rpt. in *The Writing Teacher's Sourcebook*. 2nd Ed. Ed. Gary Tate and Edward P. J. Corbett. New York: Oxford UP, 1988. 140–48.

———. "The Writing Student as Researcher: Learning from Our Students." Miami University Conference on the Teacher as Researcher. Oxford, Ohio: July 1988.

Reither, James A., and Douglas Vipond. "Writing as Collaboration." *College English* 51:8 (December 1989). 855–867.

Rorty, Richard. "Introduction: Pragmatism and Philosophy." *Consequences of Pragmatism (Essays: 1972–1980)*. Minneapolis: U of Minnesota P, 1982. xiii–xlvii.

Rosenblatt, Louise M. *Literature as Exploration*. 1938. 3rd ed. New York: Noble and Noble, 1976.

———. *The Reader, the Text, the Poem: The Transactional Theory of the Literary Work*. Carbondale: Southern Illinois UP, 1978.

———. "Towards a Transactional Theory of Reading." *Journal of Reading Behavior* 1:1 (Winter 1969): 31–49.

———. "Viewpoints: Transaction Versus Interaction—A Terminological Rescue Operation." *Research in the Teaching of English* 19 (1985): 96–107.

———. "What Facts Does This Poem Teach You?" *Language Arts* 57 (1980): 386–94.

———."Writing and Reading: The Transactional Theory." *Reader: Essays in Reader-Oriented Theory, Criticism, and Pedagogy* 20 (Fall 1988): 7–31.

Suleiman, Susan R., and Inge Crosman, eds. *The Reader in the Text: Essays on Audience and Interpretation*. Princeton: Princeton UP, 1980.

Vipond, Douglas, and Russell A. Hunt. "Literary Processing and Response as Transaction: Evidence for the Contribution of Readers, Texts, and Situations." *Comprehension of Literary Discourse: Interdisciplinary Approaches*. Ed. Dietrich Meutsch and Reinhold Viehoff. Berlin: de Gruyter, 1988. 155–174.

———. "Point-Driven Understanding: Pragmatic and Cognitive Dimensions of Literary Reading." *Poetics* 13 (1984): 261–77.

———. "Shunting Information or Making Contact? Assumptions for Research on Aesthetic Reading." *English Quarterly* 20 (1987): 131–36.

Vipond, Douglas, Russell A. Hunt, James Jewett, and James A. Reither. "Making Sense of Reading." *Becoming Readers and Writers During Adolescence and Adulthood*. Ed. Richard Beach and Susan Hynds. Norwood, N.J.: Ablex, in press.

Wimsatt, William K., and Monroe C. Beardsley. "The Affective Fallacy." *Sewanee Review* 14 (Summer 1946): n.pag. Rpt. in *The Verbal Icon: Studies in the Meaning of Poetry*. By W. K. Wimsatt. Lexington: U of Kentucky P, 1954. 21–39.

———. "The Intentional Fallacy." *Sewanee Review* 14, Summer 1946: n.pag. Rpt. in *The Verbal Icon: Studies in the Meaning of Poetry*. By W. K. Wimsatt. Lexington: U of Kentucky P, 1954. 3–18.

Zöllner, Klaus. " 'Quotation Analysis' as a Means of Understanding Comprehension Processes of Longer and More Difficult Texts." *Poetics*, in press.

8

"First Steps" in "Wandering Rocks": Students' Differences, Literary Transactions, and Pleasures

Kathleen McCormick

> There is no such thing as a generic reader or a generic literary
> work. . . . The reading of any work of literature is, of necessity,
> an individual and unique occurrence involving the mind and emo-
> tions of some particular reader. . . . The teacher of literature, above
> all, needs to keep a firm grasp on the central fact that he is seek-
> ing always to help specific human beings—not some generalized
> fiction called *the student*—to discover the pleasures and satisfac-
> tions of literature.
>
> —Louise Rosenblatt (*Literature as Exploration* 34)

In these lines from Louise Rosenblatt, written in 1938, we see the
anticipation of three significant issues with which contemporary theories of the reader and the reading process are still forcefully grappling.
First, Rosenblatt argues that we should analyze and write about real,
not hypothetical, readers, suggesting the impracticality, if not, as she
later states, the "downright condescension" (*The Reader, the Text, the
Poem* 138), of constructing ideal reading models to teach students how
to read literature. Contemporary reader-response critics still are
divided according to whether they study real readers, as Norman
Holland and David Bleich do (though their "subjective" criticism

is clearly at odds with Rosenblatt's more socially oriented approach), or whether they postulate ideal constructs such as Wolfgang Iser's "implied reader," Michael Riffaterre's "superreader," Stanley Fish's "informed reader," and Jonathan Culler's "competent reader."[1] Rosenblatt's less lofty term, "generic reader," more successfully connotes the intellectually suspect theorizations and (not incidentally) the repressive teaching practices such concepts can engender.

Second, Rosenblatt's remarks foreshadow what she is perhaps best known for, her transactional theory of reading. In *The Reader, the Text, the Poem* she argues that, as opposed to a theory of "interaction" which "implies separate, self-contained, and already defined entities acting on one another," a theory of "transaction" designates an "ongoing process in which the elements or factors are . . . aspects of a total situation, each conditioned by and conditioning the other" (17). In the transactive experience, therefore, both readers and texts are "produced" by the reading context. Rosenblatt suggests that different readers will produce different texts in the reading transaction and that teachers can legitimate and help students give voice to their readings if they recognize that their students' responses are in no way "generic."

Finally, Rosenblatt's lines also legitimize "pleasure" as a reading goal for student readers of literature. Pleasure is an unusual concept in Anglo-American literary analysis. Since Rosenblatt's work, a number of theorists, most notably Norman Holland and Roland Barthes, have developed theories of reading pleasure. Norman Holland argues, for example, that all acts of interpretation result from the reader's "transforming" the text to meet his or her own fantasies and expectations, thereby avoiding "unpleasure" and anxiety, and achieving pleasure and gratification ("Unity Identity Text Self" 125). While Holland connects his theory closely to classroom practice, its general applicability is limited because it is bound by an adherence to a (rather narrow) reading of Freud and because it sees the individual as possessing an "unchanging essence," a unique "identity theme" (121). By contrast, in *The Pleasure of the Text,* Roland Barthes develops a more extended theory of reading pleasure. He distinguishes between pleasure (*plaisir*) and bliss (*jouissance*), and connects them with readers' literary and cultural experiences. He also establishes a psychoanalytic typology of reading pleasures. His theory, however, has not been linked to classroom practice. I will argue in this essay that Barthes's theory can be applied to the teaching of literature, particularly if we see it as complementing and being complemented by Rosenblatt's more pragmatically and pedagogically based transactional theory of reading. Rosenblatt, more than any literary critic, has taught us the need for and the value of theorizing our students' reading processes.

Barthes's theory of pleasure and bliss can be adapted to extend, in poststructuralist terms, some of the theorizing that Rosenblatt has developed. Rosenblatt is rightly critical of Barthes's approach to reading in *S/Z*, in which he distinguishes between readerly and writerly texts, noting "what starts out as an affirmation of the importance of the reader ends as a distinction between two kinds of texts" (*Reader* 169). As we shall see though, Barthes's text characteristics, if read through Rosenblatt's theory of reading, can be equally (or better) expressed as characteristics of *reading*.

An emphasis on the differences among student readers, on the transactive nature of reading, and on the pleasures students take in reading literature typifies Rosenblatt's approach to reading and, as well, strongly influences the approach of this essay. It is unfortunate that the developments in American reader-centered criticism ignored Rosenblatt's work for so long. Thus it is all the more important now, when poststructuralist modes of criticism are so dominant, that we bring Rosenblatt's work into dialogue with them. Not only can such dialogue provide some compensation for earlier injustice, but (as I shall argue) Rosenblatt's work acts to critique and complement the pedagogical gaps in Barthes's thinking. In this essay, I will therefore deliberately start from where Rosenblatt pointed us—in real students' responses. I will analyze three sets of my students' responses to the "Wandering Rocks" episode of Joyce's *Ulysses*, which were written in an undergraduate class over the course of a week and a half. None of the students had read *Ulysses* before. In *The Reader, the Text, the Poem*, Rosenblatt insists that "much greater concern than is usual should be accorded the 'first step,' the registering or savoring of the literary transaction" (136). It is on the "first steps" of students' beginning to read "Wandering Rocks"—on their differences, their literary transactions, and their pleasures—that this essay will focus. I will then use Barthes's theory of pleasure both to account for my students' diverse reading pleasures and to demonstrate the benefits that can be derived from combining insights from reader-response and poststructuralist theory.

It has been a long time since most teachers of *Ulysses* have read the novel for the first time, and it may be impossible for us to remember what our early reactions to the text were. But much of what we do is probably greatly influenced by those early readings. What kinds of things about the text "hooked" us, intrigued us, frustrated us, made us want to read it again and again? What kinds of readers were (and are) we? What designs did (and do) we feel *Ulysses* has on us and we on it? And why do some people find *Ulysses* a bore while others are endlessly stimulated by it? Of course, answers to these questions are overdetermined, but our "first steps" in reading *Ulysses*, whether alone or with a teacher, may have played a significant role in our choosing to pay extra attention to it, and as well, to read criticism on it.

I can't, of course, re-create our "individual" (let alone "collective") first reading experiences of "Wandering Rocks," but I can offer a close study of some highlights and low points of my students' reading and responding to "Wandering Rocks" for their first, second, and third time. It is important to recognize that this essay is not a search for origins or an investigation of the exact cognitive processes by which these readings were constructed. While I cannot objectively construct my students' reading experiences, I can explore *how* they reported responding to "Wandering Rocks" and attempt some speculations as to *why* they responded as they did.

As a teacher, my primary goal is to encourage students to enjoy the experience of reading Joyce. I think "Wandering Rocks," the tenth and central chapter of *Ulysses*, is an excellent text for introducing students to the process of negotiating reader traps of various kinds and to the pleasure and play that reading such a text can engender. Divided into eighteen separate vignettes and a coda, each of which focuses on a different character or group of characters generally wandering the streets of Dublin, "Wandering Rocks" defies traditional unities of plot and character and creates a labyrinthine experience for readers and characters alike. One of its major structural features is its thirty-one interpolations, lines that appear out of context in one vignette but that generally occur in context somewhere else in the text, frequently in another vignette. The insertion of an interpolation into a vignette indicates that two events are occurring simultaneously, and many critics—and some student readers—further suggest that the interpolations help to establish causal or thematic connections among the vignettes.[2]

"Wandering Rocks" is not inherently "pleasurable" or even coherent: it can be read and, indeed, encourages its readers to read it in a variety of ways. To use Barthes's terms, which I will explore throughout this essay, it can be read for pleasure or bliss. According to Barthes, the text of *pleasure* is one that can be naturalized or easily mastered; it is linked, he states, to a "*comfortable* practice of reading" (*Pleasure* 14). We will see that turning "Wandering Rocks" into a text of pleasure is a satisfying achievement for many readers, fulfilling a desire to master and create coherence in the texts they read. While the text of *pleasure* "contents, fills, [and] grants euphoria" to the reader because it conforms to cultural practices with which the reader is familiar, the text of *bliss* "unsettles the reader's historical, cultural, psychological assumptions, the consistency of his tastes, values, [and] memories" (*Pleasure* 14). In addition to imposing a state of loss and discomforting the reader, the text of bliss also provides the reader with *jouissance*. *Jouissance* is a difficult word to translate into English. As Barthes's translators and editors point out, it has a distinctive sexual suggestion and is clearly related, by analogy, with orgasm. It suggests what becomes so important in Barthes's work, the metaphorical equating of the text with the body, the reader with the lover. The usual translation is, however, the broader term *bliss*. That term, of course, still retains a rich sexuality. Barthes contends that the reader, like the lover, wants to know every part of the beloved, wants to be able to name it, understand it, control it (the desire for pleasure). And yet the greatest enjoyment—what keeps the lover fascinated—is the unexpected gesture, the ambiguous sign, the uncertainty of the beloved (the desire for bliss). It is only in recognizing that signs will always be conflicting—while still feeling the pain of that recognition—that the reader/lover can experience bliss.

Barthes has been criticized for implying at times that pleasure and bliss are intrinsic properties of texts rather than reading experiences. Rosenblatt's transactional theory of reading and indeed her own distinction between efferent and aesthetic reading can help us to extend Barthes's notions of pleasure and bliss from characteristics of *texts* to characteristics of *reading*. In developing her analysis of efferent and aesthetic reading, Rosenblatt contends that the distinction between the two "derives ultimately from what the reader does, the stance that he adopts and the activities he carries out in relation to the text" (*Reader* 27). Rosenblatt argues forcefully that those who seek in "texts alone the elements that differentiate between the aesthetic and the nonaesthetic [will] arrive at only partial or arbitrary answers" (*Reader* 23). She recognizes that in trying to categorize types of texts, theorists miss the crucial point—"that the text may be read either efferently or aesthetically" (*Reader* 25). If we apply Rosenblatt's insights to Barthes's distinction between pleasure and bliss, we can only enrich it—both theoretically and in terms of its pedagogical implications.

Barthes, in effect, suggests that pleasure and bliss are not completely dichotomous: they can supplement each other. But surely this can only be true if pleasure and bliss are characteristics of reading rather than of texts. Barthes hints at this but does not quite have a vocabulary to express it. It is clearly possible, according to Barthes, for readers to read for both pleasure and bliss. He, indeed, argues that the reader who sustains both ongoing pleasure and flashes of bliss is "a subject split twice over, doubly perverse" because he simultaneously "enjoys the consistency of his selfhood (this is his pleasure) and seeks its loss (that is his bliss)" (*Pleasure* 14). Again the analogy he is using is not unrelated to the erotic. To produce a text that continually creates a tension between pleasure and bliss is to combine mastery and mystery, hedonism and loss, comfort and frustration, and for some readers, but not all, to insure excitement and challenge, and an infinite desire to reread. Rereading is the result of bliss—we want to return again and again to the site of that bliss, our encounters with the text.

Barthes's distinction between the reader of pleasure, the reader of bliss, and the doubly perverse reader of pleasure and bliss is not a "scientific" one but provides a highly suggestive analogy. Moreover, it proves useful to explore the great diversity of reading pleasures that student readers might experience in the act of reading a challenging text like "Wandering Rocks." Barthes' psychoanalytic typology of the pleasures of reading—fetishistic, obsessive, paranoid, hysterical— can also help us to analyze students' responses, not to categorize them rigidly, but to help us savor and perhaps better understand the array of factors that might enter into a reader's early literary transactions with a difficult text. It can also encourage us and our students to incorporate into our analysis "as much as possible the personal matrix within which the work crystallized" (*Reader* 136). As Rosenblatt has taught us, we can expand students' repertoires of reading pleasures only by allowing them to display their own pleasures and observe the pleasures of others. This display of pleasure (and, indeed, pain)—and perhaps more importantly the debates about how they were constituted—was the primary goal of our class discussions on "Wandering Rocks."

Rosenblatt (like I. A. Richards before her, but within a richer educational context) argued fifty years ago that we should begin with real readers. Over the course of a week and a half I asked my students to read "Wandering Rocks" three times. After each reading, I asked them to write a response statement in which they discussed the text strategies to which they most responded, the reading strategies they employed, and their overall reading experiences. I also asked them to relate their reading experience either to other texts they had read or, on the second and third responses, to their earlier readings of "Wandering Rocks." Following Rosenblatt, however, I tried to "avoid placing undue importance upon the particular form" in which students couched their responses (*Literature* 82), so that students were free simply to write a general response if these guidelines were not helpful to them. From their discussions, debates, and responses, I can loosely identify five moments of pleasure or displeasure that my students experienced—adapting Barthes's distinctions—pleasure, negative pleasure, negative bliss, bliss, and (doubly perverse) pleasure and bliss. I call these "moments" of pleasure, implying that they are fleeting, unstable, and alterable experiences, not rigid categories. Such terminology helps us to remember that a text is, as Rosenblatt points out, "an event in time . . . not an object" (*Reader* 12). It further requires us to recognize both that students' pleasures shifted over their three readings of "Wandering Rocks" and that one reader's cause for contentment may be another's cause for anguish, that what evokes pleasure or pain is not an intrinsic, predetermined property of the text. As Rosenblatt notes: "We must . . . avoid imposing a set of preconceived notions as to the proper way to react to any work. The student must be free to grapple with his [or her] own reaction" (*Literature* 80).

Most students at one time or another during their three responses expressed pleasure in reading "Wandering Rocks." For some students, pleasure occurred on a first reading, but for many others, it came only after some initial discomfort, when they suddenly discovered that they could naturalize the text and apparently master it quite easily. Readers who experience pleasure are obviously gratifying to the teacher. I often discovered, however, that underlying their expressions of pleasure was a reluctance to reread the text, and many of these students needed a fair amount of encouragement from me to do so. For out of a combination of fear that they will be unable to interpret the text and sudden relief that they have found some way to do so, they may prematurely break off their relationship with it. They generally tended to adopt one reading strategy, and if it appeared to work, did not try others, feeling for the most part quite satisfied and relieved. Given the strong institutional pressures on students to build immediate textual coherence, which Rosenblatt criticizes in *Literature as Exploration* but which still prevail in many classrooms today, such responses are hardly surprising. Many of these students, particularly those whose first response was negative, were extremely proud to have discovered on their own some strategy whereby they could naturalize the text, i.e., make sense of it, make it "natural," or reduce its strangeness. From these student responses, we glimpse the comfort of reading for *pleasure*, the satisfaction and the personal sense of fulfillment that comes from creating but believing that you are really finding coherence in a seemingly incoherent text.

Students who achieved such moments of pleasure by naturalizing the text diverged greatly in the nature of their reading pleasures. Some, for example, took what Barthes call *fetishistic* delight in the text's invention of new words, unusual usages, puns, odd descriptive phrases. These are readers who single out "quotations, formulae, turns of phrase," who take pleasure in "the word" itself (*Pleasure* 63). "One of my favorite lines," said one student, "is 'a tiny yawn opened the mouth of the wife of the gentleman with the glasses.' All he was saying was 'she yawned,' but what a way to say it!" Another said he "liked the use of unfamiliar, but playful and interesting words. For instance, 'The boys sixeyed Father Conmee and laughed.' I reread the line wondering 'what was that word?' Then I realized six eyes—three boys (with two eyes each) looking at Father Conmee." These students seemed fascinated by the language of "Wandering Rocks," and I should note that more students commented on language than any other feature of the text in their first response, and the majority of the responses were positive. Why might this be? One student wrote that in her reading of "Wandering Rocks" she "picked out certain lines or words which seemed unique, interesting, or meaningful. This was a necessary process since the plot seems to be disjointed. Thus [she] focused on comprehending specific lines or words rather than the chapter as a whole." If this student is at all representative, then perhaps teachers need to recognize the extent to which students can enjoy linguistically challenging texts. It seems as if many students fetishized the language of the text in part because it was what they could best understand, but also, and not to be underestimated, what they could best *enjoy*, at least at a given reading moment. Rosenblatt argues powerfully for the value of allowing students to explore what they have "lived through" in reading a text rather than forcing them to impose a set of preconceived notions on it (*Literature* 82; *Reader* 143). I think it is primarily because students recognized that they did not have to develop a definitive reading of "Wandering Rocks" that they felt free to enjoy the text's language.

Other students who experienced pleasure tended to be more *obsessive* than *fetishistic*—taking pleasure in what Barthes terms the *return*, the repetition, of language. These students focused on individual lines in the text, particularly the interpolations. Some, for example, noticed the repetition of the interpolated lines in and out of context, but did not attempt to explain their oddity, even if they found them very disconcerting. One student, after commenting in her first response that all of the out-of-place sentences in the chapter had made her feel "helpless," wrote in her second response that she thought herself "extremely clever" when she recognized a character from a phrase previously mentioned. She wrote, "This odd repetition can be really confusing, but when you remember the references you're fine. It's just like a memory test and I'm happy to report I passed." This student offered no interpretation of the possible significance of these lines; she was satisfied simply to have noticed their repetition. Nonetheless, while she closed off all other interpretive problems, the fact that she was able to become pleasurably engaged with the text at all constituted a significant step forward in her becoming an active, self-confident reader, and she needed to be told not that she was being overly simplistic, but that perhaps she might derive even more pleasure if she became more adventurous. This student may be ready to begin what Rosenblatt calls the "dual process of clarification" of her response—to study the text more closely and to examine her reading experiences and basic assumptions (*Literature* 146). But she will be motivated to do this only because she found herself capable of experiencing the pleasure of mastery.

For *fetishistic* readers, then, the pleasure of mastery arose from understanding the meaning of new or unusual words and phrases, for *obsessive* readers from recognizing the repetition of particular lines. For what Barthes calls *paranoid* readers (again, the term is provocative rather than scientific) to take pleasure in the text, however, they must, unlike fetishistic or obsessive readers, develop an interpretation of some kind. But characteristic of these readers, like all who experienced pleasure, was the almost instantaneous stopping of inquiry when they felt they had mastered the text. They saw, for example, that the interpolations indicate simultaneity of action, and this recognition led them to feel pride and satisfaction, and to close off all further questions. "Normally," said one, "I prefer a clear sequence of events. But instead of being frustrated, I was so proud of myself when I made a connection that it encouraged me to look for more cross-references. I figured that I must be doing something right because that 'orderly story' I want in a novel was developing after all." This student was surprised that she liked the text on her second reading, and I, as a teacher, had to be careful not to mitigate either her surprise or pleasure. She responded positively to "Wandering Rocks" because she found a way to make sense and order out of it. When we look at what she actually did, however, the picture is not quite so dramatic as she suggested: she complained in her first response about the separate sections and the misplaced lines; in her second response, she noticed four interpolations, came to the conclusion that the events were occurring simultaneously, was thrilled with herself, and promptly stopped looking further. Her third response was basically a recapitulation of her second, with increased emphasis on her pleasure and pride in enjoying the text.

In comparison to those of many students, some of which I'll discuss subsequently, these students' responses may seem relatively superficial. And yet we see that they could be encouraged, slowly, to perform deeper investigations so long as they are allowed to enjoy a certain reassuring contentment that they achieve from turning "Wandering Rocks" into a text of pleasure. Most of these students are not interested or perhaps not ready to confront the "unreadability" of the text—this is exactly what they are trying to avoid. Thus they remain in the world of pleasure. And, indeed, they may always remain readers of pleasure, which is not to imply that their readings

can't be deepened or that they will, of necessity, be inferior to readings of bliss. (After all, many fine upstanding literary critics avoid
jouissance like the plague!)

There were students whose responses were characterized by
what I am calling "negative pleasure." I use the term both to suggest
the general lack of enjoyment that these students felt while reading
and also to indicate that this lack of enjoyment occurred specifically
because they desired pleasure in the Barthesian sense—the comfort
and satisfaction of mastery—and were thwarted. Readers who experienced negative pleasure tended by and large to be text bound. They
made the mistake Rosenblatt helps us to characterize in her distinction between *aesthetic* and *efferent* reading. Beginning readers too often
try to read for content, hoping to summarize the "correct" meaning or
"facts" of a text.[3] These students tried to do just that. They encountered and observed text strategies but waited for the text to explain
them. If it didn't, they eventually gave up. Most had little sense of
their active roles in the reading process, and many had a minimal
sense of reading as play. They wanted the text to encourage them to
have feelings of mastery and control in their reading without their
having actively and self-consciously to take control. After an extended
period of patience, many responded with violence and anger to
"Wandering Rocks" for not finally exposing itself to them. They feel
about "Wandering Rocks" as Joyce's character Miss Dunne does about
The Woman in White, that it has "too much mystery business in it"
(*Ulysses* 10.371: 229.13).[4]

We should, at this point, heed one of Rosenblatt's useful warnings
and not imagine that these students are somehow all alike, all
"generic" readers. Their degrees and kinds of displeasure varied significantly. "It really 'gets my goat,' " wrote one, "when I see non-
words such as 'sunny winking,' 'tall white hatted,' or 'stickumbrella
dustcoat'—they contradict my specific knowledge about the English
language." This mild displeasure or annoyance—for it does not
appear to be violent disappointment or anger—may seem naive, but
it appears to be characteristic of those would-be *fetishistic* readers who
want to take pleasure in the word itself or who miss that pleasure
when they do not find it in the words they read. These readers, as
opposed to the fetishistic readers discussed above who enjoyed
Joyce's language, obviously require a certain kind of language—
apparently clever usages of *Standard English*—as part of their reading
pleasure. Implicit in their comments is that the writer establishes a
contract with the reader in which an agreed-upon lexicon is used: it is
the reassurance of familiarity that gives them pleasure. Such language
affords them a sense of mastery, and in violating his linguistic contract, Joyce has obviously violated the trust of some of his readers:

"Did he use the James Joyce Dictionary when he wrote this? Sorry James, but we all don't have that version," wrote one student. The condescending use of Joyce's first name appears to constitute an attempt to level and dismiss the threatening Joyce before he dismisses the reader.

Implicit in these readers' responses is that the text has consciously done something to exclude them, that they feel rejected and are acting this out by rejecting it. Neither of these students, however, was as explicit about this alienation and sense of rejection as the students whose responses are closest to Barthes's *hysterical* reader who *"throws himself* [sic] across the text" (*Pleasure* 63). One such student wrote: "Wandering is what this chapter did all right, and with no apparent goal. I was patient, waiting for Mr. Joyce to tie it together, but he didn't oblige . . . there is nothing in this hemisphere that will drive me to read another word." Another wrote: "If I ever met James Joyce, I'd slap him! Who does he think he is manipulating readers into recognizing that their textual assumptions are conventional? So what—I like nice, neat, tied-up stories and I hate this meaningless fragmentation." The violence of such comments suggests that these students are objecting to a lot more than textual techniques. Their main reading strategy was to wait for comfort and so achieve closure; such students feel betrayed, threatened, somehow shown up by the text, or even by Joyce himself.

Rosenblatt observes that "the teacher's personal love of literature . . . has not always been proof against the influence of the routine, pedantic notions concerning teaching methods" (*Literature* 80). Even a theoretically innovative pedagogy provides no insurance that students will enjoy the texts the teacher may love best; but it can, as Rosenblatt suggests, help students better grapple with their own responses. While I, like most of us, would like my students to enjoy the texts in which I take most pleasure, focus most closely on the textual strategies about which I obsess, develop complex interpretations of what I feel are the most significant aspects of the text, if students are going to react negatively, I prefer that it be in the extreme, for such reactions are interested, interesting, and sometimes negotiable.

Although these students were angry about different aspects of the text (its language, its fragmentation, its general lack of conventional strategies), and the violence of their anger necessarily spanned a great range, their written responses and comments in class discussion indicated a general confusion about the issue of textual mastery, about the kinds of texts that allow them to feel a sense of mastery, and the kinds of reading strategies they "naturally" adopt to effect that end. Most students argued—and we see evidence for this even in the brief comments quoted here—that they prefer classical realist texts in which, supposedly, "it all fits together in the end." Such "texts of pleasure" give readers a profound sense of control: they employ language that is accessible (or at least in some dictionary); they frequently confirm the reader's cultural (and almost always literary) values; they appear to reveal all their secrets in the end. "Wandering Rocks" did none of this for these students, and what particularly disconcerted some of them who tried to remember various cross references was that they had been tricked into believing that the text would finally cohere. The students, therefore, were hostile to the text because it seemed to have mastered them.

But when I asked such students what their primary strategy was for interacting with the text, they responded, quite unaware of the paradox they were setting up, that it was "patience." Patience is a stance that is best suited to texts whose language is transparent, and from which the reader can easily develop closure, unity, and significance. Such a stance is not passive, but is rather *cooperative*—especially with certain text strategies: it is, to adapt Barthes, a "readerly" way of responding to a text. If the text conforms to the reader's expectations, the reader is frequently not conscious of exerting any effort in the reading process at all, for such cooperative strategies seem "natural." "Wandering Rocks," however, is a text that foregrounds its manipulative nature, in Barthes's term its "writerliness," its unwillingness to cooperate in the meaning-making process, and it did not reward many students who waited for it to reveal itself to them. I suggested to these students that alternative, more "writerly," and apparently confrontative strategies (which we will discuss subsequently) existed for interacting with an aggressive text like "Wandering Rocks." But more persuasive than my remarks were those of other students who had themselves been more confrontative in reading "Wandering Rocks." Many students experiencing negative pleasure were quite aghast in class when they heard that other students actually enjoyed the chapter, but as Rosenblatt states: "A free exchange of ideas will lead each student to scrutinize his own sense of the literary work in the light of the others' opinions. The very fact that other students stress things that he may not have noticed, or report a different general impression, will suggest that perhaps he has not done full justice to the work" (*Literature* 129). Some students strongly resisted doing anything that might change their negative reaction to "Wandering Rocks," but others tried to develop different types of reading transactions and did experience pleasure on their next reading, which seemed to them (and at times to me) like an interpretive leap of tremendous magnitude.

The students we have just discussed experienced what I am calling negative pleasure, an unsatisfied yearning for the comfort, coziness, completion, and satisfaction of traditional texts and traditional interpretations. They acknowledged the goal of pleasure as desirable and approved—it is a goal announced and reinforced by the established rules and procedures of traditional reading. When pleasure is not experienced, but still desired, then the reader experiences negative pleasure. "Negative bliss," the reading moment I shall discuss next, is somewhat more complex. Readers experiencing negative bliss are yearning for something more than pleasure—something other than comfort entices and beckons them. Negative bliss is evidenced by dislocation, disruption, frustration, even rejection, but coupled with fascination: "there must be something more." Whereas for Barthes this reading that disturbs and fascinates can lead to *jouissance*, the bliss of recognizing the unattainability of complete meaning, for my student readers, such experiences resulted only in frustration, in negative bliss. None of my students experienced *jouissance*—at least not in their reading pleasure! Bliss is perhaps only detectable in its absence, but for readers to experience *jouissance*, it seems that they must, as Barthes does, take pleasure in the self-conscious knowledge that they will forever experience a sense of lack. Student readers who found themselves caught in such a recognition desired strongly to find some way out of it. This is why Barthes's "doubly perverse" reader sums up the best *attainable* pleasure of reading—the alternation between the discomfort/thrill of promised bliss and the coherence of pleasure, a systole and diastole that never ends. One always breaks with comfort because it is too satisfying; one can never stay, except momentarily, in bliss because it is impossible.

Those students who experienced moments of negative bliss were, I believe, the most challenging pedagogically. Their reading experiences were almost the opposite of readers who experienced pleasure: they developed distinctive reading strategies and interpretations of the text but felt continually dissatisfied with them, assuming that there was something more that they were "missing." Here, once again, Rosenblatt's concern with the pedagogical, not just the theoretical, context of reading is helpful. She comments, with regard to readers' desire for coherence, that "if such a putting-together, such a com-position, does not eventually happen, the cause may be felt to be either a weakness in the text, or a failure on the reader's part" (*Reader* 55). While readers who experienced negative pleasure seemed always to blame the text, readers experiencing negative bliss blamed themselves for not making the text fit together. Readers of negative bliss also appeared to feel minimal pleasure in the mastery they did gain over the text. They can be seen as extreme examples of Barthes's paranoid readers, seeing the text as a kind of game, discovering some of its secret constraints, but always believing that there are more secrets that the text is hiding. They gained the discomfort and the sense of loss of the reader of bliss but none of the pleasure because they were on an intellectual borderline—they saw that things cannot all work out smoothly, but they would still have preferred that they would. They appeared to want to be active readers who create meaning but, contradictorily, they were still bound to the idea of finding meaning in the text. Hence, the text continually discomforted them, continually imposed a sense of loss upon them, and it truly brought to the fore what Barthes terms the "crisis" of their "relation to language" (*Pleasure* 14): To what extent is language simply a conduit through which meaning will pass? To what extent does language infinitely defer meaning? Rosenblatt comments that "we shall not help the student to understand if we keep him functioning merely on the plane of verbalization, or translation of the literary work into generalizations and abstractions" (*Literature* 130). Her argument is addressed to teachers, but it frequently needs to be translated to our students, particularly those students experiencing negative bliss whose interpretive frustration can make "generalizations and abstractions," at least when presented by an authority figure such as the teacher, all too appealing. These student readers, unlike Barthes's sophisticated readers who might turn such a sense of loss into *jouissance*, are upset and frustrated at their inability to find a consistency that can satisfy them. Without knowing it, they are enacting a major debate in recent literary theory and criticism: whether meaning is always infinitely deferred. Their current reading experiences suggest that it is, but much of their education, their prior literary experiences, almost always with realist texts, as well as their "nonliterary" reading experiences, all tell them that meaning is somehow "present" to them in texts.

Compare the student who was happy just discovering cross-references with the following student who observed a large number of the interpolations and comments: "[I] scratched and clawed and pushed and stretched to find any meaning which may exist . . . however I was successful in finding interpretations for only a few. But all I come up with is real Mickey Mouse, and . . . no interpretations may even exist. It's killing me that I don't know." This student's fascination and frustration is clear. He discovered two-thirds of the interpolations on a second reading; he saw that they indicated simultaneity almost immediately when he first read the chapter; and he wanted to take the next critical step—developing causal or thematic connections between interpolations and vignettes. But without some absolute reassurance from the text of the correctness of this approach, he was inhibited.

Confronting the unreadability of the text made him nervous: he did not feel sufficiently confident to play with that unreadability and simply go ahead with his "Mickey Mouse" connections. Though he is an active and perceptive reader, he wanted more information to come from the text. While performing a reading of bliss and infinitely deferring meaning by, as Barthes says, recognizing that *"everything signifies,"* this student did not realize, as Barthes puts it, that "by this proposition, I entrap myself, I bend myself in calculations, I keep myself from enjoyment" (*Lover's Discourse* 63).

In discussing the diversity of ways in which readers re-create a work, Rosenblatt argues that readers "vary greatly in the extent to which they hold fast to a central structure of ideas and attitudes while sensing a penumbra of overtones and associations" (*Reader* 60). We can see in the distinctions I have made thus far some of the ways in which Barthes's theory of pleasure can help us to tease out some of this variation among readers that Rosenblatt observes. Readers experiencing pleasure and negative pleasure were willing to overlook almost any overtone or association in order to perceive some structure in the text; they differed only in whether they were successful in discovering (or inventing) that structure. Readers experiencing negative bliss, in contrast, were so overwhelmed with the number of associations they can develop that they were unable to perceive or create a structure. Unlike students who experienced contentment at seeing language repeated or at recognizing that the interpolations indicate simultaneity, students experiencing negative bliss, such as the one quoted above, sensed that negotiating "Wandering Rocks" is much more difficult than solving a single puzzle, but they resisted seeing that all puzzles do not have to be solvable in a single way or even solvable at all for reading to be enjoyable. My goal with these students, therefore, was to help them relinquish their belief in the text as the final determinant of meaning—to help them to confront the text's unreadability and do with it what they will—to take pleasure in the strategies by which they temporarily master the text, to attain bliss from the text's refusal to be pinned down. Facing and challenging the very unresolvability of a text can be a source of extreme pleasure (bliss) and need not result in a definitive naturalization of the text. Such a recognition seems necessary for such students in order to prevent them from becoming so frustrated that they give up on the text completely. These students, unlike others I have discussed so far, appeared to require models of reading that run counter to classical realism in order to be able to interact with pleasure and satisfaction with writerly texts like "Wandering Rocks," and they seemed ready to experience the doubly perverse moment of both pleasure and bliss.

Readers who did experience such moments enjoyed both feelings of mastery and feelings of mystery. They were able both to "hold fast to a central structure" and to sense "a penumbra of overtones and associations" because they did not find the central structure threatened by their associations or their associations threatened by the central structure. Unlike readers experiencing negative bliss, these readers reveled in the active role they must take in the creation of meaning. Readers who experienced doubly perverse pleasure and bliss were able to naturalize the text in ways that gave them some sense of mastery, but unlike readers of pleasure, they did not stop there. These readers saw the process of rereading as motivated by a desire to discover, not the "correct" meaning of the text, but rather new ways of reading it. They did not wait for the text to give answers and, unlike the reader who anticipates but cannot achieve bliss, they were pleased that the text did not solve all the problems it raised. They realize that reading and interpreting any text is theoretically an endless process. The doubly perverse reader was open to new possibilities and desires to reread, not out of dissatisfaction with past readings, but out of pleasure and the wish to continue the process of creating a plenitude of meaning.

Let's look at one of these readers on her first and second reading. In her first response, she noticed the interpolations, connected them with larger contexts, saw that they indicate simultaneity, and attempted to generalize about their overall effect on her, their contribution to the theme of the chapter, and the relationship of this theme to our everyday lives. This mode of reading is, of course, a traditional one, pleasurable in that it deals with textual techniques, plot, character, and theme. But as well she noted, even in this initial response, that "Joyce includes both the relevant and the irrelevant." Her first response indicated that her reading pleasure combined Barthes's notion of the paranoiac and the hysteric: on the one hand, she wanted to produce a complicated text and discover its secrets; on the other, she was willing to go beyond critical scrutiny and join in "the bottomless, truthless comedy of language" (*Pleasure* 63). While she knows that language is "truthless," this student does not forsake the pleasure of the paranoiac for the bliss of the hysteric: she truly sought both and was thus a doubly perverse reader. Her perspective was developed more clearly in this extract from her second response:

> Interpreting an interpolation is much easier when the reader has read through the chapter twice (or even three times). Since there are both forward and backward looking interpolations, a thorough knowledge of earlier and later events and characters is very helpful. . . . The second reading of "Wandering Rocks" forces the reader to notice these connections. The forward looking interpolations now shout out to be

noticed and interpreted. The episode becomes much more complex with a second reading instead of much simpler. There is more information to process and each piece brings several more alternative meanings with it, when one is able to use hindsight analysis. I think perhaps a good reading strategy to be learned from this reading is to realize that a seemingly simple piece can become as complex as the reader is willing to make it.

On her second reading, we can see this student self-consciously choosing particular reading strategies to master aspects of the text: this was her pleasure, her moment of mastery. But she was combining pleasure with a recognition that she was creating, not discovering, meaning and a sense that the process will go on forever, because there will always be those moments where, as she write later in her second response, "at times you just can't think of a single interesting thing to say—and that's OK by me." This was her bliss, her recognition of the unreadability of the text.

We see, therefore, how the doubly perverse reading moment differs from the other four reading moments I have isolated. While readers experiencing pleasure claim to enjoy the whole text simply by mastering a fragment of it, readers experiencing doubly perverse pleasure are spurred on by discovering fragments that don't fit into the whole. While readers experiencing negative pleasure are irritated by textual incongruities and wait patiently for the text to resolve itself, readers experiencing doubly perverse pleasure actively and self-consciously plunge into the text, reveling both in their own ingenuity at mastering the text and the text's ingenuity at refusing to be mastered. While readers of negative bliss refuse to acknowledge the active role they take in the production of the text (even as they confront the unresolvability of the text, they wish that the text would somehow take control and close off meanings), readers experiencing doubly perverse pleasure and bliss actively acknowledge their role in creating the text and rejoice that there is always more meaning to come.

Looking at the five moments of student readers' pleasure in reading "Wandering Rocks," we can perhaps glimpse the vast diversity of readers, texts, and poems that can be created in the reading transaction. In the past fifty years, two methodological traditions within literary criticism and theory have attempted to account for this diversity. In this paper, I have tried to sketch some of the ways in which these two traditions might—in a more detailed treatment—be brought into a productive dialogue. I have chosen, moreover, perhaps the pioneering theorist of one of these two traditions to help me focus on my students' reading practices. It is the achievement of Louise Rosenblatt to have recognized the flux and fluidity of the reading process well before other American literary theorists and educators. While the reader-response movement of the seventies legitimized the discussion of readers, returning (belatedly and often without acknowledgment) to her work, the project of analyzing the complex processes involved in reading is far from completion. One of the most exciting challenges we face now as scholars and educators is filling out the picture of readers that emerges through Rosenblatt's work and that of later reader-response critics in order to include some of the insights of poststructuralist theories of culture, language, history, and the subject. In this paper, I have sketched what I will elsewhere treat in more detail—the development and cultural situating of a taxonomy of reading pleasures of real readers. Rosenblatt herself argued that her transactional concept of reading could "only reinforce interest in the dynamics of the relationship between the author, the text, the reader, and their cultural environments" (*Reader* 174). Barthes's theory of the pleasure of the text is just one of many theories that can help us explore our students' reading processes, but it is a crucial one: it emphasizes and problematizes pleasure and mastery—two subjects of inquiry that are all too often neglected in the literature classroom, but that are significant factors in the reading transaction, and that themselves exist in a transactional relationship. In the students' "first steps" I have outlined here, we can see the material that lies waiting for the kind of analysis that Louise Rosenblatt initiated.

Notes

1. Another, more scientific, direction of investigating the reading process of real readers would be to incorporate some of the powerful insights of cognitive psychology on schema theory by such researchers as John Bransford and Nancy McCarrell, Marcel Just and Patricia Carpenter, and Allan Collins, et al., and on metacognition by such researchers as Linda Baker and Ann Brown, Shirley Wagoner, Peter Winograd and Peter Johnson. For an example of the analysis of reading literary and discursive texts that points in such a direction, see Linda Flower's "Interpretive Acts: Cognition and the Construction of Discourse."

2. For critical studies of "Wandering Rocks" and especially the interpolations, see in particular Marilyn French, Stuart Gilbert, Clive Hart, Leo Knuth, Paul Van Caspel, David Hayman, Edward Cronin, Mervin Lane, Michael Seidel, and Erwin Steinberg.

3. See McCormick et. al., *Reading Texts*, chapter 3.

4. The first parenthetical reference is to the episode and line number in the Gabler 1984 Garland edition of *Ulysses*; the second, to the page and line number in the 1961 Random House edition.

Works Cited

Baker, Linda, and Ann L. Brown. "Metacognitive Skills and Reading." *Handbook of Reading Research*. Ed. D. Pearson, M. L. Kamil, R. Barr, and P. Rosenthal. New York: Longman, 1984, 353–94.

Barthes, Roland. *A Lover's Discourse*. Trans. Richard Howard. New York: Hill and Wang, 1978.

———. *The Pleasure of the Text*. Trans. Richard Miller. London: Cape, 1976.

———. *S/Z*. Trans. Richard Miller. New York: Hill and Wang, 1974.

Bleich, David. *Subjective Criticism*. Baltimore: Johns Hopkins UP, 1978.

Bransford, John D., and Nancy S. McCarrell. "A Sketch of a Cognitive Approach to Comprehension: Some Thoughts About Understanding What It Means to Comprehend." *Cognition and the Symbolic Processes*. Hillsdale: Erlbaum, 1974. 189–229.

Cronin, Edward J. "Of Mirrors and Maps and Houses with Gardens: Joyce's 'Wandering Rocks,' Chapter X, *Ulysses*." *North Dakota Quarterly* 48 (1980): 40–52.

Culler, Jonathan. *Structuralist Poetics: Structuralism, Linguistics, and the Study of Literature*. Ithaca, N.Y.: Cornell UP, 1975.

Flower, Linda. "Interpretive Acts: Cognition and the Construction of Meaning." *Poetics* 16 (1987): 108–130.

French, Marilyn. *The Book as World: James Joyce's* Ulysses: Cambridge: Harvard UP, 1976.

Gilbert, Stuart. *James Joyce's* Ulysses: *A Study*. New York: Knopf, 1952.

Hart, Clive. "Wandering Rocks." *James Joyce's* Ulysses: *Critical Essays*. Ed. Clive Hart. Berkeley: U of California P, 1974.

Hayman, David. Ulysses: *The Mechanics of Meaning*. Englewood Cliffs: Prentice Hall, 1970.

Holland Norman. *5 Readers Reading*. New Haven: Yale UP. 1975.

———. "Unity Identity Text Self." *Reader-Response Criticism: From Formalism to Post-Structuralism*. Ed. Jane Tompkins. Baltimore: Johns Hopkins UP, 1979. 118–33.

Iser, Wolfgang. *The Act of Reading: A Theory of Aesthetic Response*. Baltimore: Johns Hopkins UP, 1979.

———. *The Implied Reader*. Baltimore: Johns Hopkins UP, 1974.

Joyce, James. Ulysses: *A Critical and Synoptic Edition*. Ed. Hans Walter Gabler et al. 3 vols. New York: Garland, 1984.

———. *Ulysses*. New York: Random House, 1961.

Just, Marcel Adam, and Patricia A. Carpenter. *The Psychology of Reading and Language Comprehension*. Boston: Allyn and Bacon, 1987.

Kain, Richard M. *Fabulous Voyager*. New York: Viking, 1959.

Knuth, Leo. "A Bathymetric Reading of Joyce's *Ulysses*, Chapter X." *James Joyce Quarterly* (1972a): 405–22.

———. "James Joyce's *Ulysses*, Chapter X: Wandering Rocks." *Language and Literature* 1 (1972b): 30–54.

———. "Joyce's Verbal Acupuncture." *James Joyce Quarterly* 10 (1972c): 61–71.

Lane, Mervin. "A Synechdochic Reading of 'Wandering Rocks' in *Ulysses*." *Western Humanities Review* 28 (1974): 125–40.

McCormick, Kathleen, and Gary F. Waller with Linda Flower. *Reading Texts: Reading, Responding, Writing.* Lexington, Mass.: D. C. Heath, 1987.

Riffaterre, Michael. *The Semiotics of Poetry.* Bloomington: Indiana, 1978.

Rosenblatt, Louise. *Literature as Exploration.* New York: Appleton-Century, 1938.

———. *The Reader, the Text, the Poem: The Transactional Theory of the Literary Work.* Carbondale: Southern Illinois UP, 1978.

Seidel, Michael. *Epic Geography: James Joyce's* Ulysses. Princeton: Princeton UP, 1976.

Steinberg, Erwin R. *The Stream of Consciousness and Beyond in* Ulysses. Pittsburgh: Pittsburgh UP, 1973.

Van Caspel, Paul. *Bloomers on the Liffey: Exegetical Readings of Joyce's* Ulysses. Baltimore: Johns Hopkins UP, 1986.

Wagoner, Shirley. "Comprehension Monitoring: What It Is and What We Know About It." *Reading Research Quarterly* 18 (1983): 246–328.

Winograd, Peter, and Peter Johnston. "Comprehension Monitoring and the Error Detection Paradigm." Technical Report No. 153. *ERIC*, 1980. ED 181 425.

9

From Transaction to Resistance: An Antipodean Journey

Bill Corcoran

A group of teachers in Adelaide, South Australia, was disconcerted about the lack of fit between what happened when the teachers read and responded to literature and the models of reading and response they presented to their students. One of their number, Lola Brown, after jotting down the strongest impressions left after her recent reading of Eleanor Spence's *A Candle for St. Anthony*, gave voice to the corporate disquiet of her fellow teachers in the form of these conclusions:

1. I've never *read* a book in the way I *teach* it. That is, what I select to talk about in class is the product of *retrospective vision*, while students are still in the process of acquiring the author's world. A mismatch!

2. Only one of my responses had a literary bent, yet what I select to talk about is often related to the literary devices, conventions, forms the author uses to construct this "reality." These I've absorbed subconsciously as I've reconstructed it for myself. My actual dialogue with the author has been at the level of *remembering, speculating, associating*.

3. No one else on earth could read this book in the way I did. (34)

There are clear and immediate echoes in these disjunctions of some of the basic tenets of Louise Rosenblatt's transactional theory of reading,

147

as Brown underlines the distance between her immediate aesthetic evocation of the text and the efferent stance she takes into the classroom.

The tangible outcome of the teachers' deliberations was *A Single Impulse: Developing Responses to Literature*, which "traces the steps of the journey taken by a group of people in search of a theory of literature teaching" (South Australia 6). I would like to critically retrace some of the stages of that journey and juxtapose some of its landmarks against those contained in a more recent document also emanating from South Australia, entitled *The Connecting Conversation*. What should emerge is as much a sense of the positioning of these Australian teachers in and across the ostensibly contradictory discourses of reader-response and cultural criticism, as it is an antipodean voyage through and beyond the writings of Louise Rosenblatt. In the end, the journey from *A Single Impulse* to *The Connecting Conversation* represents an exemplary case study of a movement from a humane, liberal form of theorizing to an even more liberal and emancipatory one.

Central to the argument will be a recognition of the positive contributions that Rosenblatt and the authors of *A Single Impulse* have made to an improved classroom practice. A focus on "the live circuit set up between the reader and 'text' " (Rosenblatt *Reader*, 14) has helped teachers provide a potential meaning space, free of their own interrogative intrusions. Through strategies such as response journals, exploratory talk, and visual or re-creative responses, students are invited to celebrate the essence of unique, evolving evocations of literature. Somewhat problematically, as we shall see, such strategies lead the authors of *A Single Impulse* to a commitment to "*ownership* of a work of literature by whoever reads, watches, or listens to it" (18) as an overriding principle in literature teaching.

However, an exclusive emphasis on the phenomenology of reading, on the "synthesizing, organizing activity of the reader in his [*sic*] evocation of a poem" (Rosenblatt *Reader*, 51), leaves essential constructs such as author, reader, text, and subjectivity culturally adrift and unproblematized. As its title implies, *The Connecting Conversation* specifically attempts to recognize acts of reading as sociohistorical events, and readers and texts as culturally constructed sites of struggle, rupture, inconsistency, and instability. What will be needed below is some sort of conceptual balance sheet to accommodate Rosenblatt's borrowing of the Jamesian notion of "selective attention" on the one hand, and Williams's account of the "selective tradition" on the other. The former will explain the psychodynamics of reading, while the latter will anticipate Giroux's (*Theories of Reproduction*) argument of the need for "theories of resistance" to challenge the ideologies of race, class, and gender embedded in texts that constitute the hegemonic selective tradition.

Toward a Redefinition of Literature

As an immediate way into continuing debates about the artificial distinction between literary and nonliterary uses of language, and monastic and social accounts of the practices of reading and writing, we need to look carefully at the redefinition of literature provided in *A Single Impulse:*

> Literature is centrally concerned with exploring and defining the value and meaning of human experience. The uniqueness of literature lies in the way it does this: through the imaginative recreating and shaping of experience in language. This definition includes oral litera-ture, drama, and film and it links children's imaginative writings with the work of published authors in that it sees them as animated by a single impulse. (8)

There is a Coleridgean agreement, first, about "the shaping power of the imagination," about the significance of the existential base of the literary transaction, and about the inevitability of what Rosenblatt calls the "conscious or unconscious reinforcement of ethi-cal attitudes" (*Literature* 16). Above all, the force of the definition, in the tradition of Britton, Dixon, Graves, and others, accords the same process status to the classroom literature produced by students and the institutionalized literature which is the "work of published authors" since they are both "animated by a single impulse" (9).

Immediately problematic in all of this are claims about the "uniqueness of literature" based on a mimetic or expressive realist view of language (Belsey). This perspective privileges subjectivity and grants individuals autonomous freedom to shape and re-create expe-rience in language. The individual's power over language and the capacity for private meaning-making preclude any consideration of language as ideology. Through transparent, innocent screens of lan-guage, perceptive readers can sense a unique vision of the author's personality and experience. Nowhere is there an acknowledgment that language predates its users, or that it is always already value-laden. As McCormick, Waller, and Flower conclude:

> We can therefore say that people's perceptions of the world are contin-gent upon their knowledge of language, not that they simply use lan-guage as a tool to describe what they perceive. In this sense we say that people are *written by* and *write* their language and their culture; that is, they in one sense form statements in language, but in another powerful sense are formed by their language. (35)

There is also an attempt, in *A Single Impulse*, to expand the textual categories of literature to include oral narratives, drama, and film. When the authors of *The Connecting Conversation* return to the question of the boundaries of literature, they explicitly refer to an even more extended field: "a much wider range of imaginative texts than those of the traditional valued canon of literature" (20). This time the list includes conversations, stories, advertisements, films, newspaper reports, television news, radio, comics, magazines, street theater, new fiction, sermons, scientific writing, and children's stories.

Unfortunately, any attempt to produce a "holdall" definition of literature by simply expanding a list of possible generic forms is just as problematic as the automatic granting of this status to student writing. Rosenblatt's objection would involve the assumption of an aesthetic stance in each instance—a not inconsiderable problem for teachers charged with the task of assessing the worth of student text. In turn, Culler offers the notion of "literary competence" as the essential prerequisite for "naturalizing" textual conventions; Hunter draws attention to learned reading practices that mark out the domain of literary discourse; and Balibar and Macherey see the production and consumption of literature as privileged bourgeois insertions into the linguistic practices of the school. Such conventional, discursive, and ideological considerations might provoke a more comprehensive analysis for the teacher who chooses not only to read the script of *Macbeth*, but also to bring Polanski's screenplay and film into the classroom.

It is therefore insufficient to hazard the generic purity and hallowed place of poetry, novels, and drama by simply placing them alongside a range of other texts. What is needed is an acknowledgment that culturally legislated literary genres share with other texts the same linguistic strategies and the same iterative possibilities for enlarging their "contextual reference by pointing toward other communicative acts, by quoting, alluding, parodying, and otherwise generating a context that is entirely semiotic and intertextual" (Scholes *Semiotics*, 33).

Rosenblatt, of course, as one of the chapter headings in *The Reader, the Text, the Poem* illustrates, is quite adamant about the futility of "The Quest for 'the Poem Itself.' " Yet her remarks throughout the chapter stop noticeably short of Barthes's characterization of the text as a "multidimensional space in which a variety of writings, none of them original, blend and clash," as a "tissue of quotations drawn from the innumerable centers of culture" (*Image* 146). For Rosenblatt, notions of intertextuality and iterability, of reading and writing as recoverable, repeatable cultural practices, are continually subordinated to her search for the transactional conditions of possibility of the "literary work of art." Even the authors of *The Connecting Conversation* accord a special place to texts, "particularly wrought and shaped to embody meaning—the artifacts of language as art—[which] are central to the work of the English teacher" (20).

This persistent desire to hold on to some patterned notion of a textual meritocracy is also implicit in Rosenblatt's treatment of the text's "openness and constraint." Her transactional analysis of the ways in which readers create idiosyncratic contexts for capitalizing on a text's meaning potential stops short of any recognition of how the semantic structure of a text contains an explicit ideology which the reader must either accept or contest. Such concerns are central to Eco's opposition of "open" and "closed" texts. The latter, be they Superman comics, James Bond novels, TV soap operas, or Harlequin romances, depend on an established formula of redundancy and repetition. Through these forms of "overcoding," closed texts delimit and relax the role of the reader. To understand textual manipulation at this level is to underscore the need for helping students deconstruct formulaic patterns in texts so that they can resist forms of ideological entrapment.

On Resituating Teachers and Students

Because they wanted other teachers to join interactively in their journey, the authors of A Single Impulse invite their readers to anecdotalize, to talk about satisfying or frustrating reading experiences, so that they can become reflexively aware of their own schema and behavior as adult readers. These shared accounts lead to six major conclusions or points of agreement: (1) that the essential prerequisite for reading literature is a drawing on the experience of living and on the cumulative experience of literature; (2) that literature expands individual perspectives on living in the world; (3) that autonomous readers exercise choice over when, what, and how they read; (4) that readers often (but not always) feel compelled to share their responses to literature; (5) that some literature, through its intensity and permanence, remains unforgettable; and (6) that there are some effects of literature that elude explanation.

Embedded in each of these points of consensus are obvious stances and propositions advanced both by Rosenblatt and a range of allied reader-response critics. As the teachers document their reliance on and movement through perception, affect, and associative responses we are reminded not only of Rosenblatt's transactional account, but also of Bleich's subjective paradigm (*Readings and Feelings; Subjective Criticism*). Reading is accompanied by "an internal, unspoken commentary of reflections, associations, anecdotes, and speculations." Literature triggers "long-forgotten memories," causes an empathy with characters, "establishes a sense of personal relationship with a particular author," and allows for a clearer recognition and knowledge of "people, places and things in our own lives." There is also more than a broad hint of Holland's "identity theme" as the teachers "recognize aspects of [themselves] in a work of literature," or when they reread the same book many times because they have found "some special point of identification with one or more of the characters in the book" (*A Single Impulse*, 14–15).

At other times they relate experiences of living and reading to the text in accounts that echo Iser's personal and textual repertoires, Rosenblatt's characterization of the text as "blueprint" or "constraint" as opposed to "norm" (*Reader*, Ch. 5) and Barthes' depiction of cultural and referential codes (*S/Z*). At a general level the South Australian teachers "match experience against the created experience, gauging its authenticity," so that negative responses to literature can be seen to result from an inability to access the cultural codes inscribed in "totally unfamiliar sets of names or environments." Equally, they relish opportunities to "gain an understanding of other individuals, social and cultural groups in other times and places," and "see [thematic] patterns in different works by the same author," and in the "connections" they are able to draw between quite disparate texts (*A Single Impulse*, 16–17).

Most obviously, perhaps, these teachers represent, through the clear exigency of their choosing to join together in a corporate task, an interesting case of Fish's "interpretive community." They are bonded less by a common allegiance to shared interpretive strategies, as for example a group of feminist, psychoanalytic, or structuralist critics might be, as by their teacherly need to understand the ways in which they characteristically write or talk about literature. They are interested in forms of informal talk about shared reading and in ways of persuading others to read or see a book or performance that has moved them. They distinguish their initial, immediate responses to literature from those "second streams of response" (Rosenblatt *Reader*, 137) that develop as a result of reflection over time. Only occasionally do the authors of *A Single Impulse* use writing, and then most often in personal letters, to capture the excitement of an initial response, and any subsequent talk or writing is used "not to engage in detailed critical analysis, but to move towards an evaluation of the literature's significance in [their] own living" (17).

There is sufficient indication already that, like Rosenblatt, the teachers involved in *A Single Impulse* are clearly situated in a professional discourse that represents the entirely compatible marriage of personal growth teaching (Dixon) and what Eagleton has called "the

Reader's Liberation Movement." The problem with this approach is its very "naturalness," its absolute dependence on autobiography and a hegemonic professional ideology, where the "experience" of teachers matches, perhaps, only a small minority of their students. Similarly, the students themselves are placed at either ends of a continuum in terms of their positive or negative attitudes and responses to literature. At no stage do the writers of *A Single Impulse* acknowledge or explore the various historical, institutional, and cultural contexts that constructed either their own homogeneity or the student variability which are their constant themes.

Again, such issues are taken up in *The Connecting Conversation*. Recognizing the need for an "inclusive curriculum," the "English classroom is [seen] as a workshop for what we call *connecting conversations*. Conversations that enable all students, inclusive of race, gender, social, or cultural background to make connections between their understanding and the knowledge of others" (23). Within this more broadly based cultural view, questions for observation and research are framed in these terms: "What makes the text what it is in its social setting? What meaning does it hold for different readers in different contexts? How does one text relate to another or others? How do readers in different communities respond to their texts? How do they take the words, images, and gestures from the text and construct meaning? What do they bring from their cultural background to their reading of the text?" (21).

Through such questions the groundwork is laid in *The Connecting Conversation* for encouraging both students and teachers to engage in resistant/strong readings as they read against the grain of dominant literary or cultural text strategies. Through explorations of the pragmatic and framing contexts that constitute the connections between, and necessary conditions for, reading and writing, they could be expected to self-consciously read from alternative perspectives of gender, class, race, or religion. They will also engage in symptomatic readings in order to seek out the absences in a text, excavating those meanings or significances that have been suppressed or marginalized through the limitations of language with its inevitably embedded ideology.

The absolute necessity of such a stance is confirmed in a range of studies that critique the operation of a consensual professional discourse, the selective tradition, or popular culture. Gilbert and Mares, for example, point to inescapable difficulties with the personal growth model of English teaching, with its assumption of the ideological neutrality of literature and its uncritical acceptance of concepts such as authorship, creativity, and personal voice. At different levels, Luke has examined Canadian basal readers to analyze the relationship between ideological content and discursive form, Christian-Smith has explored the gender-related marketing practices of the commercial romance novel, and Taxel ("The Black Experience") has studied the realities of growing up Black and female in the early part of the twentieth century as presented in Taylor's *Roll of Thunder, Hear My Cry* and Sebestyen's *Words by Heart*. Indeed, after proposing a model for a cycle of research into children's literature that would embrace in turn the cultural contexts of production, dissemination, and reception, Taxel acknowledges a significant gap in the reader-response stage of the cycle: "Little attention has thus far been given to how such crucial factors as gender, ethnicity and socioeconomic status influence response. How, for example, would the responses of a middle-class Black child differ from those of a white child from a fundamentalist family to books like *Roll of Thunder, Hear My Cry* and *Words by Heart?*" ("Children's Literature" 40).

A further warrant for a critical sociology of reading emerges if we question the sufficiency of Rosenblatt's argument that an aesthetic stance, coupled with collaborative teaching and learning, will automatically provide the means for recognizing, transcending, and resisting specific normative positions. Rosenblatt variously asserts:

> Precisely because every aesthetic reading of a text is a unique creation, woven out of the inner life and thought of the reader, the literary work of art can be a rich source of insight and truth. ("The Literary Transaction" 276–77)

> In transactions with texts we may transcend our own limitations of gender, age, temperament, environment, place, or time to discover undreamed of affirmations of, or distinctions in, values. We may participate in whole societies of men and women living by values very different from our own, and we may be helped to sense more keenly the structured human meanings of our society. ("Language, Literature and Values" 74).

> [Students] should try to understand what values are affirmed or rejected by their own reactions. They should become aware of how the attitudes they brought to the text differ from the values dominant in the world of the work, or how their own values have been illuminated, reinforced or modified by the literary experience. In short, they should develop the habit of thinking rationally about things that engage their emotions. (*Literature as Exploration* 77)

As I have indicated, the confident expressionist rhetoric that Rosenblatt shares with the writers of *A Single Impulse* has had a salutary impact on literature classrooms, releasing them from the objectivist shackles of New Criticism. There appears to be no arguing against the potential for liberating the imagination of the student reader, for tolerating the necessary messiness of individual searches for meaning, or for enfranchising the culturally and academically disadvantaged, until one runs up against a structuralist and poststructuralist wall of language as material, cultural, and historical practice. As Giroux contends, the capacity for critical thinking and learning extends immediately beyond illusory promises of freedom to a consideration of how power and resistance inevitably reside in the "structured silences" of the humanist account of transaction:

> The pedagogical value of resistance lies, in part in the connections it makes between structure and human agency on the one hand and culture and the process of self-formulation on the other. Resistance theory rejects the idea that schools are simply instructional sites by not only politicizing the notion of culture, but also by analyzing school cultures within the shifting terrain of struggle and contestation. ("Theories of Reproduction and Resistance" 292)

Ownership and Choice: Two Unstable Principles

When the institution of literature is seen in turn as an arena for "struggle and contestation," and the reader's role takes on the form of Foucault's "agonism," the strongest pedagogical claims of *A Single Impulse* are brought into relief. What are we to make of two interrelated principles—*ownership* and *choice*—as the twin pillars on which the dynamics of the classroom are to be based? If, as I have been arguing, other teachers are to embark on a similar journey of theory building based both on Rosenblatt's version of reader response and the forms of cultural criticism embraced in *The Connecting Conversation*, they will need to understand the potential instability and ambiguity nested in these principles.

Ian Reid has met the ownership issue head on, preferring to see what happens in classrooms as a series of reciprocal "exchanges" between reader and text, between student reader and teacher reader. He concludes:

> I don't find it satisfactory to conceive of any aspect of this in terms of ownership; a literary text is not a possessible object any more than the two-way flow of classroom discourse is. Each is an interpersonal semantic transaction, not belonging to anyone. Its significance is neither inherent within its form of words nor governed subjectively by any single participant (author or reader, teacher or student) but rather is the unstable product of its situation of all that is brought to it. ("Beyond the Cindarella Syndrome" 19)

While it is impossible to argue against this fully contextualized view of the way meanings are constructed in literature classrooms, it is easy enough to understand the sources of teacher guilt. Having in the past appropriated texts from students, having intimidated students with the power of their own rereadings of familiar texts, the authors of *A Single Impulse* set out their own injunctions, defining what *they* mean by ownership:

- Stop being definite about "meanings" in literature and allow lots of tentative exploration of text.
- Allow time for talking and writing about responses to literature of the "this reminds me . . . " kind.
- Model the means by which [teachers] themselves are making sense of a work of literature.
- Allow and encourage pauses for reflections on the literature as it is being studied.
- Engage in drama/imaginative writing/drawing/oral/designing/imitating/predicting activities as a particular work is being studied and in this way enrich the experience of entering the world of that literature making it compelling to the student. (33–4)

In fairness, Rosenblatt had dealt with most of the items in this, and an expanded agenda, when *Literature as Exploration* was first published in 1938. Fifty years later, Probst proposes a "Dialogue with a Text," which takes account, among other things, of students' initial reactions to the text, their immediate perceptions, associations, feelings, and ideas, the textual elements that were prominent or problematic in the initial encounter, and invitations to test the adequacy of an evolving reading against the readings of other group members. Similarly, the essays in the collections by Corcoran and Evans, and Nelms continue the attempt to document a range of classroom practices that take full account of the interactions of readers, texts, and contexts.

The question of choice might seem less problematic, given the variability among students and alternative forms of response proposed throughout *A Single Impulse*. But as soon as the possibility of expanding the range of literature to allow for student choice is mooted, there is an inevitable recognition of the need for heavy and responsible forms of mediation. Where this involves getting to know one's students, or making space for open exchanges about books that have been recently read, the teacher is quickly cast in the role of mentor or guide. Quite often, alternative texts might need to be suggested in classrooms where the literary diet has become stereotypically racist or sexist. This inevitably raises the universal problem of censorship and the exact extent to which a classroom can become the site for an unlimited series of intersecting narratives. The problem, as always, with the sanitized classroom that excludes pornographic, sexist, or violent voices is that it simply negates the discursive forms and therefore the social practices that surround it. It is unreal.

Green approaches the heart of the problem when he claims that reading is treated in *A Single Impulse* in a "psychologistic manner," which results in the "privatization of readers and reading: each is looked into, and constructed as, his or her own individualism, as essential isolation" (64). There is little recognition in *A Single Impulse* that beyond the present reading "experience," beyond "ownership" and "choice," there is a fermenting world of countertheory, where subjective accounts of the act of reading have to struggle for survival against structuralist and poststructuralist attacks on the very existence of the reading subject. "There is no sense," Green continues, "of teachers' *and* students' choices as both structured and, from the outset, delimited: selections on the basis of prior selections, interpretations of what is already interpreted" (63).

Similar difficulties emerge when Rosenblatt senses that Barthes might prove a useful ally for her transactional theory. In the end, she remains opposed to his depiction of "readerly" and "writerly" texts, his characterization of literature as "institutionalized subjectivity," and his translation of reader and text into a network of intersecting codes. "The implication to be rejected," according to Rosenblatt, "is that the individual consciousness is somehow a kind of construction, something to be seen as merely a collection or intersection of patterned forces" (172). For Rosenblatt, there will be no denial of "the vital, dynamic, active, empirical self" (*Reader* 172).

Neither Rosenblatt nor the authors of *A Single Impulse* have looked far enough afield for a poetics that would take sufficient account of the dialectic between agency and structure, between the individual and systemic poles of language. Bakhtin's dialogism specifically acknowledges the cultural grounding of language without necessarily impoverishing or effacing the possibility of individual creativity in language:

> The word in language is half someone else's. It becomes "one's own" only when the speaker populates it with his own intentions, his own accent, when he appropriates the word, adapting it to his own semantic and expressive intention. Prior to this moment of appropriation the word does not exist in a neutral and impersonal language . . . but rather it exists in other people's contexts, serving other people's intentions: it is from there that one must take the word, and make it one's own. (*Dialogic Imagination* 293–94)

Far from "owning" literature, what students gain from reading is a right of reply, a dialogic possibility of creating "a counter-discourse to the discourse of the utterer" (Todorov 22), which will bespeak differential positions of race, gender, or class. In this sense, Bakhtin's dialogism, like Giroux's resistance, presents an image of classroom readers empowered not only to transact with texts, but also to understand their own constructed subjectivities and the validating systems that privilege certain readings and marginalize others.

Some Final Landmarks

For other teachers wishing to find their particular way from transaction to resistance, Rosenblatt and the South Australian teachers have provided an invaluable chart of the territory and useful vehicles for traversing the terrain. But we still need some alternative methods of mapping that allow for both more sweeping and more microscopic views.

To this end, the members of the Alternative English Co-operative, an independent watchdog group in South Australia, have underlined some of the local and universal problems associated with the status of *A Single Impulse* and similar "official" curriculum documents. They analyze its means of production, structural organization, and purpose and ultimately reject its closed narrative structure: "With the relentless pressure of the revivalist meeting or television documentary, *A Single Impulse* continually claws the reader back to *its* central concerns. Structurally, readers are led through its content; it is the Only Way" (16). This single-minded evangelizing, so characteristic of other contemporary revolutions be they of the genre or writing-process type, runs the risk of imprisoning teachers in quasireligious forms of commitment that oversimplify and exclude alternative views (see, for example, Reid *Place of Genre;* Rodrigues; and Hart).

What is most obviously missing in *A Single Impulse* but quite explicitly highlighted in *The Connecting Conversation* are analytic frameworks that enable a close scrutiny of their central metaphors. Observation and intuition, the methodology of *A Single Impulse,* are just sufficiently liberating to unearth a common principle to connect reading and writing, but they lead inevitably to intellectual and ideological closure. The category "literature" exists as a pre-existent given, either in the form of products taken into the classroom or as "works" formed in the classroom. At one level this formulation just manages to take account of the prior, willed determination of the reader to adopt an aesthetic stance, to create the "poem" in a moment-to-moment transaction with the text (Rosenblatt *Reader*). But the reader, as Scholes suggests, may not be "free" at all: "The 'free' reader is simply at the mercy of the cultural codes that constitute each person as a reader, and of the manipulative features of the text, the classroom and the whole reading situation as well" (*Semiotics and Interpretation* 14).

The teacher readers of *A Single Impulse* are caught in a double bind, since they have failed to examine either the historical nature of their own cultural definition as readers or the contextual limitations placed on their subsequent attempts to read student texts as literature. And again, Rosenblatt's promise that "a critical framework" can be adduced from transactional theory, "with its sense of the individual reader and the individual text as bearers of culture creating new cultural events in unique transactions" ("Viewpoints" 106) falls far short of a perspective on resistance that might guarantee the radical, critical pedagogy outlined by Giroux and the authors of *The Connecting Conversation*. Despite the "terminological rescue operation" in which Rosenblatt winches her dynamic, organismic concept of transaction free from the rocks of an information-processing model of interaction, she is still trapped, in Giroux's terms, in an individualist, interactionist ideology that fails to politicize knowledge, culture, and power in any of the essential senses demanded by reproductive ideology (Giroux, *Theory and Resistance*).

When particular texts or authors are guaranteed a place both on private bookshelves and in school bookrooms, it is important to examine not only "private" motives for reading, but also the motivations of publishers or the compilers of canonical lists guaranteed to promote cultural literacy (Hirsch) and the composition of mandating curriculum committees. Part of the broader view of a cultural theory of literature should enable teachers to see their unwitting complicity in academic and economic forms of literary production, sharpen up their awareness of the culturally constructed ways in which they read, and allow them to escape from the imprisoning arguments embodied in either "art for art's sake" thinking or the "intentional fallacy" with all its uncritical acceptance of "the more or less transparent allegory of the fiction, the voice of a single person, the *author*, 'confiding' in us" (Barthes *Image*, 143).

Vestiges of the author "fiction" attacked as well by Derrida and Foucault can be found in the distaste evinced by both Rosenblatt and the authors of *A Single Impulse* for any precipitate move from response to analysis, from aesthetic reading to efferent writing. Of course, the alternative of "dependent authorship" (Adams) allows for immense possibilities as students fill in the gaps of existing texts through writing additional chapters or through imitative writing and parody. Yet these often powerful transformations that emerge from immersion "in the author's world" may still need to be explained as deconstructionist or semiotic "re-writings," as Scholes's principle of " *'scribo ergo sum'*: I produce texts therefore I am, and to some extent I am the texts that I produce" (*Semiotics and Interpretation* 4). And that will still mean, as Rosenblatt herself acknowledges, bringing at some stage critical texts into the classroom so that students can expand their own discursive personalities. In both the interpretive and imitative processes, students must make "connections between a particular verbal text and a larger cultural text, which is the matrix or master code that the literary text both depends upon and modifies" (Scholes *Textual Power*, 33–34). In this way, they will find critical and cultural benchmarks beyond the limiting evidence of their own lives and memories, or the literary tropes they are trying to explicate or emulate.

In the more culturally grounded version of a response-oriented classroom proposed in *The Connecting Conversation*, there is no basis for the exclusion of possible voices or possible worlds. Its writers call on Oakeshott's version of education as an unending conversation, which continuously holds both private and public worlds up for inspection:

> Education, properly speaking, is an initiation into the skill and partnership of this conversation in which we learn to recognize the voices, to distinguish the proper occasions of utterance, and in which we acquire the intellectual and moral habits appropriate to conversation. And it is this conversation which, in the end, gives place and character to every human activity and utterance. (199)

When classrooms are seen as places for disciplined conversation, the teacher's questions and the authority of texts can hardly be denuded of political, social, and ideological significance. In this form of "connecting conversation," nobody's experience is valorized or left unexamined, no text is shrouded in an aura that obscures its iterative resonances or its struggle into production, for due heed is taken of Barthes's warning that "what is oppressive in our teaching is not finally the knowledge or culture it conveys—but the discursive forms through which we propose them" (Inaugural Lecture 476).

The residual challenge offered by this situating of Rosenblatt in the territory occupied by *A Single Impulse* and *The Connecting Conversation* is an invitation to see how teachers (and their texts) have been "written" through conflicting discourses. The potential dialogue, or "disciplined conversation," that these texts set up will allow no easy resolution of the privileged status of readers, literature, or subjectivity. By analyzing the cultural situation of both text and reader, teachers and students will escape from the merely personal and anecdotal to a fuller understanding of the social contexts, purposes, and functions of a theory of literature teaching. The movement from transaction to resistance abjures the assumption that literature provides a stable platform from which the authentic voice of the self may speak by reasserting the place of history, and by restoring that other "live circuit" that necessarily connects language and power.

Works Cited

Adams, P. "Writing from Reading—'Dependent Authorship' as a Response." Corcoran and Evans 119–52.

Alternative English Co-operative. " 'A Single Impulse' or The Only Way? A Critique of a South Australian Curriculum Document." *Category B* 8 (1984): 15–23.

Bakhtin, M. *The Dialogic Imagination.* Trans. Caryl Emerson and Michael Holmquist. Austin: U of Texas P, 1981.

Balibar, E., and P. Macherey. "On Literature as an Ideological Form." *Untying the Text: A Post-Structuralist Reader.* Ed. R. Young. London: Routledge & Kegan Paul, 1981, 79–99.

Barthes, R. *Image, Music, Text.* Trans. R. Miller. New York: Hill & Wang, 1977.

———. Inaugural lecture, College de France. *A Barthes Reader.* Ed. Susan Sontag. New York: Hill & Wang, 1982, 471–82.

———. *S/Z.* Trans. R. Miller. New York: Hill & Wang, 1975.

Belsey, C. *Critical Practice.* London: Methuen, 1980.

Bleich, D. *Readings and Feelings: An Introduction to Subjective Criticism.* Urbana, Ill.: NCTE, 1975.

———. *Subjective Criticism.* Baltimore: Johns Hopkins UP, 1978.

Britton, J. N. *Language and Learning.* Harmondsworth, England: Penguin, 1970.

Brown, L. "Do We Teach the Way We Read?" *English in Australia* 62 (1982): 33–36.

Corcoran, B., and E. Evans, eds. *Readers, Texts, Teachers.* Portsmouth, NH: Boynton/Cook; London: Open UP, 1987.

Christian-Smith, L. "Power, Knowledge and Curriculum: Constructing Femininity in Adolescent Romance Novels." *Language, Authority and Criticism: Readings on the School Textbook.* Ed. S. De Castell, A. Luke, and C. Luke. Lewes, England: Falmer Press, 1988.

Culler J. *Structuralist Poetics.* London: Routledge & Kegan Paul, 1975.

Derrida, J. *Writing and Difference.* Chicago: U of Chicago P, 1978.

Dixon, J. *Growth Through English: Set in the Perspective of the Seventies.* London: NATE for Oxford UP, 1975.

Eagleton, T. "The Subject of Literature." *English Magazine* 15 (1985): 4–7.

Eco, U. *The Role of the Reader: Explorations in the Semiotics of Texts.* Bloomington: Indiana UP, 1979.

South Australia. Education Dept. *The Connecting Conversation: Literacy, Language and Learning in the English Classroom.* Adelaide: Publications Branch, Education Dept. of South Australia; London: Methuen, 1987.

———. *A Single Impulse: Developing Responses to Literature.* Adelaide: Publications Branch, Education Dept. of South Australia; London: Methuen, 1983.

Fish, S. *Is There a Text in This Class? The Authority of Interpretive Communities.* Cambridge, Mass.: Harvard UP, 1980.

Foucault, M. *Language, Counter-Memory, Practice: Selected Essays and Interviews.* Ithaca, N.Y.: Cornell UP, 1977.

Gilbert, P. *Writing, Schooling and Deconstruction: From Voice to Text in the Classroom.* London: Routledge & Kegan Paul, 1989.

Giroux, H. "Theories of Reproduction and Resistance in the New Sociology of Education: A Critical Analysis." *Harvard Educational Review* 53 (1983): 257–93.

———. *Theory and Resistance in Education: A Pedagogy for the Opposition.* South Hadley, Mass.: Bergin & Garvey, 1983.

Graves, D. *Writing: Teachers and Children at Work.* Portsmouth, N.H.: Heinemann, 1983.

Green, B. " 'Yes, but. . . . ' A Single Impulse." *English in Australia* 68 (1984): 60–66.

Hart, K. ed. *Shifting Frames: English/Literature/Writing* Centre for Studies in Literary Education: Deakin UP, 1988.

Hirsch, E. D., Jr. *Cultural Literacy: What Every American Needs to Know.* Boston: Houghton Mifflin, 1987.

Holland, N. N. *5 Readers Reading.* New Haven: Yale UP, 1975.

Hunter, I. "The Concept of Context and the Problem of Reading." *Southern Review* 15 (1982): 80–91.

Iser, W. *The Act of Reading: A Theory of Aesthetic Response.* Baltimore: Johns Hopkins UP, 1978.

Luke, A. *Literacy, Textbooks and Ideology.* Lewes, England: Falmer Press, 1988.

McCormick, K., G. Waller, with L. Flower. *Reading Texts: Reading, Responding, Writing.* Lexington, Mass.: D. C. Heath, 1987.

Mares, P. " 'Personal Growth' as a Frame for Teaching Literature." Hart, 6–18.

Nelms, B., ed. *Literature in the Classroom: Readers, Texts, and Contexts.* Urbana, Ill,: NCTE, 1988.

Oakeshott, M. *Rationalism in Politics.* New York: Basic Books, 1962.

Probst, R. "Dialogue with a Text." *English Journal* 77 (1988): 32–38.

Reid, I. "Beyond the Cindarella Syndrome: Other Sides of the Story." *Opinion* 13 (1984): 13–26.

———., ed. *The Place of Genre in Learning: Current Debates.* Geelong, Australia: Deakin UP, 1987.

Rodrigues, R. J. "Moving Away from Writing-Process Worship." *English Journal* 74 (1985): 24–27.

Rosenblatt, Louise. "Language, Literature and Values." *Language, Schooling, and Society.* Ed. S. Tchudi. Portsmouth, N.H.: Boynton/Cook, 1985. 64–80.

————. "The Literary Transaction: Evocation and Response." *Theory into Practice* 21 (1982): 268–77.

————. *Literature as Exploration.* New York: Noble & Noble, 1968.

————. *The Reader, the Text, the Poem: The Transactional Theory of the Literary Work.* Carbondale, Ill.: Southern Illinois UP, 1978.

————. "Viewpoints: Transaction Versus Interaction—A Terminological Rescue Operation." *Research in the Teaching of English* 19 (1985): 96–107.

Scholes, R. *Semiotics and Interpretation.* New Haven: Yale UP, 1982.

————. *Textual Power: Literary Theory and the Teaching of English.* New Haven: Yale UP, 1985.

Taxel, J. "The Black Experience in Children's Fiction. Controversies Surrounding Award Winning Books." *Curriculum Inquiry* 16 (1986): 245–81.

————. "Children's Literature: A Research Proposal from the Perspective of the Sociology of School Knowledge." *Language, Authority and Criticism: Readings on the School Textbook.* Ed. S. De Castell, A. Luke, and C. Luke. Lewes, England: Falmer Press, 1988. 32–45.

Todorov, T. *Mikhail Bakhtin: The Dialogical Principle.* Trans. Wlad Godzech. Minneapolis: U of Minnesota P, 1984.

Williams, R. *Marxism and Literature.* London: Oxford UP, 1977.

10

Rosenblatt and Feminism

Elizabeth A. Flynn

At first glance, or even at second glance, Rosenblatt's *Literature as Exploration* and *The Reader, the Text, the Poem* do not appear to be feminist works. In neither book does she emphasize that gender is an important factor in the reading transaction. Nor does she use gender-neutral language.[1] Furthermore, most of the theorists cited or the authors discussed in both books are male. In the bibliography appended to *Literature as Exploration*, for instance, there are ninety items listed only seven of which are by women. Of the 173 individuals referenced in the index to *The Reader, the Text, the Poem*, only eight are women. When Rosenblatt speaks of literature, she usually seems to be referring to that written by white males, with an occasional reference to George Eliot, Jane Austen, Emily Brontë, or Virginia Woolf, or to Richard Wright or Ralph Ellison.

Discussions of Women's Issues

A third glance, though, reveals a somewhat different picture. *Literature as Exploration* has numerous references to women's subordinate position in society and explicit or implicit suggestions that both women and men need to develop an awareness of the changing status of women in society. The attitudes toward women expressed in the book are surprisingly progressive given that it was published four decades ago. In the chapter "Some Basic Social Concepts," for instance, she makes the point that "the individual will be liberated from blind subservience to the norms of his group, not by throwing overboard all standards, but by seeing them in relation to the whole complex of attitudes and values into which they fit." She illustrates the point by saying it was not enough for women to resent the norms set up by the Victorian image of the submissive, self-effacing female. Women had to learn in what ways this image was linked with economic dependence and the habits of mind derived from acceptance of political and intellectual authoritarianism (152).

Later in the same chapter she discusses the impact of emotionally rooted attitudes on behavior in moments of indecision. She illustrates the point by discussing the hypothetical situation of a young man who has become familiar, in history and sociology courses, with modern ideas concerning women's potential equality with man. He becomes convinced of the desirability of the new ideal of marriage as a partnership and a mutual give-and-take. Rosenblatt says, though, "The success with which he carries out his program for a modern marriage, however, will largely depend on the degree to which these intellectual convictions have been translated into emotional attitudes and have displaced the old automatic sets" (178).

In the chapter "Personality," Rosenblatt makes the point that old patterns of behavior can be surmounted only because conditions have so changed that there is a pressing need for a new adjustment. The new image will probably need to be reinforced by constant repetition over a long period of time. She uses as an example the image of the emancipated woman, which appears in literature at least from the time of Shelley and Mary Wollstonecraft. It was not until early in the twentieth century, though, that the image was translated into the practical lives of an appreciable number of women (198).

Later in the chapter she makes the point that literary images are not always liberating ones but are sometimes irrelevant to actual life. She suggests, for instance, that literature can sometimes be held responsible for instilling in women emotional obstacles to their sincere ambition to be independent emotionally and intellectually: "Throughout their entire experience with literature, they have been led to identify themselves most often with the older image of woman as temperamentally, as well as economically, subordinate and dependent" (221).

There are fewer such discussions of women's issues in *The Reader, the Text, the Poem*. At one point, though, in a discussion of the limitations of professional critics, scholars, and teachers, she observes that ordinary readers may bring to the text experiences, awarenesses, and needs that have been ignored in traditional criticism. She illustrates the point by explaining that women are finding their own voices as writers and critics. She rejects the idea, though, that only women can speak about women in literature and concludes, "The aim should be to widen the range of critical voices—not to reject the contributions of the professional students of literature but to strengthen the affinities between them and ordinary readers" (143). And some of the examples Rosenblatt uses in *The Reader, the Text, the Poem* are woman oriented. She illustrates efferent reading, for instance, by citing the example of the mother whose child has swallowed a poisonous liquid and who frantically reads the label on the bottle to discover the antidote to be administered (24).

Rosenblatt is clearly deeply committed to women's equality in the home and in the workplace, and aware, to an extent, of issues that feminist literary critics have been grappling with. Furthermore, she writes as a woman. Both the style and the content of her work reveal a feminine sensibility, a particularly female way of conceiving problems and working out solutions to those problems.[2] Patrocinio Schweickart in her "Reading Ourselves: Toward a Feminist Theory of Reading" argues that mainstream reader-response theory is a male enterprise and is primarily concerned with issues of control and partition—how to distinguish the contribution of the author/text from the contribution of the reader (55). Schweickart suggests that a female model of reader-response would focus not on control or partition but on managing the contradictory implications of the desire for relationship and the desire for intimacy. The problematic is defined by the drive to "connect" rather than to "get it right" (55).

Rosenblatt's work exemplifies this female approach. Everything she writes has an implicit or explicit pedagogical motive. Students must be taught to connect with the texts they are introduced to. They must learn to experience and appreciate literature before they learn to analyze it. For Rosenblatt, literature is a powerful tool in the socialization process. Students learn about life, about themselves, by experiencing literary events. Too often, though, according to Rosenblatt, classroom literary instruction has the opposite effect. Students are introduced to literary texts as if they were structures to be dismantled rather than experiences to be relived. They are taught that literary texts are objects rather than subjects. Traditional instruction in literature has an alienating rather than a healing effect.

Rosenblatt and Iser

The extent to which Rosenblatt departs from mainstream, male-oriented reader-response theory becomes clear when her position is juxtaposed with that of Wolfgang Iser. The two are ideally suited for a detailed comparison because their positions are so similar in so many ways. *The Reader, the Text, the Poem* and Iser's *The Act of Reading* were both published in 1978.[3] Both books emphasize the importance of the reader in the act of interpreting a literary text, though both recognize that the text also plays a significant role in the interpretive process. Both eschew the extreme subjective position that eliminates the possibility of distinguishing between valid and invalid interpretations.

Rosenblatt and Iser, though, use different terms to describe the act of reading. For Rosenblatt, reading is a "transaction" between reader and text, whereas Iser sees it as an "interaction." Rosenblatt rejects the term "interaction" because she sees it as dualistic and implying "separate, self-contained, and already defined entities acting on one another—in the manner . . . of billiard balls colliding" (17). For her, transaction designates an ongoing process in which the elements or factors are aspects of a total situation, each conditioned by and conditioning the other (17). The metaphor is an organic one and emphasizes merging, loss of separate identity. She sees the model as an "ecological" one in which "sharp demarcation between objective and subjective becomes irrelevant" (18).

Iser's conception of interaction sometimes sounds a lot like Rosenblatt's conception of transaction, certainly because he, too, was influenced by the work of John Dewey. At one point, for instance, he speaks of past feelings, views, and values being "made to merge" with the new experience (132). Dewey is only a minor influence on Iser's work, though, and more often Iser employs the more mechanistic language of the German phenomenologists. Reader and texts more often appear to be separate entities that do not lose their separate identities. Later in *The Act of Reading*, for instance, he says, "Reading is an activity that is guided by the text; this must be processed by the reader, who is then, in turn, affected by what he has processed." He goes on to say, "the two partners are far easier to analyze than is the event that takes place between them" (163). There is little sense that the "two partners" lose their separate identities and merge. Later in the same section he discusses "contingency" as a constituent of interaction and speaks of the "behavioral plans" of the two partners as being "separately conceived" (164). And since the two partners never really lose their separate identities, one partner can control the other. Ultimately, for Iser, texts control readers. Readers play an active role in the interaction by allowing themselves to be stimulated by the text, by responding appropriately to the textual cues that are provided. Iser says that the constitutive activity on the part of the reader "is given a specific structure by the blanks and the negations arising out of the text, and this structure controls the process of interaction" (170).

Texts, which are composed of "blanks" and "negations," control readers' responses through structures that are created in the act of reading. Presumably, these structures stimulate interpretations that are the same for all readers. We are back to issues of control and partition and a long way from the language of merging stimulated by a discussion of Dewey's work.

Rosenblatt's emphasis on the event, on the ecology of the act of reading, allows for a consideration of the importance of context in the literary transaction. The concept is really only latent in her work—the title, after all, is *The Reader, the Text, the Poem*, not *The Reader, the Text, the Context*. But she does observe that the situation within which reading takes place has an effect on the "poem" that is evoked. Her position allows, then, for a consideration of historical, social, and political factors that affect the literary transaction. A feminist theory can be built on the framework she provides.

Iser, in contrast, says very little about the situation within which reading takes place. He is primarily interested in characteristics of texts that structure responses. The phenomenological processes that a reader undergoes—responding to images, filling in blanks and gaps, "wandering" from one perspective to another, consistency building—are largely reactive ones, responses that are triggered by the text. There is virtually no discussion in *The Act of Reading* of the context within which reading takes place.

Rosenblatt's position is different, too, in that she places her discussion within the context of practical concerns. She begins *The Reader, the Text, the Poem* with a discussion of student response statements, and her purpose in writing the book at all seems to be to improve classroom pedagogy. Rosenblatt wants to empower student readers, to disrupt the traditional hierarchy whereby critics and teachers have greater interpretive authority than nonprofessional readers.

Iser reinforces established hierarchies. He is interested in how professional critics read texts and does not concern himself at all with the concerns of developing readers or with the problem of misreading or misinterpretation. He does not need to take up the problem of validity of interpretation because he assumes that his reader is competent, trained, able to respond appropriately to the signals within the text. Iser's reader is a kind of ideal reader—perhaps Iser himself.

Rosenblatt emphasizes that reading is an emotional as well as an intellectual experience. She discusses the effect that literature can have on the development of emotional maturity of adolescents in *Literature as Exploration* (42) and argues that literature offers us an emotional outlet (36, 74). In *The Reader, the Text, the Poem* she emphasizes that aesthetic reading entails emotional involvement in the text, a fusion of the cognitive and the emotive (46). Rosenblatt's reader is an individual who feels as well as thinks, who has emotional as well as intellectual needs.

Iser says very little about the emotional dimensions of reading and describes an activity that seems to be almost entirely cognitive. In a discussion of the "emotive theory" of psychoanalysts such as Norman Holland and Simon Lesser, for instance, he transforms emotion into cognition. He sees that Holland's approach is little different from the eighteenth-century concept of *beau desordre*, "which indicated the aesthetic pleasure derived from a temporary disturbance of order accompanied by the expectation that in some unforeseeable way order would be restored" (44). For Iser, reading involves the restoration of order after a temporary disturbance. Order is restored, we learn later, through the cognitive activity of consistency building.

Rosenblatt and Feminist Literary Criticism

Rosenblatt's work, then, while not overtly feminist, is distinctly feminine and does provide a healthy alternative to mainstream reader-response theories. And because it is already feminine in orientation, it is well suited to profit by the insights of feminist literary criticism, especially the idea that reading can be an alienating experience for women readers. In turn, Rosenblatt's approach can enrich feminist theories of reading. Her concept of aesthetic reading can be developed into a strategy for reading women's texts, and her transactional approach to reading can contribute substantially to the attempt on the part of feminist literary theorists to explain how gender affects reading.

Rosenblatt assumes that all works are potentially liberating. The problem with our educational practices, according to Rosenblatt, is that students are being taught to read incorrectly. They are not being encouraged to enjoy literature or to partake of its therapeutic powers. If they were encouraged to read literature within the context of social scientific knowledge, and to read it aesthetically, they would learn from it, build better lives on the basis of it. Feminist literary theory demonstrates, though, that this is not always the case. Too often, the experience of reading canonical male texts is counterproductive, even dangerous. Students do not only need to learn to merge with texts, to partake of their wisdom. They also need to learn to defend against them, to recognize when their messages are threats to their own sense of self. Here feminist criticism is helpful and would add a very useful dimension to Rosenblatt's work.

The work of Judith Fetterley is particularly helpful in demonstrating that reading male texts can be an alienating experience for women readers. Fetterley argues in *The Resisting Reader* that female readers are "immasculated" by canonical male texts, forced to identify against themselves. In reading works by Hemingway, Fitzgerald, and others, female readers actively participate in the construction of a world that excludes them. Much of the reading that women readers do, Fetterley suggests, results in estrangement from the self. Sandra Gilbert and Susan Gubar also focus on the effects of male texts on women readers, though they are especially interested in the woman reader/writer. In *The Madwoman in the Attic* they argue that nineteenth-century British and American women writers devised revisionary myths and metaphors in an effort to come to terms with the institutionalized misogyny of their male precursors.

In turn, feminist critics should find Rosenblatt's discussion of aesthetic reading useful, especially as it bears on approaches to the reading of texts by women writers. Schweickart in "Reading Ourselves" argues that women must learn to read texts by men and women differently. The feminist reader of a male text must defend against it, resist it, sit in judgment of it. Feminist readers of a female text, in contrast, should speak as a witness in defense of the woman writer. Schweickart says, "The feminist reader takes the part of the woman writer against patriarchal misreadings that trivialize or distort her work" (46). According to Schweickart, feminist readers should also construe the work not as an object, but as the manifestation of the subjectivity of the absent author, another woman (47). If readers need to learn to read women's texts sympathetically, Rosenblatt's aesthetic reading provides a useful model. Readers can serve as witnesses in defense of women writers by suspending judgment initially and attempting to relive the experience conveyed in the work and to partake of the reading event fully. Here, the reader also suspends analytical skills, all knowledge of literary categories. The reader attempts to merge with the work of women writers, to become it. Such a strategy would be especially useful in attempting to teach male student readers to read women's writing appreciatively, to suspend judgment of it. My own research suggests that male students sometimes dominate texts, impose their own meanings on them, and judge them too harshly.[4] If this is so, then they need to learn to read aesthetically, empathically, nonjudgmentally.

Rosenblatt's work can also be useful to the feminist literary theorist because it offers a solution to the dilemma of attempting to determine just how gender affects reading. Feminist reading theorists agree that gender plays an important role in the reading process. They haven't fully worked out precisely what that role is, though, because they haven't fully worked out what the category "gender" is. This is a problem for feminist theory generally, an "identity crisis," to use

Linda Alcoff's terms. In her essay, "Cultural Feminism Versus Post-Structuralism: The Identity Crisis in Feminist Theory," Alcoff discusses the limitations of both cultural feminism and poststructuralism and argues for a "positionalist" view, an approach that bears a remarkable resemblance to Rosenblatt's transactional theory of reading.

According to Alcoff, the cultural feminist position of Adrienne Rich, Mary Daly, and others assumes, implicitly, if not explicitly, a kind of essentialism, a belief in an innate female essence. They tend to invoke universalizing conceptions of woman and mother in an essentializing way—to offer "an essentialist response to misogyny and sexism through adopting a homogeneous, unproblematized, and ahistorical conception of woman" (413).

At the other extreme is poststructuralism with its attack on the authenticity of the subject, of the essential identity of the individual. French feminists, strongly influenced by Lacan, Derrida, and Foucault, argue that the subject is not a locus of authorial intentions or natural attributes or even a privileged, separate consciousness. Individual practices and experiences are entirely social in origin. Alcoff objects to the seeming erasure of any room for maneuver by the individual within the social discourse or set of institutions: "It is that totalization of history's imprint that I reject. In their defense of a total construction of the subject, post- structuralists deny the subject's ability to reflect on the social discourse and challenge its determinations" (417). Alcoff argues that gender is not a point to start from, not a given, but is a construct, formalizable in a nonarbitrary way through a matrix of habits, practices, and discourses (431). She finds it both possible and desirable to construe a gendered subjectivity in relation to concrete habits, practices, and discourse while at the same time recognizing the fluidity of these (431). The way to avert the tendency to produce general, universal, or essential accounts of gendered subjectivity is to emphasize the historical dimension, according to Alcoff. The way to avert the tendency to negate the possibility of identity at all is to recognize that one's identity is always a construction yet also a necessary point of departure (432). Alcoff finds it useful to see the concept "woman" as defined by the external context within which a woman is situated (433). She summarizes her positionalist view as follows: (1) that the concept of woman is a relational term identifiable only within a (constantly moving) context; (2) that the position that women find themselves in can be actively utilized as a location for the construction of meaning, a place where meaning is constructed, rather than simply the place where meaning is discovered (434).

Rosenblatt's transactional view of the reading process bears some resemblance to Alcoff's positionalist view. Rosenblatt emphasizes that reading is an event in time that subsumes the individual participants so that they are no longer recognizable as individual entities. She also emphasizes that reading is an active process, one in which meaning is constructed rather than simply discovered. Rosenblatt's rejection of the extremes of the objectivity of the New Criticism and the subjectivity of certain forms of reader-response criticism is similar to Alcoff's rejection of the extremes of cultural feminism and French feminism. Meaning, for Rosenblatt, does not reside in the text as it does for the New Critics, or in the reader as it does for reader-response critics such as David Bleich[5], but in the transactional process that is the result of the merging of reader and text. The term "reader," then, is a shifting category and is best defined in relation to reading events, motives for reading.

Alcoff's positionalist view and Rosenblatt's transactional view suggest that there is no transcendental category "woman reader," just as there is no transcendental category "woman's text." Feminist literary criticism reminds us that all reading is gendered reading and can be analyzed as such. We can only do so, though, in terms of transactions, contexts, processes, positions. The gender of the reader—a myriad of experiences, attitudes, ideas, memories, and feelings before the reading event—is reconstructed in the act of reading. The reader becomes a woman as the text is encountered. That becoming can take multiple forms, though. If the text is one that should be resisted, becoming can mean either alienation or active resistance. If the text is one that should be embraced, becoming can mean either passivity or active acceptance. What we need to do is to teach male and female students effective reading practices, effective ways of constructing gender in the process of reading. A good way to begin is to make them aware of the specificities of the processes they presently employ.

When I claim, then, as I did earlier, that Rosenblatt writes as a woman I do not mean that she shares an essential interpretive framework with all other women or that her gender allows her to transcend history and the particularities of her own educational background. For one thing, I made it clear that in many ways she also writes as a man, having been trained by men and socialized into an educational institution that is androcentric. She *sometimes* writes as a woman, and then in ways that are specific to her particular historical situation. We do not look to Rosenblatt for advancements in feminist literary theory, though, as I have demonstrated, her work does have useful applications here. We look to her as a foremother, a strong woman aware of the implications of gender in her own life and the lives of her colleagues and students, a woman who was influenced by Ruth Benedict and who was a friend of Margaret Mead, a woman who chaired a department, won a distinguished teaching award, bore and raised a child, wrote books, but whose work has not, until quite recently, received the recognition it deserves. Hers is the kind of story feminists need to tell.

Notes

1. In a postscript to a letter to me Rosenblatt explained her use of the generic *he* in both books:

> You might be amused at my troubles with the generic "he." When I wrote the first edition of *Lit. as Ex* (that goes back at least to 1936), I was reacting against the fact that whenever the subject was "teacher," the literature used "she." My use of the generic "he" was a feminist gesture, to counteract the notion that teaching was a feminine, and hence rightfully lower-paid, occupation!
>
> And as I wrote much of *The Reader, the Text, the Poem* in the fifties (the second chapter was published in 1964, but I sent it out to a journal and it was refused in 1956, as I recall) [sic]. Fighting the New Critics, I couldn't carry on that particular linguistic battle at the time, and couldn't start to rewrite the whole manuscript when it finally was published in 1978. And as I don't like any of the simple substitutions for "he," it would mean a complete rewriting. My more recent articles meet the problem by eliminating it, but it does require a different approach, a difficulty since I stress the individual reader as belonging to various groups (and certainly sex-stereotyping is something I was pointing out from *Lit as Ex* on) but still as being unique.

2. For a discussion of Rosenblatt as a woman reader-response critic see my essay, "Women as Reader-Response Critic," published in the *New Orleans Review.* In the article I also discuss the positions of Jane Tompkins and Susan Suleiman.

3. Iser's *The Act of Reading* was first published in German in 1976.

4. See "Gender and Reading."

5. See especially *Subjective Criticism.*

Works Cited

Alcoff, Linda. "Cultural Feminism Versus Post-Structuralism: The Identity Crisis in Feminist Theory." *Signs* 13 (1988): 405–36.

Bleich, David. *Subjective Criticism.* Baltimore: Johns Hopkins UP, 1978.

Fetterley, Judith. *The Resisting Reader: A Feminist Approach to American Fiction.* Bloomington: Indiana UP, 1978.

Flynn, Elizabeth A. "Gender and Reading." *College English* 45 (1983): 236–51.

———. "Women as Reader-Response Critics." *New Orleans Review* 10 (1983): 20–25.

Flynn, Elizabeth A., and Patrocinio P. Schweickart, eds. *Texts, and Contexts.* Baltimore: Johns Hopkins UP, 1986. 31–62.

Gilbert, Sandra, and Susan Gubar. *The Madwoman in the Attic: The Woman Writer and the Nineteenth-Century Literary Imagination.* New Haven: Yale UP, 1979.

Iser, Wolfgang. *The Act of Reading: A Theory of Aesthetic Response.* Baltimore: Johns Hopkins UP, 1978.

———. *Der Akt des Lesens: Theorie aesthetischer Wirkung.* Munich: Wilhelm Fink, 1976.

Rosenblatt, Louise. Letter to the author. 5 May 1987.

———. *Literature as Exploration.* 1938. New York: MLA, 1983.

———. *The Reader, the Text, the Poem: The Transactional Theory of the Literary Work.* Carbondale, Ill.: Southern Illinois UP, 1978.

Schweickart, Patrocinio P. "Reading Ourselves: Toward a Feminist Theory of Reading". *Gender and Reading: Essays on Readers, Texts, and Contexts.* Ed. Elizabeth A. Flynn and Patrocinio P. Schweickart. Baltimore: Johns Hopkins UP, 1986, 31–62.

11

Louise Rosenblatt:
A Woman in Theory

Temma F. Berg

Louise M. Rosenblatt is a rare bird. She is a woman in theory. She is an anomaly. Women, we have been told (by women and men), do not do theory. At least, they do not do it well enough to be remembered. Or is it just that whatever women do, we will not remember it? In 1979, Susan Sniader Lanser and Evelyn Torton Beck looked at the status of women in theory and decided that the woman critic is "ignored, undervalued, or dismissed if at all possible, especially if she challenges the status quo" (85). They were troubled by this treatment and concluded that "though she may be well known in her lifetime, in time her name will be forgotten, her work unread."

While this may have been true in 1979, when Lanser and Beck wrote their germinal article, "[Why] Are There No Great Women Critics? And What Difference Does It Make?," is it still true nearly ten years later? Does such a fate still await the woman in theory? In an essay written about a decade after Lanser and Beck's, Elisa Kay Sparks concluded that not much had changed. Women were still not being taken seriously as theorists and were underrepresented in critical anthologies. "What was missing from mainstream, historical anthologies of literary criticism then—theoretical work by women . . . —is to a large degree still missing now" (51). Women are not included in critical anthologies, according to Sparks, except in those that have a decidedly practical and/or pedagogical bent.

Some critics have speculated that theory is inherently a masculine enterprise because it relies on such masculine qualities as abstract reasoning and detached analysis. As a woman in theory myself, I feel threatened by such a division of the world into "feminine" practicality and "masculine" theorizing, for I enjoy reading and writing—theoretically—about such male (masculine?) theorists as Sigmund Freud, Jacques Derrida, and I. A. Richards, and I do not see why theory and practice need to be treated as a binary opposition. However, whatever the relationship between the masculine and feminine and the theoretical and practical, I am even more deeply distressed at the possibility that Rosenblatt's work may be forgotten because it is written by a woman, and therefore (perhaps) different from the theory written by men and therefore (perhaps) ineligible for canonization or even serious consideration.

I would like to help keep Rosenblatt's work alive, but how is that possible? We know what happens to women in theory. In the critical canon, women and the feminine have been deplored when they have not been simply overlooked. We are now in the midst of a refeminization of the literary domain and we have a new mob of scribbling women, but we have, I hope, no false confidence about the future of our endeavors as women in theory. Theory does not have a good history in that respect. Even today, theory and theoreticians resist including women or the feminine.

How Are Women (Mis)Treated in Theory Today?

What follows is a practical, personal, and necessarily very truncated look at women in theory today. Other women will have different stories, but though the individual anecdotes might vary, I doubt whether the overall purport would. All would lead to the inevitable conclusion that women are not welcome in theory.

In 1984, I was a member of the first feminist seminar to be held at the School of Criticism and Theory. Taught by Sandra M. Gilbert, we quickly found ourselves in a bind: we were part of the theoretical enterprise and we were not. We felt that what was happening in Sandra's class was different from what was happening in the other classes. (Something special *must* have happened, for we are the first SCT seminar to have produced a book together based on our seminar work. It was the first book and, to my knowledge, still the only book to be written by a seminar at the school.) I believe that our unusual energy was fueled by the resistance to our ideas we felt at the school. When it came time to write an introduction to the book, we wanted to write about what we experienced during the summer; we wanted to give our readers some idea of how our book happened. Predictably, the first reader of the book objected that our introduction was too "personal." We faced again the question that would not go away. If the feminine (the emotional, the personal) must be kept out of theory, can women do theory? There we were again—outsiders because we did it differently. We revised our introduction, toned ourselves down, put in weak qualifiers, but still Sandra, when she wrote a preface, resisted even that show of force. According to Sandra, if we felt uncomfortable at the school, it was not because of anything people at the school did, but because we were doing it to ourselves:

> Were we "marginalized" at the School? Here I tend to disagree with the editors of *Engendering the Word;* I don't think we were. To be sure, the intellectual and social adventures of our communal summer were sometimes stressful. I have to confess that occasionally I felt as though I, personally, was in Evanston, Illinois, to represent not just feminism but womankind—a nasty feeling for a critic committed to the plural rather than the monolithic, to the liberating variety facilitated by cultural constructionism rather than the false unity imposed by biological essentialism. But how much of that uncomfortable feeling was simply my own self-consciousness and how much was really inflicted by the situation? I suspect more was due to the former than to the latter, and I suspect it because many of the issues that were crucial to our seminar were also central to most of our other colleagues at the school. (ix)

I'm sorry, Sandra, we were not doing it to ourselves. You were not doing it to yourself. We *were* uncomfortable. Yes, you felt you had to represent all "womankind"; we all did and one gets tired of that. But we *were* marginalized, even as close to the center as we were. I'm not saying that Hayden White, Stephen Greenblatt, Jurij Striedter, and Geoffrey Hartman did not respect you (and us); I think they did. But we were not doing it right; our history was unsophisticated; our attitude toward poetry as product was wrong; what we were doing was just not as important.

My sense of our displacement at SCT was reconfirmed when I read Jane Tompkins's "Me and My Shadow," an essay which, among other things, describes her experience at SCT the following summer. Jane writes the article from two perspectives—the perspective of "Professor Tompkins" and the perspective of "Jane." From the first she writes abstractly and theoretically about Professor Messer-Davidow's essay on a new feminist epistemology. From the second, she writes concretely and personally about Ellen and their experience at SCT and their "exclusion from the discourse of Western man" (177). Sandra, we were not imagining it in 1984, and we are still not imagining it. We are being silenced even as we speak. Look over (once more) your (and Susan's) exchange with Frank Lentricchia in *Critical Inquiry*. What does that have to tell you/us? Even if you had tried to be more circumspect in your response to his essay (and—like a woman?—I thought that you might have given him too much room to confront/ affront you), he would have answered you the same way. He may claim that his (aggressive) pose is only a pose, but irony is a slippery distance to put between yourself and your Self and he takes that pose too often. Look at his pose/picture in the *New York Times Magazine* of June 5, 1988, and place it next to Jane's picture in that same issue. Yes, of course, she also self-consciously chose her pose, but look at the pose she self-consciously chose as opposed to the one he self-con- sciously chose. Maybe he's taken that pose once too often; we begin to believe he is as frontally aggressive as he looks. He does not want to be questioned.

I learned this when I questioned his reading of a Frost poem ("Mowing") at another theoretical watering hole—the Georgetown University Literary Criticism Conference and Graduate Seminar (summer, 1988). In examining the possible literary influences on Frost's poem, Lentricchia pointed out lines and images that seemed to reflect on the poet's engagement with Wordsworth and Shakespeare. I noticed a line ("and scared a bright green snake") that suggested to me that Frost might have read Emily Dickinson. Lentricchia's first response to this suggestion was that it was historically impossible. Not knowing enough about Frost's and Dickinson's dates I was silenced by his certainty. However, that night when I went home, I called my local Emily Dickinson expert (Martha Nell Smith, University of Maryland) and she insisted that it was very likely that Frost read Dickinson. Armed with dates of editions, etc., from her, I went back to challenge Lentricchia the next day. I finally got him to agree that he could not prove Frost had *not* read Dickinson, but then again no one could prove he had because the evidence was just not there in his letters and journals. I wonder if it states in Frost's letters and journals on what days he read the appropriate Wordsworth poem or Shake- speare play? Or does Lentricchia just assume Frost read Wordsworth and Shakespeare while he needs unassailable proof that Frost read Dickinson before he will revise his Dickinsonless history of Frost?[1]

Actually, the first question I silently proposed to ask Lentricchia has more to do with the argument of this essay. It struck me, as I listened to his talk, that his view of Modernism, especially inasmuch as he views it as a flight from femininity, is very like Gilbert and Gubar's. I was, at first, tempted to ask him if he knew of their work and if it had influenced him (thereby exposing my ignorance of their exchange in *Critical Inquiry*, which I had not yet read). I passed by that question to ask the one I did about Frost and Dickinson, but, actually, the two questions were the same, for Lentricchia is as anxious to relieve Frost of any debt to Dickinson as he is to relieve himself of any debt to Gilbert and Gubar. As Lawrence Lipking wrote in *Critical Inquiry*, years before Gilbert and Gubar and Lentricchia's quarrel appeared there, "Many debates between male and female critics seem to have the same structure: a logic that masks the real issues of power and desire" (70). Lipking, it seems to me, is right; many male theoreticians desire to disempower women and to keep them (women) out of whatever critical picture they (men) are painting.

Gilbert and Gubar's argument with Lentricchia is very important. Moreover, it is a continuation of an argument they alluded to during our summer at SCT. In class one day Sandra jokingly said she didn't mind being a footnote in Jonathan Culler's book. But you did mind. And you mind being even less than a footnote in Lentricchia's work. You should mind. Because what you are fighting is what women are always fighting: being ignored, being omitted from anthologies, being, ultimately, forgotten. You are fighting extinction, and you should not give up the fight.[2]

The same fight you fight Louise Rosenblatt has fought, even with Jane Tompkins, who did not include Rosenblatt's work in her anthology of reader-response criticism. In her introduction to the anthology, Tompkins (in a footnote that addresses the issue of exclusions and inclusions) suggests that "Louise Rosenblatt deserves to be recognized as the first among the present generation of critics in the country to describe empirically the way the reader's reactions to the poem are responsible for any subsequent interpretation of it" (xxvin). Going on to link Rosenblatt's work with Walter Slatoff's, Tompkins asserts that their work raises "issues central to the debates that have arisen since." However, Rosenblatt's work was excluded not only from the Introduction but also from the body of essays "chosen to provide a conceptual framework for organizing the ever-growing quantity of reader-oriented work." Rosenblatt has occasionally been acknowledged in a footnote by various reader-response theorists, but her work has, in general, not been considered as important, as central to the reader-response movement, as the work done by such men as Stanley Fish, Wolfgang Iser, David Bleich, and Norman Holland.

Women are not welcome—even by other women—in theory. Why? Do we write theory so differently that it is not recognized as theory? In *Beyond God the Father*, Mary Daly writes about the problem of method in philosophy and how it interferes with her ability to ask certain questions. What she writes bears on my present argument: "The tyranny of methodolatry," she suggests, "hinders new discoveries. It prevents us from raising questions never asked before and from being illumined by ideas that do not fit into pre-established boxes and forms. The worshippers of Method have an effective way of handling data that does not fit into the Respectable Categories of Questions and Answers. They simply classify it as nondata, thereby rendering it invisible" (11). I think theory, like philosophy, has a method that has served as a strait gate, letting through only certain questions, certain ways of answering, certain styles of investigation. Women at places like SCT have been trying to widen that gate and enter into that male enclave called theory, without having to pass certain tests (pass over certain texts?), write certain ways, answer certain questions, but it is questionable whether we have at all succeeded. The gate, it seems, has kept many out. I begin to suspect that the only ones welcomed in are the ones who write theory "like the guys."

Do I want to suggest that there is a man's and a woman's way of writing theory? Perhaps, but before I can even begin to propose such a possibility, we need to know what women in theory have written.

Yes, Virginia, There Are Women in Theory

In 1753, Charlotte Lennox published *Shakespear Illustrated: or the Novels and Histories, on Which the Plays of Shakespear are Founded, Collected and Translated from the Original Authors, with Critical Remarks*. While most theorists are familiar with Johnson's *Preface to Shakespeare*, few are acquainted with Lennox's work, even though her work predates Johnson's and, like his, very much reflects eighteenth-century tastes. She judges works for their adherence to poetical justice, lifelikeness, and propriety. Overall, Lennox is much harder than Johnson on Shakespeare; she usually finds his transformations of earlier stories faulty, and his plots more inconsistent and absurd than the originals on which they are based.

Though Lennox might, almost relentlessly, find the originals superior to Shakespeare for consistency, naturalness, and poetical justice, she did devote three volumes of very arduous scholarly work to Shakespeare, so we cannot accuse her of trivializing or underestimating the Bard. She was, in her own way, recognizing his genius, but perhaps trying to show us that geniuses are, like all wo(men), fallible. Perhaps she felt that the men around her were too reverential, and someone needed the courage to point out the Elizabethan playwright's faults.

I also found refreshing Lennox's astonishment that other critics find it necessary to establish Shakespeare's classical knowledge: "It is really surprising to see the Admirers of Shakespear so solicitous to prove he was very conversant with the Antients; they take all Opportunities to find in his Writings Illusions to them; Imitations of their

Thoughts and Expressions; and will not scruple to allow their Favourite to have been guilty of some little Thefts from their Works, provided it will make out his Claim to an Acquaintance with them" (I, 240). Elsewhere (*Engendering the Word* 25n), I have argued that perhaps the debate about the level of Shakespeare's education has always been important to literary historians because they are anxious to protect the canon against invasion by women. If greatness depends upon classical training, then, since women were generally excluded from classical training, women could be depended upon not to be great. On the other hand, if Shakespeare could achieve greatness without classical training, then perhaps a woman could. I admired Lennox's subversive insistence that Shakespeare was a natural genius lacking acquaintance not only with ancient tongues but with modern Italian and French as well.

Like Lennox's *Shakespear Illustrated*, Clara Reeve's *The Progress of Romance* (1785) is a work of excavation. Reeve wants to uncover as many works of Romance as possible, their dates, their authors, their countries of origin. Also, she wants to determine what are the characteristics of Romance and what are the effects of reading one. Like many modern feminist critics of Romance, Reeve seeks to demonstrate the value and purpose of such a genre and reproves her male contemporaries for their narrow vision: "The learned men of our country have in general affected a contempt for this kind of writing, and looked upon Romances, as proper furniture only for a lady's Library" (I, xi). Because she values the Romance form, she does not see why men insist on maintaining a distinction between Epic and Romance to the favor of the former and the disparagement of the latter. She insists that Romances, like Epics, have influenced men to become heroes. Reeve judges those Romances and novels best that instill virtue by recording the pleasures to be won by being virtuous; she does not approve of books that show virtue (through no fault of its own) in distress. "Virtue," according to Reeve, "stands in need of every encouragement" (II, 26).

Like Clara Reeve, Mrs. Jameson is also very concerned with the effects of reading, especially on women. She put women at the center of her book on Shakespeare, *Characteristics of Women, Moral, Poetical and Historical* (1832), for as she explains in her introduction, she hopes to reform the education of women. However, unlike her predecessor, Mrs. Jameson does not believe that virtue must necessarily be rewarded. In fact, Jameson finds Johnson's definition of poetic justice narrow and rigid. A play does not necessarily promote morality by mathematically apportioning good to good and evil to evil. Her estimation of a "moral" play is much more complex than that. For example, when looking at Katherine of Aragon in *Henry VIII*, Jameson does not expect that good will receive good, only that good will be good despite undeserved adversity and thus serve as a beacon to us all. Not only does Shakespeare do justice to our sense of reality in that respect (that the good suffer sometimes through no fault of their own), but he also does justice, according to Jameson, to the ability of women (even those deeply divided against one another) to love one another: "How nobly has Shakespeare done justice to the two women and heightened our interest in both by placing the praises of Katherine in the mouth of Anna Bullen!" (421).[3]

Throughout her book, Jameson insists on an essential difference between men and women. She believes this difference has much to do with the differences in their intellectual work: "The essential and invariable distinction appears to me this: in men the intellectual faculties exist more self-poised and self-directed—more independent of the rest of the character, than we ever find them in women, with whom talent, however predominant is in a much greater degree modified by the sympathies and moral qualities" (53). Virginia Woolf uses playful metaphors to make the same serious point: "The student who has been trained in research at Oxbridge has no doubt some method of shepherding his question past all distractions till it runs into its answer as a sheep runs into its pen. . . . But if, unfortunately, one has had no training in a university, the question far from being shepherded to its pen flies like a frightened flock hither and thither, helter-skelter, pursued by a whole pack of hounds" (28). When Jameson and Woolf make such stylistic distinctions, they seem to agree with those contemporary arguments that insist there is a distinct difference between men's and women's ways of writing. Men write directly, forcefully, and with a tighter grip on their argument. Women write diffusely, confuse aesthetic and personal issues, and cannot stick to the theoretical point. "Almost inevitably," according to Lipking, "the male critic comes round to Telemachus' manner of argument: women take literature too *personally*" (67; Lipking's emphasis). Jameson would agree with Telemachus, except she would not see this need to take things personally as a problem, just as a difference. Like Lipking, she might want to assert that women employ a different poetics, though I doubt that she would agree with Lipking's suggestion of a "poetics of abandonment." She might prefer a "poetics of empathy."[4]

Women critics, especially feminist critics, are often criticized for treating women in literature as real people rather than as textual constructs, but perhaps that is just another important way women in theory differ from men. They cannot so easily separate the worlds we live in through art from the worlds we live in experientially. As Jane Marcus has so forcefully expressed it, "*A real woman's poetics is a poetics*

of commitment, not a poetics of abandonment. Above all, it does not separate art from work and daily life" (84).

The next woman in theory I would like to discuss is perhaps the
least theoretical of them all. Mary Cowden Clarke writes fictional
narratives of *The Girlhood of Shakespeare's Heroines* (1850). However,
because she seems to continue what begins to look like a woman's
tradition in theory, I think her work is important. Like her predecessors, Mary Cowden Clarke insists on the continuity rather than the
disjunction between art and life. The distance between the literary
creation and the reader can always collapse. Shakespeare's heroines
are not simply literary creations; they are living people who have a
history that can, at least, be imagined.

Like her predecessors, Clarke insists on the interconnectedness
not only of life and art but of all experience. Everything that happens
to us contributes to shaping us; therefore, in order to understand an
adult heroine, we need to understand what she might have been like
as a child. This is true not only in life but in art. To understand
Shakespeare's heroines, we need to understand what they might have
been like as girls. The girlhoods of Shakespeare's heroines are meant
to demonstrate what incidents might conceivably have led to the
formation of their characters as they emerge in the plays. Particularly
interesting in this respect is Clarke's tale of Lady Macbeth, which
begins with the scene of her birth. Her father and mother want a son,
not a daughter. It would seem that Clarke here anticipates modern
readings of the play, which see Lady Macbeth as a woman repressing
her feminine side in an attempt to help her husband accomplish
her/his goal, but ultimately succumbing to it (expressing it?) in her
inability to kill the sleeping Duncan ("Had he not resembled/My
father as he slept, I had done't") and in the sleep-walking scene;
however, unlike modern critics of the play, Clarke feels free to
locate—in parental rejection—the source of Lady Macbeth's desire to
repress her womanly self.

Another particular incident in the life of Lady Macbeth vividly
demonstrates Clarke's concern (an ongoing concern, it would seem, of
women theorists) with the powers of the reading process. When she
is a young girl, Lady Macbeth's old nurse tells her a tale of a woman
who revenges the death of her son by enticing the King into her castle
"in seeming loyalty" only to cunningly kill him (I, 138). While the old
nurse tells the tale as a cautionary tale (the queen had "to abide in exile
and concealment" [I, 140]), the young Lady Macbeth interprets it as a
tale of success ("But she gained her end!" [I, 140]) and later is pleased
to learn that the woman in the story was her ancestor. Obviously this
tale, brought in by Clarke to suggest what caused Lady Macbeth's
traitorous behavior toward her King, also suggests that reading is a

powerful charm not to be used lightly. We are what we read. At least, we may become (act out) what we read.

Women in theory have always been concerned with reading, how it shapes us, how we shape it. In that respect, Louise Rosenblatt's work culminates a tradition of which she may not even have been aware. While she saw her work as a rejection of the New Critical emphasis on close reading (" . . . having written a critique of the art-for-art's-sake theorists, I was also disillusioned with the engrossment in technique and so-called purely literary matters" [*Literature* viii]), it can also be seen as a continuation of women theorists' insistence on the interconnectedness of all things, or, as Louise Rosenblatt so aptly puts it, "the mutual interdependence of all facets" (*Literature* viii). Rosenblatt's concerns are the concerns women have, over the centuries, shared. Like the women theorists who have preceded her, she wants very much to prove to us that reading and literature are not separate from but a part of every other aspect of life. She wants to question what the prevailing critics of the day assert; she wants to be heard, but, like the women in theory who have followed as well as preceded her, she often wonders if anyone is listening.

Rosenblatt does not write about reading as an abstract phenomenological process, but as something that students do and teachers need to guide. Reading has enormous consequences for teacher and student. Reading is not an isolated act; it has many repercussions. Reading gives us attitudes, and it is our responsibility, as teachers and students of literature, to see how this happens. Reading is a social as well as an aesthetic experience. The theory of reading can never be separated from its practice.

If our institutions of higher learning fail students (and Rosenblatt believes that they sometimes do), it is because they cut literature off from life, deny its capacity to affect us emotionally. Response, if it exists, is formulaic not personal. Students too often feel compelled to read critics rather than the works themselves. Students have, literally, lost their voices, and Rosenblatt wants to give them back what they have lost.

Rosenblatt never apologizes for the practicality of her models of reading. She is writing to teachers to tell them how to teach better and how, in the process, to make themselves better, more flexible readers. She wants to bring out the fullness of the reading experience for, inevitably, when that experience is performed responsibly, the reader will be able to bring out the fullness of the text:

> Challenged to establish the validity of his interpretation and judgment of the work, he will be stimulated both to examine the text more closely and to scrutinize the adequacy of his own past experience and basic assumptions. He will test whether what he brings to the text has

> enabled him to do justice to all that it embodies. This may lead him to probe further into literary techniques and forms. It may also impel him to acquire various types of knowledge—literary and social history, biography, philosophy, psychology, anthropology—that may deepen his understanding of the work. Such a process of clarification and enrichment of successive literary experiences will foster sound critical habits. From this kind of literary study there should flow, too, enhanced understanding of himself and the life about him. (*Literature* 124)

If we would only begin to do justice to the literary work, we might begin to bring justice into our lives.

First published in 1938, *Literature as Exploration* sought to help us learn to use literature as a survival mechanism in a world on the brink of war. In this book, Rosenblatt presents literature as an empowering force and as a place where all the facets of our world can be brought into play. Everything counts. Everything helps us understand the literary text and the literary text helps us understand everything— about ourselves, about our world. We cannot throw out the personal, the irrational, the merely historical, the contingent, the practical. Reading is a profoundly complex experience, which draws us both into and out of the worlds we inhabit.

Like other women in theory before her, Louise Rosenblatt insists on the personal nature of the reading experience: " . . . a reading is of necessity a participation, a personal experience" (*Literature* 278). Rosenblatt's insistence on the personal nature of the reading experience makes her a wonderful forerunner of contemporary feminist literary theory. By looking at her insights and convictions, we can see not only a continuation and elaboration of what may begin to look like a tradition of women in theory, but a proleptic look at what concerns us now. By looking closely at her work, we might even be able to begin to define the outline of a feminine (feminist?) aesthetic.[5]

Of primary importance to any feminine/feminist aesthetic would be the twin assumptions that literature is deeply interconnected with life and that we need to understand just how much this is so. For example, our images of ourselves come from the books we read, and while sometimes these images can be liberating and empowering, sometimes they can be debilitating. Louise Rosenblatt insists on this negative possibility: "The human complications that are recognized as important and valid enough to be given explicit attention in fiction, in the newspapers or other mass media, reflect overwhelmingly the stereotyped notions of masculine and feminine nature and behavior. The man, dominant, masterful, superior; the woman, emotional, dependent, clinging, are the images most often and most forcibly presented even in this supposed age of woman's emancipation. These stereotypes will affect in some way the actions, feelings, and choices

188   The Experience of Reading

of the individual" (*Literature* 91). Women in theory insist again and
again on this important connection. Though we may be accused of
taking literature too personally, we must remember that critics like
Rosenblatt have insisted that we have not yet taken it personally
enough because we have not yet estimated just how personally literature takes us: "To what extent, for example, can the influence of
literature be held responsible for the fact that many women today find
within themselves emotional obstacles to their sincere ambition to be
independent emotionally and intellectually? Throughout their entire
experience with literature they have been led to identify themselves
most often with the older image of women as temperamentally, as
well as economically, subordinate and dependent" (*Literature* 221n).
We have begun to examine the part that literature plays in the formation (and transformations) of our psychic life, but we must not forget
that Louise Rosenblatt pioneered in this effort.

If one hallmark of a feminine/feminist aesthetic is its belief that we
cannot separate literature from life, then another would have to be
that we cannot separate our intellectual reactions to literature from
our emotional reactions: ". . . if we are to keep literature alive, we
cannot completely separate the technical, the esthetic, from the
human meanings of the work" (*Literature* 289). Women in theory often
insist on this need to accept and examine our emotional responses to
the characters and situations re-presented in fiction to the extent that
we are often accused of naively confusing the women we read about
with ourselves and the women we know, thereby undermining the
nature of representation. When we are told we need to separate
ourselves from the women we read about and from the emotional
responses we have to them, we should remember that theorists like
Rosenblatt have encouraged us to explore those very connections that
we are so often urged to sever. For example, when, in *Literature as
Exploration*, Rosenblatt tells us about a class discussion of Ibsen's
Nora, she does not find it at all strange that "the young women had
obviously identified very strongly with Nora" (228). In fact, Rosenblatt goes on to observe that "the discussion seemed to have personal
immediacy for them." Such identification and immediacy is not only
not naive, according to Rosenblatt, it is imperative: "More significant
than any statements made by the students was the fact that these
ideas grew out of emotional tension and lively personal feeling. There
is no proof that the insights achieved were retained. But it can safely
be said that they were more likely to be retained than if the same idea
had been encountered in an impersonal way in a traditional psychology or sociology course" (230). The personal lived-through experience
of literature is what makes it valuable. We learn to understand ourselves by learning to understand literature. Literature is the best
access to (and corrective of) our emotional life.

In the above citation, Rosenblatt also alludes to another of her central beliefs, a belief that would also have to be part of any feminine/feminist aesthetics just as it is already a part of many practical women's studies programs. The best learning experience is interdisciplinary. Not only can we not separate literature from life, we cannot separate it from psychology, sociology, economics, anthropology. In the above excerpt from *Literature as Exploration*, the inference is that literature gives us a better, because more personal, access to ourselves. Elsewhere Rosenblatt drops the above implied hierarchy and unambivalently asserts that the different disciplines depend on one another: "The anthropologist's idea of the interdependence of the various aspects of any culture can be related to the study of literature. An understanding of what happens in the realm of literary activity *requires* the study of the accompanying economic, social, and political conditions" (*Literature* 257; my emphasis). Stressing here what has served as one of the key assumptions in women's studies, Rosenblatt very much espouses what begins to look less and less like a poetics of abandonment and more and more like a poetics of inclusion.

Women in theory insist on inclusiveness in still another way. Not only is there an attempt to dismantle any hierarchy among disciplines or between reason and feeling but there is also an attempt to undermine the traditional evaluation processes, which privilege certain texts or styles of reading over others. Rosenblatt, because she insists on reading as a personal experience, also insists on the authority of each reader's experience and on its value: "Absorption in the quality and structure of the experience engendered by the text can happen when the reader is enthralled by the adventures of the Hardy Boys or by the anguish of *King Lear*. In either case, in my view, the text has given rise to a literary work of art" (*Reader* 27). Rosenblatt wants to empower, not disable, the ordinary reader: ". . . there is a sense in which [the ordinary reader's] reading is indeed as 'good' [as G. W. Knight's]: drawing on the reservoir of his own past life and reading, he has lived through the experience himself, he has struggled to organize it, felt it on his own pulses. It is now part of the life experience with which he encounters the future" (*Reader* 141–42). Systems of value, Rosenblatt insists, like women in theory before and after her, should not be used to enrich some at the expense of others. Toward the end of *The Reader, the Text, the Poem*, Rosenblatt makes her most radical contribution to the possibility of a feminine/feminist aesthetic:

> Readers may bring to the text experiences, awarenesses, and needs that have been ignored in traditional criticism. Women, for example, are finding their own voices as writers and critics, as are the ethnic minorities and special cultural groups. Workers . . . are themselves becoming articulate and self-aware. (142)

Rosenblatt goes on to worry that as a result of their alienation from the dominant tradition these special groups seem to threaten the empathy that she believes is at the heart of the reading experience. If only women can speak for women, blacks for blacks, and so on, then we are closing off rather than opening up, fragmenting rather than making more inclusive, the reading experience. Rosenblatt is right to worry about this phenomenon, but these various groups are right to suspect misappropriation. Many contemporary feminists worry that now that men have entered feminism, women and women's issues will disappear even from the feminist theoretical enterprise. As Janet Todd has warned us, "Women's voice from experience needs to remain at its [feminist criticism's] base and, until men listen to it as well as imagining costumes and modalities for themselves, there cannot really be male feminism or men in feminism, simply men using feminism" (134). Significantly, Todd's insistence on the importance to feminist theory of women's personal experience seems to echo Rosenblatt's insistence on the authority of personal experience.

Ultimately, Rosenblatt provides a solution to the dilemma both Todd and she see. Readers must acknowledge their situatedness—by ethnic identification, sexual orientation, class, and the like. Men can be feminists, but they must acknowledge their maleness. White women can read and interpret (is there any difference between these two activities?) a text by a black woman, but they must acknowledge their whiteness. A white woman's reading is not a black woman's reading. A man's reading is not a woman's. However, we must not give up the hope that by reading each other we can learn from each other.

Is There a Women's Theory?

At this point, I may be seen as wanting to insist on two traditions in critical theory—a woman's and a man's. I do not mean to do so. The women quite obviously see themselves as part of a single developing tradition. They quote men (and women), cite others' ideas copiously, do not feel antagonistic to (though they may disagree with) their male contemporaries. However, the men rarely mention the women. Thus, it seems as if women are forced to become part of a developing tradition of their own; they are the part that is systematically suppressed, ignored, forgotten, not cited by the dominant tradition. If I seem to be creating a woman's tradition in critical theory, it is only because the men have refused (and continue to refuse) to let women in.

If women are ever to be included, we need to start looking at why they have been excluded, which means we may have to look at the possibility that the way women write and what they write about may have something to do with why they have been neglected. Women, perhaps, have asked different questions, found different answers when they asked the same questions, emphasized different aspects of the literature under consideration. That is why they have been excluded, and if we are going to include them, we may need to revise our view of critical theory, what it should be and what it should do.

Men in theory do not believe that they are putting themselves at the center of their theory. They, they insist, are talking about universals, humankind, mankind, men. They veil their self-absorption in universal drapery. As Lawrence Lipking suggests, "[A women's poetics] reveals how much literary theory serves exclusively masculine interests" (78). And if we look at women's theory as a tradition of its own, we see that what is marginalized (when not attacked) in men's theory is put at the center of women's theory. Whether the critic is Lennox, Reeve, Jameson, Clarke, or Woolf, woman moves to the center—her concerns, her experiences, her representations in literature. And because talk about women cannot be universal, but must be seen as personal, then theory written by/about women cannot be universal, it can only be personal. It then becomes very easy to discredit and overlook the work of women in theory.

Although Rosenblatt did not focus as steadily on women and women's issues as some of her predecessors did, I believe that her focus on the personal can be seen as a substitute for more direct engagement. Certainly, her beliefs were subversive of the priorities in traditional (male) literary theory, which, when it was not overlooking or transforming the personal and the emotional aspects of the aesthetic experience, was actively repudiating them. I know I am in danger of distorting Rosenblatt's work; she never saw herself as part of a tradition of women in theory. None of the women I have written about did. Nevertheless, there is a way in which they can be seen as part of a tradition that is just beginning to emerge. And certain characteristics seem to emerge as part of this tradition. Though she and the other women I have written about may not have seen themselves as shaping an aesthetics in opposition to the dominant (male) culture, the shape of a feminine/feminist poetics begins to be discernible through her (and their) work. Central to this aesthetic is a belief in the power of the aesthetic experience to affect, indeed create, our emotions. This power is such that it threatens the boundary between art and life. Art enters our life and becomes one with it. It becomes impossible to separate out the various elements in aesthetic experience. As Rosenblatt suggests, "The mark of the reader's aesthetic activity is precisely that he . . . fuses the cognitive and the emotive, or perhaps more accurately, apprehends them as facets of the same lived-through experience, thus giving it its special meaning and quality" (*Reader* 46). The personal, the emotional, cannot be separated from the intellectual, the cognitive. A woman's poetics is a poetics of inclusion—we cannot exclude anything as extrinsic to the experience of reading. A woman's poetics is a poetics of empathy—reading fosters our sympathetic insight and makes us better.

Rather than assume that we are distorting literary theory when we suggest there are two separate critical traditions, perhaps we need to reconsider whether critical theory has been distorted by the omission of women's thought. Lanser and Beck insist, and I think rightly so, that it has: "If women's work were at the center of our definitions, our hierarchy of values would very likely be changed" (87). Before we can see a single line of theory that includes both men and women, we need to see more clearly *what* has been left out. Also we need to be more persistent in our attempts to answer the question Why has women's work been kept out?

Why, for example, has Louise Rosenblatt's work been kept out? She asked important questions and tried to subvert the status quo, which devalued the authority of personal experience, yet her contribution never has been recognized. What would be the effect of recognizing her work as part of a tradition of women in theory? Her work, which might seem marginal and idiosyncratic and untheoretical when viewed from the perspective of male literary theory, seems much more pertinent and central when viewed from the perspective of a woman's tradition in literary theory. Unlike men, who want to avoid (or at least transmute) the personal, the emotional, the individual, Rosenblatt insists on returning to it again and again. We must understand the emotional effects of reading and the individuality of the experience. We must value every reader's experience (no one can read for you). We must emphasize the continuity rather than the disjunction between art and life.

However, I do not so much seek to validate a female line running parallel to, never touching, the male line, as to show what had to be left out so that the history of literary criticism could take the shape of a simple, single male line. The male line of theory is a construction of literary history. But to see just how much this is so, we may need to construct an alternative female line of theory. Both lines are unnecessarily exclusive, but we will not believe this until we see what has been invisible for so long—women in theory.

Notes

1. Of course, I did not think of these questions at the time. I have never been very good at quick retorts. They inevitably come to me days later.

2. Two years before Gilbert and Gubar and Lentricchia's exchange, Lisa Jardine published a paper which suggests that Gilbert and Gubar's position

vis-a-vis Lentricchia is analogous to the position of British feminists vis-a-vis "the [British] Left." Presented at the Southampton Sexual Difference Conference, her paper, wittily titled " 'Girl Talk' (for Boys on the Left), or Marginalising Feminist Critical Praxis," discusses the growing rift between British feminist theorists and their male Marxist counterparts and suggests that while men like Eagleton and Williams seek to claim marginality, they are not, in fact, marginalized. On the other hand, women and feminist theory are: "When women obtrude their feminist politics, there is no possibility of blending—their being 'other than' *all* the male members of the institution is out in the open, and there is no possibility of going back on that" (214). Women are no more welcome in British theory than they are in American. The concluding line of Jardine's essay—"She is hopelessly confused (he says)"—uncannily looks forward to the cartoon that accompanies Gilbert and Gubar's response to Frank Lentricchia. Under the heading "Famous Bozos No. 3 Cathy's Clown," a man speaks to a woman. The balloon above his head reads: "Believe me, Kate, as a feminist myself, I'm only trying to point out areas where lack of theory perhaps prevents you from perceiving the true nature of your oppression." She, quite aware of "the true nature of her oppression" and perhaps locating it in the hand caressing (threatening?) her throat, thinks (as indicated in the cloudy bubble above her head): "Will no one rid me of this patronising smoothie?" We cannot dismiss our feelings as women or as feminist theorists.

3. If there is one theme that seems to run almost universally through the writings of women in theory, it is this insistence on women's love and support of one another. Charlotte Lennox also noted Anne Bullen's "most tender concerns for the Sufferings of her Mistress, Queen Catharine . . . " (III, 230). And, of course, there is Virginia Woolf's passionate insistence that Olivia liked Chloe.

4. In "Still Practice, A/Wrested Alphabet: Toward a Feminist Aesthetic," Jane Marcus plays havoc with the narrowness of Lipking's suggestion: " . . . one could offer instead a feminist aesthetics of power with, say, Judith beheading Holofernes and Artemisia Gentileschi's depiction of the scene as its paradigm. Or, an aesthetics of maternal protection, an aesthetics of sisterhood, an aesthetics of virgin vengeance from the Amazons to Joan of Arc to Christabel Pankhurst, an aesthetics of woman's critique of male domination" (82). Certainly Marcus is correct to point out the limitations of Lipking's "poetics of abandonment," but I would also agree with Laurie Finke that we cannot simply dismiss men and theory: "If feminist criticism is to claim women as oppressed or repressed subjects, it must lodge that claim within a theory of the subject; if feminist writing is to represent women's experiences, it must do so within a larger framework of a theory of representation; and if feminist critics are to examine the uniqueness of women's relation to language, they must ground that examination in a persuasive theory of language" (267–68). Theory must continue to inform practice and practice must continue to acknowledge its theory. Women and men must continue to write literary history together; otherwise, we continue to write histories that miss the mark of difference altogether.

5. At this point I would like to make special mention of the work of Rachel Blau DuPlessis. Although I do not cite her directly anywhere in this chapter, her work indirectly informs the whole of it.

Works Cited

Atlas, James. "The Battle of the Books." *New York Times Magazine* 5 June 1988: 25.

Berg, Temma F., Anna Shannon Elfenbein, Jeanne Larsen, and Elisa Kay Sparks, eds. *Engendering the Word: Feminist Essays in Psychosexual Poetics.* Urbana: U Illinois P, 1989.

Clarke, Mary Cowden. *The Girlhood of Shakespeare's Heroines, in a Series of Tales.* 5 vols. 1850. New York: A. C. Armstrong & Son, 1891.

Daly, Mary. *Beyond God the Father: Toward a Philosophy of Women's Liberation.* 1973. Boston: Beacon Press, 1985.

DuPlessis, Rachel Blau. "For the Etruscans." Showalter 271–291.

———. *Writing beyond the Ending: Narrative Strategies of Twentieth-Century Women Writers.* Bloomington: Indiana UP, 1985.

Finke, Laurie. "The Rhetoric of Marginality: Why I Do Feminist Theory." *Tulsa Studies in Women's Literature* 5 (1986): 251–72.

Gilbert, Sandra M., and Susan Gubar. "The Man on the Dump Versus the United Dames of America; or, What Does Frank Lentricchia Want?" *Critical Inquiry* 14 (1988): 386–406.

Jameson, Mrs. Anna. *Characteristics of Women, Moral, Poetical and Historical.* 1832. Boston: Houghton-Mifflin, n.d.

Jardine, Lisa. " 'Girl Talk' (for Boys on the Left), or Marginalising Feminist Critical Praxis." *Oxford Literary Review* 8 (1986): 208–17.

Lanser, Susan Sniader, and Evelyn Torton Beck. "[Why] Are There No Great Women Critics? And What Difference Does It Make?" *The Prism of Sex: Essays in the Sociology of Knowledge.* Ed. Julia A. Sherman and Evelyn Torton Beck. Madison: U of Wisconsin P, 1979.

Lennox, Charlotte. *Shakespear Illustrated: or the Novels and Histories, On which the Plays of Shakespear Are Founded, Collected and Translated from the Original Authors, with Critical Remarks.* 3 vols. 1753. New York: AMS Press, 1973.

Lentricchia, Frank. "Andiamo!" *Critical Inquiry* 14 (1988): 407–13.

———. "Patriarchy Against Itself—The Young Manhood of Wallace Stevens." *Critical Inquiry* 13 (1987): 742–86.

Lipking, Lawrence. "Aristotle's Sister: A Poetics of Abandonment." *Critical Inquiry* 10 (1983): 61–81.

Marcus, Jane. "Still Practice, A/Wrested Alphabet: Toward a Feminist Aesthetic." *Tulsa Studies in Women's Literature.* 3 (1984): 79–97.

Moers, Ellen. *Literary Women: The Great Writers*. New York: Oxford UP, 1976.

Reeve, Clara. *The Progress of Romance and the History of Charoba, Queen of Aegypt*. 1785. New York: Facsimile Text Society, 1930.

Rosenblatt, Louise M. *Literature as Exploration*. 1938. 3rd ed. New York: Noble and Noble, 1976.

——. *The Reader, the Text, the Poem: The Transactional Theory of the Literary Work*. Carbondale, Ill.: Southern Illinois UP, 1978.

Showalter, Elaine. "Feminist Criticism in the Wilderness." *Critical Inquiry* 8 (1981): 179–205.

——. *The New Feminist Criticism: Essays on Women, Literature and Theory*. New York: Pantheon Books, 1985.

Sparks, Elisa Kay. "Old Father Nile: T. S. Eliot and Harold Bloom on the Creative Process as Spontaneous Generation." Berg 51–80.

Todd, Janet. *Feminist Literary History*. New York: Routledge, 1988.

Tompkins, Jane P. "An Introduction to Reader-Response Criticism." In *Reader-Response Criticism: From Formalism to Post-Structuralism*. Ed. Jane P. Tompkins. Baltimore: Johns Hopkins UP, 1980.

——. "Me and My Shadow." *New Literary History* 19 (1987): 169–78.

Woolf, Virginia. *A Room of One's Own*. 1929: New York: Harcourt Brace Jovanovich, 1957.

12

A Transactional Affair

John Rouse

Surely there is a seductive element in the relations we have with students, in our effort to help these younger ones enter into new experience or take it in. And their response to the material we present must be mixed with their response to the person presenting it, for whatever a teacher may say is taken first as commentary on himself or herself. So we plan our first meeting with them carefully, knowing that their resistance to our line of inquiry will be lessened in the degree to which they feel this new person standing there can be taken seriously as a partner in the new life-adventure, as they have taken others.

In her memoir of Freud, H. D. tells of an episode that occurred during the first week of her analysis, perhaps during the first session. She was stretched out on that famous couch in the consulting room, languidly stirring the waters of the unconscious but holding herself back from the plunge, when suddenly Professor Freud, as she called him, lost his temper and began beating his fist on the headpiece of the old-fashioned sofa. Startled, she veered round, sitting stark upright, feet on the floor. "The trouble is," he said, "I am an old man—*you do not think it worth your while to love me.*" Freud was, in fact, seventy-seven at the time. And from long experience he knew that what a client chooses to tell the analyst is given as a gift, as testimony to their secret understanding, their unspoken interest in each other. He knew, shall we say, that there must be an erotic element in such a relationship, for without it the work will not go well at all—the client will not take him seriously enough, will lack the emotional impetus for making the gift. He lost his temper, was passionately angry as a would-be lover can be—surprising her, making her feel guilty. And so on another day, when no one else would come to him because of soldiers everywhere, the threat of violence, she came through the silent streets thinking that if he remembered what he had said, then surely her coming was the answer to it (Dolittle 15–16, 62).

Perhaps every preceptorial relation requires an erotic element for its success, some personal interest the individuals feel for each other that makes them want to reach out, either to challenge or to stroke. Even during lessons conducted in the most impersonal manner some such dynamic must be at work. As teachers we reach out first, give our students a poem perhaps, inviting their response—and they give us their response as a gift testifying to their interest and commitment. But then, what form should that response take and how should we answer it?

Until recently, there was no problem here; we were sure of the relations among teacher, text, and student. The status of the poem as a verbal object was certain, and in the New Criticism we had a method for knowing it—a method taught by teacher critics to their student apprentices. We knew where we stood with each other. But now a proliferation of critical methods suggests that the old way no longer satisfies, that we would know our students in a different way. The choice we make of critical method may well depend on the kind of relation we now wish to have with young people—on the particular erotic quality that method implies.

The relation Louise Rosenblatt would have with her students is one that depends on what both student and teacher bring to it—and so the result cannot be specified in advance. It is not an instructional relation, in which the teacher adds knowledge to a student who is otherwise unchanged by the encounter, but rather a transactional relation, in which each contributes to the developing experience and from which each learns something. This transactional relation is a direct consequence of her critical approach to a text, for she holds that a poem exists only when it is enacted by a reader, a process or transaction to which both reader and text contribute. And the results of this transaction may not be known immediately, for only with time do individuals assimilate the poetic experience and the meaning of what they have done together.

If a poem exists only when a text is lived through by a reader, then what happens within that reader during the reading is of great interest. In the New Criticism, by contrast, any move away from the text to a reader's inner states involved an "affective fallacy" and was to be avoided. The teacher was to maintain an impersonal, objective distance from both text and student. But Rosenblatt, by insisting on the contribution of the reader, anticipated the development of reader-response criticism, which now encourages us to take a more personal interest in students by drawing out their experiences with a text. The teacher may still be at the front of a classroom, separated from the student by a desk or lectern—but they both may talk much more about themselves. And sometimes the text may seem to fade away, dissolve in the wash of feelings and memories it evokes. The individual reader's experience of a text *is* the text in some classrooms.

Stanley Fish, who teaches an "affective stylistics," tells about a student who finished his course and went on to another, where she asked the professor, "Is there a text in this class?" "Yes," he answered, "it's the *Norton Anthology of Literature.*" "No, no," she said, "I mean in this class do we believe in poems and things, or is it just us?" (Fish 305). In some classrooms it is just us, just our individual responses to the stimuli on the page. There is no poem to interpret or argue about, as if printed words have a meaning independent of their readers, but only individual subjectivities or private realities to be revealed and accounted for.

In a psychoanalytic classroom, for example, the text is used to elicit a stream of associations which can then be interpreted as a therapist interprets the report of a dream. Response replaces text as the center of interest. And to understand a response we must understand the individual's language, since "the meanings of commonly held words necessarily vary from person to person," as David Bleich tells us, and "every individual has his own idiosyncratic language system" (148–9). We have, that is, private etymologies for all the words that make a text, since we first learned those words while learning to live with others, and their emotive character remains inseparable from the feelings involved in our experiences at the time. And because those experiences have varied from person to person, it follows that we each read a different poem even when we have the same text before us—we subjectively transform that text into the terms of our past experience. In reporting their responses, then, readers must talk about what the text suggests to them or reminds them of, and this students will do under the "analytic guidance" of their teacher. They can even be shown how they read their own ego themes into the text—if, as Norman Holland says, we have "sophisticated students, ideally those with some insight into themselves arrived at in a clinical setting" (216–17). So the classroom becomes an extension of the consulting room as students learn a confessional style and become, for all their independence of vision, dependent on their teacher in a very personal way, as the analysand depends on the analyst.

Rosenblatt, however, likes to keep a text between her and the student, so to speak, for she insists on the active part a text will play in the transaction that makes a poem. So she gives her students a text—an unfamiliar one separated from its provenance so that these readers have no clues outside the page itself to guide response. And this first response, the feelings, sensations, images, and ideas that come to us with the unfolding of events, this immediate lived-through experience—for this pleasure we read. But some readers, often professional readers, move on so quickly to making scholarly comments or to recounting their previous experiences, that one hardly knows if they took any immediate pleasure or satisfaction in the reading itself. For Rosenblatt this first encounter with a text is of absorbing interest, and she would like to know how readers feel and think their way through those words on a page to gain from them a satisfying experience. So she gives her students a text, asking them to keep a running account of their first reading—and the result is a record, a partial record at least, of the ways they managed their first impressions. Using such records gathered over many years, Rosenblatt has explored (in *The Reader, the Text, the Poem*) how we read a work of art, how we achieve a poetic experience from our reactions to words on a page.

She finds that readers taking up an unfamiliar text respond just as they do in any new situation. Immediately, from the very first words, they begin making assumptions about what is going on here, what they can expect—and they respond accordingly with the memories, feelings, and thoughts that come to them intuitively. But then events may take an unexpected turn, new elements appear that seem not to fit, that are strange, ambiguous, even upsetting—that cause one to reflect, perhaps to reread. Now those earlier expectations are modified as the reader "feels his way towards a vital principle of coherence for his own inner responses," looking for a context or persona or level of meaning that gives a sense of unity to the reading (54–67). Experiencing a work of art, then, means living through the frustrations and fulfillments of one's expectations until a sense of culmination or completion has been achieved. We live facing forwards as we read, expectantly, preparing for what is to come.

Rosenblatt takes the individual not as finished but still in the process of becoming, still capable of new growth given new experience. She is less concerned with the motives of readers, with uncovering those past experiences that may have determined a reading, than with the individual reader's possibility. Poetry commands the possible, Kierkegaard said, and in that spirit Rosenblatt would ask: How may a person be changed by the lived-through experience of a poetic fiction?

For her the answer lies in the immediacy and emotional persuasiveness of the esthetic experience, which involves us in other ways of living, of feeling and thinking, in a different pattern of expectation. She finds that readers, in their accounts of a first reading, move back and forth between text and self, drawing on their previous experience to fill out the indications of a text which guides their response by presenting words, images, and events in a particular order. So the reading patterns us, rearranges elements of our past experience according to another point of view. In the immediacy of the reading, we move with people who by their actions live according to certain values, and we are implicated in the human consequences of holding those values. Such new experience can supplement our limited history, and in its light we may begin to clarify our own values and revise our understanding of what life can be. Only when this happens "has there been a full interplay between book and reader, and hence a complete and rewarding literary experience"—an experience that returns us to our usual world with a renewed sense of its possibility (*Literature* 107).

And with a renewed sense of our own emotional capability. Not because we can name emotions felt while reading, since the names available are few while feelings are as various as their objects, and so the names tell us very little. Love, we know, is a word of many meanings, as many as there are loving situations, and the feeling it names is not of the moment only but develops in time. All emotions, as John Dewey said, "are qualifications of a drama and they change as the drama develops," so that while experience is emotional, "there are no separate things called emotions in it" (41–42). Our feelings as we read are summed up in the interest with which we follow the indications of the text, ordering elements in our past experience in this new way to realize the unfolding drama. A poetic text is itself the naming of significant feeling, and by enacting this naming in our reading we experience new emotional possibility. So reading is a performing art, Rosenblatt insists, and the instrument on which one plays a text is oneself—with every performance an expression of one's emotional responsiveness or understanding (*Literature* 277–91).

But some readers have difficulty performing a poetic text. Moving between text and self they become attracted to some element in their past experience and go off on a train of associations, leaving the text and passing into reverie. Unable to yield themselves to the discipline of the text, they miss the possibilities it offers, remaining rapt in themselves, unmoved, untouched. But the text is the object of our response, and to abandon it is to lose all sense of the emotions possible in our reading. Every emotion has an object, as John Casey points out (in his study of Wittgenstein): we are afraid of something, in love with someone, ashamed of having done something—but the object of an emotion is not always its cause. We can identify an emotion without ever knowing its cause, but *there is no way to identify an emotion without knowing its object*. If a child is afraid of the fire, then that fire is the object of the child's fear; the cause of that fear, however, lies in some earlier experience. A child's behavior, taken by itself, might indicate fear or sullen anger or shyness, but given that behavior in a context—in the presence of fire—we can name the emotion at once without any seeking for a cause in past experience (94–99).

This suggests how we can justify our emotional response to a poem: we can give *reasons* for feeling as we do about it. The child has a reason for being afraid of the fire, and we have reasons for thinking *King Lear* sad, an attitude we justify by describing the play as we see it. Feeling does not exist apart from thinking in a world of its own, ineluctably private and arbitrary, for how we feel about something is closely connected with what we think about it. There is a conceptual connection between feeling and its object, there is a logic of the emotions. This does not mean, however, that response is simply a matter of logical inference from the facts, or that a work of art compels a particular interpretation. We respond to a text in our individual ways, according to our individual experiences with life and art. What is required of us by other readers is a justification of our response—and we justify response by giving reasons for it, by describing the text so that others may be persuaded to see it as we do. And as readers begin to see a text in the same way, they begin to feel and value it in the same way. There is no gap between knowledge and an appropriate esthetic or emotional response, for a failure of feeling is often a failure of understanding.

Readers can fail a text, then, by misunderstanding it—by seeing in it only their habitual concerns and responding accordingly, for example. A young woman who finds in the opening scene of *King Lear* her own selfish, autocratic father may dearly wish to see Lear humbled, and so may see only those elements in the play that allow her the satisfaction she seeks. Her experience is narrowed by an automatic response previously conditioned. But understanding a work of art is not a matter of reacting to the stimulus of each word or image or event in this automatic way, Rosenblatt points out, but of reacting to the patterns of feeling and thought they make, of perceiving a context. Words happen into meaning within a context. This young woman may have an experience of *King Lear* that feels satisfying and complete, but unless those feelings aroused in the beginning have been further shaped by the developing context, her response has been immature or inappropriate or even irresponsible. True, she can have only her own experience of the text—but we can still ask if that experience was appropriate, given the events of this text.

Suppose, for example, that you experience in the course of your day, suddenly, a feeling of fear. That feeling would be justified by whatever actual danger is present or anticipated. But if this fear has some wholly private or inexplicable cause, you may be suspected of suffering a neurotic impulse. So also one's response to a text is justified by what one can point to in that text that provides reasons for the response. In other words, a work of art presents a series of events to be lived through, and Rosenblatt would ask if the reader has experienced those events as presented, if the "work-as-evoked corresponds to the text" (*Reader* 19). If not, then one's response may be taken by other readers as unsophisticated or idiosyncratic or perhaps self-indulgent, even neurotic. For insofar as we share common perceptions of events in life or in art, we are able to invoke common criteria for the evaluation of response. Poetry is a public art.

A group of readers, then, should be able to compare and evaluate their individual responses to the same text—just as we can judge individual reactions to a fire. We may not agree in our judgments, each having seen the event from a different perspective, but our possession of a common language allows us to share impressions and enlarge both our individual and our common understanding. Learning to live and work with others is learning to survive on the same terms as they do, with the same language—and the words of a poetic text are part of this language by virtue of their potentiality for evoking referents we commonly recognize. "Just as the personality and concerns of the reader are largely socially patterned," Rosenblatt remarks, "so the literary work, like language itself, is a social product" (*Literature* 28). However, she also reminds us that language must be internalized by each individual human being "with all the special overtones that each unique person and unique situation entail," and "this quality of language—essentially social yet always individually internalized—makes the literary experience something both shared and uniquely personal" (*Reader* 20, 53). So she holds that personal response is central in literary experience, while denying that esthetic judgment is ultimately subjective.

But for those critics who, like Holland and Bleich, hold that language is a private affair, esthetic judgment must be subjective, a matter of personal feeling. And without a common language for our feelings we have no way of identifying common experience and making common judgments, and so must live isolated within our individual subjectivities. There are no special *King Lear* emotions that we can share, these critics would say, because there is no *King Lear*—only words on a page reminding us each of our past experience, which supplies the emotions we "add" to the text. Even so, one might wonder if the sadness you felt while reading *King Lear* was the same sadness you felt when years ago Grandfather was packed off to the nursing home.

The basic problem here is the notorious difficulty of using words to describe feelings, for they cannot do so with any precision—or so we are told. But in fact words often express our feelings very precisely, or otherwise there would be no point in spoken intimacies. Of course there are times when our nonverbal behavior can express our feelings as fully as anything we could say, but words differentiate feeling into those more subtle and complex forms we call emotions. As feeling becomes less and less primitive, Casey points out, "so the verbal expression of it becomes more and more the natural expression, until finally we come to those emotions which can only be expressed verbally." He goes on to describe a continuum from

> rather simple and primitive feelings which seem capable of being expressed in a number of different ways, to other less simple feelings which can only be expressed verbally but for which any one of a number of verbal expressions would be suitable, to those complex structures of thought and feeling—such as works of literature—where any substitution would be, for all practical purposes, impossible. (107)

Casey offers this example: Macbeth's capacity to feel as he does when he hears of his wife's death is bound up with his capacity to speak as he does; the feelings expressed in the "tomorrow" speech are inseparable from a command of language. And if we wish to talk about those feelings, we must talk about their verbal expression. There is no way we can separate the emotional meaning of a work from its language (106).

This suggests that a work of art shapes new emotional response. It does not simply elicit feelings that are already in the reader, feelings that are then added to the text; rather, in art new forms of feeling are bound up with new forms of expression. And if we wish to describe those emotions experienced while reading, we must describe the text, giving an account of what we see in it. And this account can be understood by others, even evaluated by them, given the words of that particular text.

To insist that "every individual has his own idiosyncratic language system" is to leave feeling with only a private and arbitrary connection with the words of a text, and so the relation between emotion and its object becomes merely contingent rather than logical, a matter of one's conditioning rather than of reasons—and so the work of art is lost as the formal object of response. And having been lost, it cannot serve as a criterion by which response is evaluated or judged. The teacher becomes, then, a totally accepting person who does not judge response; feelings and memories come surging up as we read and their validity is not to be denied.

But the poetic text is for Rosenblatt a public object, the formal object of response, and in the "transaction" between person and text the poem comes into being. No two readers will experience precisely the same poem, of course, but as they compare their responses they may discover further possibilities in both self and text, and move in conversation from their immediate isolation toward a communion of meanings.

The part Rosenblatt would play in this conversation is that of one who is still trying to understand. She assumes no priority for her own experience, keeping that to herself, but rather asks questions as though she hopes to learn what these young readers know that she does not, namely their responses to this text. She encourages them to speak freely of the feelings and thoughts evoked, of the expectations fulfilled or disappointed, of the judgments made—until the differences or disagreements that emerge make it necessary for them to reconsider both self and text. Then she will ask how the text has prompted a particular reaction, returning the students to the page for its justification. And she will ask them what personal value is implied in a particular judgment, helping them clarify and make explicit the assumptions about human nature, morality, and justice by which they order and understand their experience—so they can recognize how the poetic text may put their values to the test or offer other possibilities in life. This conversation, in short, simply continues the reading process itself, the "active, self-ordering and self-corrective process" manifested in those running accounts readers have given of their first experience with a text (*Reader* 11).

And it continues, then, the emotional interest felt during that experience as each reader speaks from a personal sense of the work, reasoning with others about it. In her study of first readings, Rosenblatt has shown how attention to qualities of feeling as we read leads to interpretation, since by means of feeling we make immediate discriminations in the flow of events; and how in conversation these readers express their personal involvement with this text by reporting the discriminations they have made, pointing out passages that others may not have used in their reading or used in the same way. Feelings are no longer just felt; they make sense, they have reasons, and we can talk about them. And if because of this exchange one begins to see the text differently, then one begins to feel and value it differently. So this conversation continues the education of feeling as these readers learn to "maintain [a] personal sense of the work and yet react to it in rational terms" (*Literature* 231). There is no separation here of feeling from reason.

Nor is there any separation here of the feeling intellect from behavior, of the inner from the outer life. A work of art, Rosenblatt insists, has a content—the lives and deaths of its characters, the issues and values they live, the particular view of life expressed—and those individual evocations of this content that become lived-through experiences can influence the attitudes of readers and hence their actions. If art were only a diversion there would be no point in regulating it, as totalitarian regimes do, but it may in fact provide, as Rosenblatt points out, "the emotional tension and conflicting attitudes out of which spring the kind of thinking that can later be assimilated into actual behavior" (*Literature* 227). In other words, she takes feeling, thought, and behavior as aspects of one movement—although, of course, not all our gestures will be completed.

So she can speak of the influence of art on habits of ethical and social judgment, of the part a teacher might play in the development of social understanding, of the role of literature in a democracy—concerns that seem rather quaint from the advanced perspective of some critics. But rather than taking the inner life as a separate world of existence, Rosenblatt is concerned with the discovery of attitudes and values in the world of common experience. And she is not so interested in tracing these back to their origins in past experience as in understanding how they guide present response. She is not concerned with uncovering the secrets of the past (for nostalgia is the enemy of present feeling) but with the reader's developing response, which may continue even after the reading. To follow the guidance of a poetic text is to submit oneself to a stringent discipline, to undertake a "self-ordering and self-corrective process" with uncertain results— and this is why a work of art is often difficult to interpret, because what it means cannot be clear when the outcome lies ahead.

This very uncertainty of result makes the relation between teacher and student uncertain, ambiguous. In some classrooms there is no uncertainty of result because the results have been specified in advance and will be tested for at the end. But Rosenblatt has a more poetic relation with her students, for just as poetry is an indirect form of communication, offering not a message but an experience, so her method is indirect—tentative, questioning, conversational. And she holds herself personally apart, so that her students follow her not out of affection or faith but rather follow the text out of faith in their own ability to appropriate for themselves the experience it offers.

Nor does she claim authority, being herself under the authority of the poetic text, which gives its own directions and makes its own demands, to which we respond in our various ways. She only insists on the obligation we have to this reality outside ourselves, knowing that one's inner autonomy is given in transaction with the outside. Those who must partner with someone in order to manage themselves, even in a classroom, may take her as they will, depending on their need for someone to like or dislike, to follow or oppose. Or they may in fact remain indifferent to her and so remain independent, free to develop their own inwardness and continue their self-revision.

With direct teaching the authority is direct, deriving as it does from the teacher's superior knowledge or insight, and each learner must enter into a personal relation with that authority by submitting to or opposing the teacher, by accepting or rejecting, perhaps even by loving or hating. But with an indirect or transactional method the erotic element has a very different character, for here a teacher without the compelling force of authority must by every artful means turn the feeling intellect of learners to issues that lie outside the preceptorial relation.

Such a method requires both art and self-control—the self-control that enables us to hold back our own ideas, insofar as the disciplined ego will allow. The teacher does not approach students directly with a proposition, but rather waits for messages from them, having persuaded them to participate together in a new experience. For they are to be changed not by the addition of ideas already prepared but through their own activity.

A moment will come, however, when these young readers feel curious about this person who is implicated in their experience and they will ask a direct question of the teacher, hoping to elicit a personal response, perhaps a personal judgment about the matter at hand. This moment is decisive in the relationship, and much depends on how that question is answered. Perhaps a teacher, now tempted to play at being an authority, settles the matter and gives certainty. But then the self-movement of the learner comes to an end, while the teacher, having assumed authority, becomes in fact the servant of students who sit back expecting further instruction in the truth. And yet some answer must be given them, some response made.

Rosenblatt, whatever she might say at this moment, will still maintain a certain distance. She has not made the separations that so bedevil some teachers or critics, the separation of feeling from thought, and of the inner from the outer life, but her poetic method requires a separation of teacher from learner so that she may win them to new experience. Then the values of eros, including interest, enthusiasm, and the discriminating power of feeling, are directed not to the teacher but to the learner's own relation with issues that matter. So she maintains the necessary separation between an erotic and a teaching presence, becoming in time even more intriguing.

Works Cited

Bleich, David. *Subjective Criticism.* Baltimore: John Hopkins UP, 1980.

Casey, John. *The Language of Criticism.* London: Methuen, 1966.

Dewey, John. *Art as Experience.* New York: Capricorn Books, 1958.

Dolittle, Hilda. *Tribute to Freud.* Boston: David R. Godine, 1974.

Fish, Stanley. *Is There a Text in This Class? The Authority of Interpretive Communities.* Cambridge: Harvard UP, 1980.

Holland, Norman. *5 Readers Reading.* New Haven: Yale UP, 1975.

Rosenblatt, Louise. *Literature as Exploration.* 1938. New York: Noble and Noble, 1968.

———. *The Reader, the Text, the Poem: The Transactional Theory of the Literary Work.* Carbondale, Ill.: Southern Illinois UP, 1978.

13

The Aesthetic Mind
of Louise Rosenblatt

Alan C. Purves

In writing about the contributions of Louise Rosenblatt to the intellectual history of the United States and to the history of the teaching and study of literature, I should like to show where I think she stands in a long stream of psychological aesthetics. As an aesthetician, she concentrates less on the nature of beauty and issues related to the genre and judgment than she does on the nature of the way in which the human mind experiences art. Rosenblatt acknowledges her indebtedness to Dewey and Bentley's *Knowing and the Known*. But her close self-identification with Dewey had the unfortunate consequence, I think, of having an aesthetic position confounded with a series of educational practices carried out in the name of Dewey. The fact that Rosenblatt was read with an eye to pedagogical implications and that she held a position in education served to confuse the unwary reader.

Her first major work in English, *Literature as Exploration*, appeared in 1938, shortly before the publication of an equally famous work on the reading of literature, *Understanding Poetry*, by Cleanth Brooks and Robert Penn Warren. To a great extent, that volume, like Rosenblatt's, shows the influence of a volume written a decade earlier, which remains one of the seminal books on the reading of literary texts, I. A. Richards's *Practical Criticism*. One of Richards's major findings was that his student readers tended to approach the works they read with what he calls "stock responses," "mnemonic irrelevancies," "doctrinal adhesions," "technical preconceptions," or "general critical

209

preconceptions." To Richards, the idea that half of the topologies of "failure in reading and judging poetry" came from the fact that readers were not blank slates when they read a poem was a matter of some concern, particularly because their particular filled slate did not match his. They tended not to be the "objective" readers that he had hoped the universities were training.

One might argue that Brooks and Warren also wrote from a concern with what was in their student readers' heads. They proceeded to demonstrate this concern by following each poem with a series of adept questions that could lead students to become dispassionate analysts of literary texts. Following from Richards's discovery, they effected a pedagogical experiment in producing close if not "scientific" readers. To a great extent, they were successful with at least two generations of American students. Their work was imitated in Europe by various structuralists and poststructuralists, particularly in France and Belgium.

Rosenblatt elaborated the same concept, that readers come to texts with a set of preconceptions, but approached it from a different perspective, concentrating on the human concerns of the texts and the readers more than on issues of style, language, and structure. Her source was not Richards but the variety of philosophers and anthropologists she had been reading since her undergraduate days at Barnard. One might say that the idea was "in the air." She tended to look for counters to the "art for art's sake" approach that she had studied in her thesis at the Sorbonne. Although some might put her in the Freudian camp and see her approach as similar to that of Simon Lesser in *Fiction and the Unconscious,* such an interpretation would be misleading, I think, for notwithstanding her focus on content and on the relationship between reader and text, she does not see the reading of literary texts so much as a form of therapy or escape as a set of mediated experiences, which can be used to challenge the mind and its values. Broadly psychological in focus, she is not, in any strict sense, a Freudian, and she rejects bibliotherapy in the classroom. More important than her concern with the substance of the text is the way in which she turns Richards's ideas around. What is in the reader's head is not erroneous, but a necessary part of reading. It becomes a given of her definition of the reader.

Rosenblatt's reversal of Richards is, to my mind, one of the main contributions of her early work. The very act of interpretation is the relating of the text to a set of known structures in the reader's head. To be sure, there can be misinterpretations and misapplications of knowledge. But the fact of erroneous interpretations does not negate the basic principle that interpretation is driven both by the reader and by the text. The idea of the active use of prior knowledge in reading literature, a main theme of *Literature as Exploration,* is the point of the reader-response critics whom Rosenblatt anticipated by some thirty years. The reading of the text is an active event; it necessarily entails the bringing of prior knowledge to bear upon what is read. What is in the head cannot be the object of censure or praise: it is, and it results from, prior experience, prior reading, and prior teaching. Readers cannot avoid using this knowledge and cannot avoid entering into a transaction with the text that makes the result particularly theirs. To say this is not to deny the possibility of general perceptions and readings but is to assert that these general readings are always modified by human individuality.

If we turn the calendar forward to the 1970s and the publication of *The Reader, the Text, the Poem*, Rosenblatt's second major text, we find that work appearing at about the same time as the work of the cognitive psychologists who advanced the theory of human thinking known as schema theory. This theory bears a remarkable resemblance to the premises underpinning the work of I. A. Richards (despite the fact that Richards was clearly influenced by behavioral psychology) and Rosenblatt's transactional theory. Schema theory states that people acquire schemata, frames, or scripts (each of these terms has been used) concerning various real-world phenomena either from prior reading or from direct experience, and these schemata affect the ways in which they read various texts. In general, the schemata set forth by the cognitive psychologists are described in terms of the context of the texts, whether they have to do with restaurants or prisons. One of the more noted experiments uses a text that can be read as a description of a prison break or a wrestling match depending upon which schema is activated by a cue in the text (Anderson).

At about the time that schema theory became ubiquitous in the psychological literature concerning reading, Rosenblatt's *The Reader, the Text, the Poem* appeared. In it, she set forth the idea that when readers read, they are indeed bringing various preconceptions to bear on the text, among which preconceptions are some that deal not solely with the content but with the form, structure, or style of the text. Just as she presented a corrective to the formalist tendencies of Brooks and Warren, so she was bringing a corrective to the content emphases of the schema theorists. They had looked primarily at contrived passages of prose and at deliberately ambiguous texts concerning prisons or wrestlers; some even denied that texts like poems were susceptible to their theory. Literary texts are not "schema driven" but imaginative. It is difficult for a literary person to understand this vague distinction, and Rosenblatt clearly shows that all texts were so susceptible.

It is clear from various empirical research studies concerning the reading of literature that Rosenblatt's formulation is correct. One may, of course, argue that research in response to literature was so influenced by her work that it managed its evidence to support her theory. I happen to think that the former is the case. Beginning with I. A. Richards, and continuing with the work of James Squire, Arthur Applebee, Norman Holland, Charles Cooper, and myself (see Purves and Beach), there is a steady stream of findings that readers bring something with them when they read texts. What they bring is a sense of the appropriate content of literary texts, as well as a sense of the structure, form, and style of literary works. The range of prior knowledge, schemata, frames, or prejudices (depending upon which terminology one employs) is broad and not confined to content as some of the psychologists would have it. Among the kinds of knowledge are that concerning content as reflected in phonology and rhythm, vocabulary, grammar, syntax, text structures of genres, emotional nuances and tones, and symbolic or mythological patterns. Readers have a vast array of knowledge in their heads, and they bring that knowledge to bear on the transaction that is the meeting of the reader's mind with the text. It is impossible for a reader to make a claim, whether it be considered right or wrong, concerning the relationship of the tall soldier in Crane's *The Red Badge of Courage* to Christ without a fair amount of knowledge concerning language and literature, not to mention knowledge of the ways in which it is appropriate to read literary texts and interpret them. Richards's categories of preconception concerning content, form, emotion, and critical stance apply today, and I think that Rosenblatt would accept all of them as aspects of the intellectual baggage that readers carry with them. She would also be less certain than others as to the superior value of one type of baggage over another. One could argue that the particular sort of prior knowledge that one brings to bear on the transaction depends upon the particular circumstances of the text, the situation of the reader, or the setting in which the transaction occurs. Whereas Richards deplores excesses of emotion and rigid application of formal precepts, I do not see Rosenblatt as arguing that there is a "best amount or type of prior knowledge."

All of what has preceded would make Louise Rosenblatt an interesting but not a formidable figure in twentieth-century aesthetics. But she is precisely formidable because she adds one important dimension to the transactional approach and the idea of prior knowledge. It is a dimension that leads from psychological aesthetics to general aesthetics. Readers bring to texts not simply critical preconceptions as Richards suggested, but, according to Rosenblatt, dispositions as to how to read texts; they can choose between *efferent* and *aesthetic* reading (to use her powerful terms). Rosenblatt here turns into a crucial aspect of psychological aesthetics the distinction that Richards had phrased in terms of referential and poetic texts, and referential and emotive language. For Rosenblatt, the aesthetic and efferent distinction refers to kinds of reading that readers make by the way they focus attention during the transaction with the text. To read efferently is to focus attention on the referential and internalize it as knowledge about something, or as a set of injunctions to belief or action. Aesthetic reading, by contrast, focuses on the experiential as well as referential elements. Message and form are totally incorporated. The reader attends to and contemplates the totality without seeking knowledge or determining consequent action. That is why some of Richards's "stock responses" are, upon further examination, misplaced efferent readings, instances where the students take as tracts what he and others see as poems. This failure is, in one sense, a failure to draw upon the appropriate procedural schema for reading certain kinds of texts. I do not think that efferent and aesthetic readings exist on a continuum, although some critics do. To me, they appear to be poles between which a reader may oscillate during the course of reading a given text, and the sum total of reading may tend on "average" to be seen as aesthetic or efferent.

From my various studies of the ways by which students respond to literary texts, I would contend that the penchant for aesthetic reading is learned; certainly it is driven out of the heads of readers by instruction. In the cross-national study of student response to literature (Purves), we found that both after reading short stories and in the abstract, students in the United States reported that the questions they would prefer addressing dealt with the surface and symbolic meaning of the text and with the moral to be derived from it. By contrast with students in England and New Zealand as well as in several European countries, United States students aged fourteen and seventeen saw the message as the most important aspect of short stories and by extension of fiction and literature in general. This tendency became more solidly advanced as one moved from the younger to the older students. These same questions were the ones preferred by secondary school teachers. A later study we undertook indicated that these questions were not the same as those addressed by much younger students (Purves and Monson). That this is a general failing among students in the United States results, I am sure, from a constant pedagogical pressure to read all texts efferently, because teachers, following the penchant of the general populace, believe that all texts have a moral. I would go so far as to assert that a large number of our literary critics have also lost the ability to read aesthetically. A great deal of academic criticism, even some that comes under the heading of "reader-response criticism," is efferent moralizing. One can see an emphasis on content in the work of critics as diverse as Lionel Trilling, Leslie Fiedler, Henry Nash Smith, and

Judith Fetterley. This criticism also tends to view literature as dealing explicitly with moral issues and themes, with messages of one sort or another. That such a view of the text is so dominant may well explain why Rosenblatt is not as well recognized as she should be. Aesthetic reading is not popular in academe.

Rosenblatt shows that *how* we read a text depends upon what is in our heads, just as much as the meaning or emotion we gain from reading the text. Aesthetic or efferent reading is, as she argues, a matter of stance. We can choose how to read a text or a portion of a text. In a study that I conducted with Harry Broudy a few years ago, we set out to examine what he refers to as the uses of learning. We used several passages from the *New York Times* on diverse topics, heavy with allusion, as well as a poem, and asked students in the first year of graduate school to read them and comment upon them as they read. The students were selected on the basis of their background, so that we had an artist, a dancer, and a student each in the humanities, in engineering, in law, in commerce, in social sciences, and in the hard sciences. The results indicated that the students tended to use various kinds of prior knowledge when they read, much of it indirectly. Broudy had hypothesized that we use knowledge replicatively, applicatively, interpretively, and associatively. The latter two are seldom tested in school, yet the use of prior knowledge to interpret new phenomena and the use of that knowledge by recalling an association with something new are clearly parts of the transaction of reading whether it be efferent or aesthetic. So it was, we found among all our readers, that those who did not have some knowledge about the text's topic found themselves unwilling to or unable to read the text with comprehension. But the finding of that study most germane to Rosenblatt's point about stance was that the sort of learning that occurred most frequently in our protocols was not *what* but *how*. In most instances, we found that our subjects had learned certain "mannerisms" of reading (for want of a better word), such as one student's immediate distrust of anything that contained metaphor, or another student's manner of reading all literature that derived from the critical theory of Maritain. On subsequent interviews these readers recalled precisely where they had learned to read certain texts in the ways that they did. If these particulars of stance are learned, it would appear plausible that one can learn to read a text aesthetically or efferently. Perhaps it is safer to assert that one can learn that it is or is not appropriate to read aesthetically. How we read is a matter of stance, which is a matter of choice.

And it is precisely here that psychology leads to aesthetic principle, for if how we read a text depends upon what is in our heads, then how we read a text can determine the individual and collective apperception of the text. It is this principle that explains how it is that there can be such phenomena as "found poems" or Pop Art as well as how it is that people can shoot actors portraying villains. That is to say, if one reader reads Martin Luther King's "I Have a Dream" speech as a prose poem, experiencing the text for itself and what it does to the mind at the time and relishing that experience, for that reader the speech becomes poetic. It is clear from recordings of the speech that although it is a political document to be taken efferently, King's style of delivery as well as the text itself led some people to listen aesthetically, at least in part. Some heard the message as a call to action concerning civil rights; others heard the "music" of the speech without taking a specific message from it. If a sufficient number of readers read aesthetically, the text may well become accepted as a part of the literary canon. The text may no longer be read efferently by a large number of readers. That has been the fate of many texts whose local origins are all but forgotten. It has not happened with King's speech as yet. But one hopes there may be a time when it need not be read efferently. To a certain extent, such has been the fate of many "topical" works such as the satires of Swift or some of the essays of Carlyle or Arnold; the information that they once contained is obscure to the modern reader, and it may be immaterial. When the works were written, the information and its relevance seemed paramount to all concerned. To be sure, these works can be resurrected for their historic topicality, but for most readers, the aesthetic reading does not depend upon that topicality. To make this argument is not to deny the importance of the content of these works, but the content has ceased to be referential, and the work is not seen as the repository of information.

Literature, then, is a body of texts that a reader, or a group of readers, finds necessary to read aesthetically. Clearly a part of the burden is on the text or group of texts; yet a part of the burden is on the readers. For readers in many cultures, certain aspects of the text serve as a cue, and the fact of wide margins and capital letters at the beginning of each line can cue a reader to be disposed to read a text aesthetically. Readers have acquired a knowledge of many of these cues which become part of their schemata and by which they associate text types with dispositions as to how to read. Yet they can also pick up a text which has none of these cues, such as a piece of prose in a newspaper, and after reading a few lines, find themselves reading the text aesthetically, making it a poem. If that happens on a sufficient number of readings by a sufficient number of readers, that text may be seen as a "work of literature." It may even become a part of the canon. The canonical properties of literature, then, arise less from the texts than from the shared perceptions of readers. Thus we cannot assert that any text is necessarily literature. We also cannot deny to any text the possibility of being considered literature.

As I remarked earlier, Rosenblatt's theory makes it possible to understand that, by the same token, a reader or a society of readers can depoeticize a text. The most common version of this sort of transformation occurs in instances where large numbers of readers choose to treat a text as a tract rather than a poem and seek to ban it. Such is the recurrent case with *The Merchant of Venice* and even with folktales such as "Jack and the Beanstalk." It would appear that a large portion of the American population does not or cannot read most texts aesthetically; it is not part of the Calvinist tradition, a tradition that pervades our schools, both common and critical. Beginning with the basal reading text, children are asked for the main idea of the text. That is the end of reading. Later on, the terms are changed to theme. In addition, teachers tend to be encouraged to see children's literature as containing a moral; that is the best justification for including it in the curriculum. Given these tendencies, no wonder that children are pushed into the efferent mode. It is hard to select the aesthetic stance when there has been no encouragement for so doing.

From Louise Rosenblatt, then, comes a more synoptic view of psychological aesthetics than from most other theoreticians of reading and criticism. She sees that the perceived text is related to the perceived world as well as to the reader. The reading of the text is a mental event determined in great part by the reader, but also clearly affected by the nature of the text. The reader is not independent of the text nor the text of the reader. More importantly, however, the way in which a text is read, which is to say the stance that one adopts toward the text, is as important as what is derived from or adduced to the text. One may see the reading of texts as an individual matter, as she clearly claims. Yet she also provides the theoretical underpinnings for our understanding that how we read texts is also a social or cultural matter. The cross-national research that we undertook in the 1970s showed that styles of responding to texts characterized national groups of students. In each of the ten countries, students tended to become increasingly alike within an educational system, but not across educational systems. They also tended to become like their teachers, who less closely resembled the leading critics of the country. It was clear that in some countries aesthetic reading tends to be encouraged, if we can assume that the questions students ask reflect the stance which they adopt while reading. Other research, such as that of Broudy and Beach, tends to support this assumption.

The expressed response to literature is a social action, and an action that often occurs in school. The reader is never an isolate save at the very best moments of aesthetic reading, when the societal pressures have been put aside in those moments of aesthetic surrender that is poem making. Even then, society may affect what happens after reading and force the aesthetic reader into being an efferent critic. Too much efferent criticism can undermine the capacity to read aesthetically. To my mind, that has happened in the United States, and it is difficult to change this state of affairs since it is very much in the American grain, as Richard Hofstadter pointed out over two decades ago. Louise Rosenblatt's aesthetic lies clearly in the mainstream of twentieth-century aesthetics, particularly European aesthetics. Its existence and its reception remind us of how we might read literature were our culture not against such reading. As an aesthetician, then, she provides us with a vision of how both the individual reader might read the variety of literary and nonliterary texts and how a culture might reinforce the broadened perspective of generations of readers. Such a vision has clear educational ramifications, some of which have been captured in literature curricula in various parts of the world.

Works Cited

Anderson, Richard C., Rand J. Spiro, and William E. Montague. *Schooling and the Acquisition of Knowledge.* Hillsdale: Erlbaum, 1977.

Brooks, Cleanth, and Robert Penn Warren. *Understanding Poetry.* New York: Harcourt Brace, 1938.

Broudy, Harry. "Report on Case Studies on Uses of Learning: Final Report to the Spencer Foundation." ED 244 016. ERIC 1982.

Dewey, John, and Arthur F. Bentley. *Knowing and the Known.* Boston: Beacon Press, 1949.

Hofstadter, Richard. *Anti-intellectualism in American Life.* New York: Alfred A. Knopf, 1963.

Lesser, Simon O. *Fiction and the Unconscious.* Boston: Beacon Press, 1957.

Purves, Alan. *Literature Education in Ten Countries: An Empirical Study.* Stockholm: Almqvist and Wiksell, 1973.

Purves, Alan, and Richard Beach. *Literature and the Reader: Research in Response to Literature and the Teaching of Literature.* Urbana: NCTE, 1972.

Purves, Alan, and Dianne Monson. *Experiencing Children's Literature.* Glenview, Ill.: Scott Foresman, 1985.

Richards, I. A. *Practical Criticism.* New York: Harcourt Brace, 1929.

Rosenblatt, Louise M. *Literature as Exploration.* 1938. New York: Modern Language Association, 1976.

———. *The Reader, the Text, the Poem: The Transactional Theory of the Literary Work.* Carbondale, Ill.: Southern Illinois UP, 1978.

Bibliography of Louise M. Rosenblatt

Compiled by Sidney Ratner

L'Idée de l'art pour l'art dans la littérature anglaise pendant la période victorienne. Paris: Champion, 1931. New York: AMS Press, 1976.

"Some Fundamental Considerations on Materials Prepared for the Use of College Students." *Parent Education* 2.4 (1935): 31–35.

" 'Marius l'Epicurien' de Walter Pater et ses points de départ francais." *Revue de Littérature Comparée*, 15.1 (1935): 97–106.

"The Writer's Dilemma: A Case History and a Critique." *The International Journal of Ethics.* 46.2 (1936): 195–211.

Literature as Exploration. New York: Appleton-Century, 1938. Rev. ed. New York: Noble and Noble, 1968. London: Heinemann, 1970. Third ed. New York: Noble and Noble, 1976. Fourth ed. New York: Modern Language Association, 1983.

With Howard Mumford Jones and Oscar J. Campbell. "Statement of the Committee of Twenty-four: The Aims of Literary Study." *PMLA* 53. Supplement (1938): 1367–71.

"Readin'—Always Readin'!" *Educational Method* 19.3 (1939): 134–41.

"Development of Reading Interests and Critical Appreciation in Secondary Schools and Colleges." *Reading and Pupil Development.* Ed. William S. Gray. Supplementary Educational Monographs 51. Chicago: U of Chicago P, 1940. 223–29.

"Moderns Among Masterpieces." *English Leaflet* New England Association of Teachers of English. 39 (1940): 98–110.

Rev. of *The Aesthetic of Walter Pater,* by Ruth C. Child. *Journal of English and Germanic Philology* 14.1 (1942): 118–21.

"Art and Western Culture." Rev. of *Art and Freedom,* by Horace M. Kallen. *Survey Graphic* 32 (1943): 265–66.

"Literary Cosmopolitanism or International Understanding?" *Comparative Literature News-Letter* 1.6 (1943): 1–2.

"Communicating Ideas Through the Teaching of Literature." *Conference on Science, Philosophy, and Religion in their Relation to the Democratic Way of Life.* Vol. 5. New York: Harpers, 1945. 849–52.

"France" in "The Underground Press of France, Belgium, Norway, Denmark, and the Netherlands." *Library of Congress Quarterly Journal* 2.3 (1945): 3–14.

"Toward a Cultural Approach to Literature." *College English* 7.8 (1946): 459–66.

Guest Editor, *English Journal*. Intercultural Relations Issue, 35.6 (1946).

Reviews of *The American Novels and Stories of Henry James*, ed. F. O. Matthiessen; *Long Anchorage*, by Henry Beetle Hough; *Albert Sears*, by Millen Brand; *You Can't See Around Corners* by Jon Cleary. *Brooklyn Eagle*. 1947.

"The Acid Test for Literature Teaching." *English Journal* 45.2 (1956): 66–74.

"International Understanding Through Literature." *Programs and Projects for International Understanding*. Ed. Lawrence H. Conrad. New York: American Association of Colleges for Teacher Education, 1956. 67–71.

"Literature: the Reader's Role." *English Journal* 49.5 (1960): 304–10, 315. Rpt. in *Education Synopsis* 12.2 (1967): 1–6.

"The Genesis of Pater's 'Marius the Epicurean.' " *Comparative Literature* 14.3 (1962): 242–60.

"Reappraisal of the English Curriculum." *Frontiers of Education*. Ed. Arthur E. Traxler. Washington, D.C.: American Council on Education (1963): 63–73.

"Research Development Seminar in the Teaching of English." Project G-009. Cooperative Research Branch of the Office of Education, U.S. Department of Health, Education, and Welfare, 1963.

"The Poem as Event." *College English* 26.2 (1964): 123–28.

"A Performing Art." *English Journal* 55.8 (1966): 999–1005. Rpt. as "Literature: A Performing Art" in *Teachers College Record* 63.4 (1967): 307–15.

"A Way of Happening." *Educational Record* 49.3 (1968): 339–46. Rpt. in Arthur Daigon and Ronald Carter, Eds., *Challenge and Change in the Teaching of English*. Boston: Allyn and Bacon, 1977. 156–69.

"Pattern and Process—A Polemic." *English Journal* 58.7 (1969): 1005–12. Rpt. in *The Use of English* 22.3 (1971): 203–11.

"Towards a Transactional Theory of Reading." *Journal of Reading Behavior* 1.1 (1969): 31–51.

"Literature and the Invisible Reader." *The Promise of English: 1970 Distinguished Lectures*. Champaign, Ill.: National Council of Teachers of English, 1970. 1–26.

"On a Review of *Literature as Exploration.*" *Journal of Aesthetic Education* 5.3 (1971): 188–91.

Rev. of *The Masks of Hate*, by David Holbrook. *English Journal* 62.4 (1973): 639–40.

Rev. of *The Politics of Literature: Dissenting Essays on the Teaching of English*, ed. Louis Kampf and Paul Lauter. *English Journal* 63.3 (1974): 110–11.

"What We Have Learned: Reminiscences of the NCTE." *English Journal* 66.5 (1977): 8, 88–90.

The Reader, the Text, the Poem: The Transactional Theory of the Literary Work. Carbondale, Ill.: Southern Illinois UP, 1978.

"Whitman's 'Democratic Vistas' and the New 'Ethnicity'." *Yale Review* (1978): 187–204.

" 'What Facts Does This Poem Teach You?' " *Language Arts* 57.4 (1980): 386–94.

"Act I, Scene 1: Enter the Reader." *Literature in Performance* 1.2 (1981): 13–23.

The Journey Itself. Leland B. Jacobs Lecture. New York: School of Library Service, Columbia University, 1981.

"The Literary Transaction: Evocation and Response." *Theory into Practice* 21.4 (1982): 268–77.

"On the Aesthetic as the Basic Model of the Reading Process." *Theories of Reading, Looking, and Listening*. Ed. Harry R. Garvin. *Bucknell Review* 26.1. East Brunswick, N.J.: Associated University Presses, 1981. 17–32.

"The Reader's Contribution to the Literary Experience." *English Quarterly* 14.1 (1981): 1–12.

"The Reading Transaction: What For?" *Developing Literacy*. Ed. Robert P. Parker and Frances A. Davis. Newark, Del.: International Reading Association, 1983. 118–135.

"Viewpoints: Transaction Versus Interaction—A Terminological Rescue Operation." *Research in the Teaching of English* 19.1 (1985): 96–107.

"Language, Literature, and Values." *Language, Schooling, and Society*. Proceedings of the International Federation of Teachers of English. Ed. Stephen N. Tchudi. Portsmouth, NH: Boynton/ Cook, 1985. 64–80.

"The Transactional Theory of the Literary Work: Implications for Research." *Researching Response to Literature and the Teaching of English*. Ed. Charles R. Cooper. Norwood, N.J.: Ablex, 1985. 33–53.

"The Literary Transaction." *The Creating Word*. Papers from an international conference on the teaching of English in the 1980s. Ed. Patricia Demers. London: Macmillan; Alberta, Canada: University of Alberta P, 1986. 66–85.

"The Aesthetic Transaction." *Journal of Aesthetic Education* 20.4 (1986): 122–28.

"Writing and Reading: The Transactional Theory." *Reading and Writing Connections*. Ed. Jana M. Mason. Boston: Allyn and Bacon, 1989. 153–76.
Earlier versions published: Technical Report No. 17. Urbana, IL: Center for the Study of Reading, 1987.
Technical Report No. 13. Berkeley: Center for the Study of Writing, 1988.
Reader: Essays in Reader-Oriented Theory, Criticism, and Pedagogy. 20. Fall, 1988. 7–31.

"Retrospect." *Responding to Literature: A Fifty Year Perspective*. Ed. James R. Squire and Edmund J. Farrell. Urbana, Ill.: National Council of Teachers of English, 1990.

"Literary Theory." *Handbook of Research on Teaching the Language Arts*. Ed. James R. Squire. Boston: Macmillan, forthcoming.

Notes on Contributors

Carolyn Allen is associate professor of English at the University of Washington in Seattle. She writes and teaches in twentieth-century studies; her most recent articles are on feminism and postmodernism. She is currently completing a book on contemporary women writers, *The Subject in the Body.*

Temma F. Berg is assistant professor of English at Gettysburg College, where she also teaches in the Women's Studies Program. She has published many essays on the subject of reading, especially of women reading, in *Studies in the Novel, Criticism,* and *Canadian Review of Comparative Literature.* She edited, as well as contributed to, the anthology *Engendering the Word: Feminist Essays in Psychosexual Poetics;* guest edited an issue of *Reader: Essays in Reader-Oriented Theory, Criticism, and Pedagogy* on the interrelationship between reader-response theory and deconstruction; and contributed the essay on reader-response theory to the anthology *Tracing Literary Theory.* She has been working on an anthology of women's literary theory.

Ann E. Berthoff is professor emeritus, University of Massachusetts at Boston, and Randolph Distinguished Visiting Professor, Vassar College, 1989–90. She is the author of *Forming/Thinking/Writing, The Making of Meaning: Metaphors, Models, and Maxims for Writing Teachers,* and *The Sense of Learning* and is the editor of *Reclaiming the Imagination: Philosophical Perspectives for Writers and Teachers of Writing* (all Boynton/Cook). She is completing an anthology of I. A. Richards's essays, *Richards on Rhetoric.* She is especially interested in the philosophy of language that informs and directs Louise Rosenblatt's theory and practice, finding in it the influence of C. S. Peirce, both his semiotics and his pragmatism.

John Clifford is a professor of English at the University of North Carolina at Wilmington where he teaches courses in literature, writing, and theory. He has coauthored several textbooks and his essays and reviews have appeared in *College English, College Composition and Communication, Reader,* and *Rhetoric Review,* as well as in several anthologies, most recently an essay on Eiseley in *Literary Nonfiction*, on Althusser in *Contending with Words*, and a piece on literacy in the proceedings of the MLA conference on the Right to Literacy. He studied with Louise Rosenblatt in the early seventies at New York University. His professional thinking was greatly influenced by this experience.

Bill Corcoran is Principal Lecturer in English Education at Queensland University of Technology, Brisbane, Australia. He is the editor of *English in Australia* and has published widely on literary theory and the teaching of literature. With Emrys Evans, from the University of Birmingham, he coedited *Readers, Texts, Teachers* for Boynton/Cook. The title of this collection of essays by Australian and English hands is as direct a steal from Louise Rosenblatt as the contents are a celebration of her work.

Emrys Evans teaches English Education at the University of Birmingham (UK). With Bill Corcoran, he edited *Readers, Texts, Teachers* (Boynton/Cook 1987), in which his own chapter, "Readers Recreating Texts," makes substantial reference to Rosenblatt and Iser. As an Oxford-educated secondary school teacher, personally influenced by C. S. Lewis and Tolkien, he was never more than a half-convinced Leavisite, and was happy to find his way to Rosenblatt indirectly under the guidance of Iser.

Elizabeth A. Flynn is associate professor of reading and composition at Michigan Technological University. She is coeditor, with Patrocinio P. Schweickart, of *Gender and Reading: Essays on Readers, Texts, and Contexts* (Hopkins, 1986) and editor of the journal *Reader*. She has published articles in *College Composition and Communication, College English, New Orleans Reader*, and *Writing Instructor*, and book chapters in *Language Connections* (NCTE, 1982) and *Writing Across the Disciplines* (Boynton/Cook, 1986). She has known Louise Rosenblatt since 1979.

Russell A. Hunt is professor of English at St. Thomas University. A specialist in eighteenth-century English literature and literary theory, he currently devotes most of his attention to the study of reading and writing considered as social acts, particularly the social dimensions of the phenomena of literary reading. He has published on these issues in *College English* and (with Douglas Vipond) in *Poetics, TEXT, Reader, Reading Research and Instruction*, and *English Quarterly*.

Kathleen McCormick is associate professor of literary and cultural studies at Carnegie Mellon. She has published a number of articles on reading theory and on adapting literary theory to the undergraduate curriculum. As well, she has published two textbooks with colleagues at Carnegie Mellon that develop these issues, *The Lexington Introduction to Literature* and *Reading Texts*. She is currently writing a book-length study integrating cognitive and cultural analyses of the reading process, entitled *Reading: Cognition, Institutions, Ideology* (to be published by Manchester University Press) and is coediting the MLA book on *Approaches to Teaching* Ulysses.

Gordon Pradl is professor of English Education at New York University where he was fortunate to begin teaching in 1971, the year before Louise Rosenblatt retired from the department. He has thus spent his academic career working in a teacher education program that has been based on her transactional model. Currently, he works as the director of staff development in NYU's Expository Writing Program and is the coeditor of *English Education*.

Alan C. Purves, director of the Center for Writing and Literacy and professor of education and humanities at the State University of New York at Albany, received his A.B. from Harvard and his M.A. and Ph.D. in English from Columbia University. He has taught at Columbia and Barnard colleges, the University of Illinois, and Indiana University before coming to Albany. He has served in many professional organizations and has held office in the National Council of Teachers of English and the International Association for the Evaluation of Educational Achievement (IEA), of which he is currently chairman. He has written or edited some twenty-five books and seventy articles dealing with literature, written composition, reading, and measurement, including *The Elements of Writing about a Literary Work* and *How Porcupines Make Love*, a text on the application of Louise Rosenblatt's approach in the classroom.

Sidney Ratner, Professor of History, Emeritus, Rutgers University is the author of books and articles on economics, American economic and intellectual history, and philosophy; he is currently writing an intellectual biography of John Dewey. He is the husband of Louise M. Rosenblatt.

John Rouse is the author of *The Completed Gesture: Myth, Character, and Education*. He teaches at Saint Peter's College in Jersey City, New Jersey.

Mariolina Salvatori is an associate professor of English at the University of Pittsburgh, where she teaches in both the composition and literature programs. She holds a degree in languages, literatures, and institutions of Western Europe from the Orientale University (Naples, Italy) and a Ph.D. in English from the University of Pittsburgh. She has written on modern Italian literature, literary perceptions of aging, the immigrants' experience, and the interconnections of reading and writing, theory and practice, literature and composition.

John Willinsky, an associate professor with the Department of Curriculum and Instruction at the University of Calgary, is the author of *The Well-Tempered Tongue* and *The New Literacy: Redefining Reading and Writing in the Schools*. His essay in this collection is part of a larger project on the relationship between literary theory and education.